READING BETWEEN THE NUMBERS

READING
BETWEEN
THE
NUMBERS

STATISTICAL THINKING
IN EVERYDAY LIFE

JOSEPH TAL

New York ... and Bogotá
Carac... Milan
...re
Sydney   Tokyo   Toronto

McGraw-Hill

A Division of The McGraw·Hill Companies

1 2 3 4 5 6 7 8 9 0   DOC/DOC   0 6 5 4 3 2 1 0

ISBN 0-07-136400-5

Printed and bound by R. R. Donnelley & Sons Company.

This publication is designed to provide accurate and authoritative information in regard to the subject matter covered. It is sold with the understanding that neither the author nor the publisher is engaged in rendering legal, accounting, or other professional service. If legal advice or other expert assistance is required, the services of a competent professional person should be sought.

—From a Declaration of Principles jointly adopted by a Committee of the American Bar Association and a Committee of Publishers

McGraw-Hill books are available at special quantity discounts to use as premiums and sales promotions, or for use in corporate training programs. For more information, please write to the Director of Special Sales, Professional Publishing, McGraw-Hill, Two Penn Plaza, New York, NY 10121-2298. Or contact your local bookstore.

To my parents Avraham and Channa
And my children Shira and David
החוט המשולש

CONTENTS

From the Tower of Babel onward, humanity has had communication problems. Still, until now, we have gotten on tolerably well. Recently, this has not been enough. Over a century ago, L. L. Zamenhof recognized the need for a universal language and devised Esperanto for it. His language never did take off, but English did. And still this has not been enough.

Much of modern-day discourse demands greater precision than conventional language affords. From biology to baseball and from marketing to medicine to psychology, we collect numbers and communicate with them. Increasingly, we require means to organize these numbers and extract their information. Statistics is one such means.

Numerous professions and disciplines converse in statistics. Whether we realize it or not, so do most of us daily. Indeed, statistics has become a sufficiently prevalent form of communication to be considered a universal language.

Today we take our ability to manipulate numbers for granted. It has not always been so. Some of the simple arithmetic that we do quickly took hours for the medieval mathematician. Moreover, we compute interest, fill out tax forms, and inspect complicated bills as a matter of course. Apparently, we live on a level of abstraction that is "altogether beyond" that of even our recent ancestors.[1] But we are not always comfortable with it.

Perhaps this very abstraction is what often makes formal statistical reasoning seem foreign to the layperson. Maybe it is our collective, traumatic experience with new and postmodern math. Whatever the reason, it is a fact that this particular language feels unnatural to most. It need not be.

Statistical thinking is indeed abstract. In many ways, however, it is no more so than the kind of thinking we do every day. *Reading between the Numbers* sets out to show this. This book represents one nonmathematician's efforts to come to terms with statistics. For me, this has meant bringing the logic of the discipline of statistics I have chosen to real-world situations I have mostly not chosen. Over the years, the connection has become clear to me. In *Reading between the Numbers* I attempt to convey my experience.

The book's progression follows loosely on that of introductory statistical texts. While modeled on standard fare, however, this is not a textbook. For one, the book avoids mathematics as much as possible—it is weak on formulas. This is not because mathematics is unimportant. It is *very* important. When focusing on concepts, however, the most useful formulas are those whose meaning is intuitive. And there are not so many of these.

The book's topics are introduced through stories, with the underlying concepts only revealed in time. With one exception, its ideas progress from concrete examples to the more abstract rules and not the other way around. In this, too, *Reading between the Numbers* differs from standard texts. But this is how our minds usually work.

ACKNOWLEDGMENTS

Reading between the Numbers encapsulates what insights I have gained into statistics and its connection to the real world. Many have contributed to it by teaching me how to think logically and then how to think statistics. I am indebted to all of them. (I am also indebted to those who have taught me how to think illogically, but this is not the book to repay *that* debt.)

I would like to thank William Sawrey, who did not throw me out of his methods course, for which I had not the prerequisites. His lucid lectures taught me the logic of science. I also would like to express my gratitude to William Revelle, a psychologist and a mathematician—and a wonderful person. Bill was a supportive and exacting advisor, and I have tried to live up to his standards ever since.

Ayala Cohen is a teacher's teacher who has taught me how to *look* at numbers. I have yet to meet anyone who can extract information from data as well as she.

Paul Feigin is simply a brilliant statistician. I am privileged to have him for a partner, teacher, and friend. A client once said of Paul that when you ask him a question, you get an answer. For some of us, this is a *tour de force*.

My father, Avraham Tal, reviewed this book as it went along. His comments on both the mathematics and the writing went a long way toward making this book what it is. My mother, Channa Tal, had exposed me to books early on and so had sown the seed for this one. As for thanking my parents for all the rest, well, there are not enough pages here for it.

Finally, I would like to thank Amy Murphy of McGraw-Hill. She believed enough in this book to accept it, and her painstaking editing improved it greatly. But the book is ultimately my own, as is the responsibility for what is in it.

CHAPTER I

Why Statistics

COMMUNICATION

. . . the two entities who might enlighten us [about birth and death], the baby and the corpse, cannot do so, because their apparatus for communicating their experiences are not attuned to our apparatus for reception.

E. M. FORSTER[1]

This book is about statistical thinking. In it you will find rules, regulations, and all manner of analytic procedure. On the face of it, there is nothing further from the way we actually *think*. Well, not entirely.

On a cloudy day a woman looks out her window and says, "I think it's going to rain. I better take an umbrella on my way out." Only the odd statistician will say, "Given the number of clouds, their color, and the season, there's an 80 percent chance of rain today. If I take an umbrella, there's a 20 percent chance that I'll have wasted my energy." An odd statistician indeed.

Yet, when we juxtapose the terms *think* and *80 percent chance,* we find that they are not so very different. In fact, we may view 80 percent as one interpretation of the word *think*. And this is precisely the problem. Such words are open to interpretation. Many interpretations.

Here then is one basic function of analytic thinking: *communication*. Formal reasoning provides the kind of precision that is rarely needed in everyday conversation. Yet there are situations in which such communication can help. There are situations in which it is crucial.

Developing a new drug is a risky business financially. On average, it costs near half a billion dollars and takes over 10 years. Once on the market, the drug's patent is protected for 7 years, during which time the company must recoup its costs. And then, only one in four new drugs show a profit.

Patent laws are designed to protect innovators—to ensure that they have the opportunity to profit by their originality and investment. While in most areas patents are given for 20 years, in pharmaceuticals the period is substantially shorter. Governments have decided that 20 years is much too long for a monopoly where life and limb are concerned. So after 7 years, it is open season. Any company wishing to produce the drug may do so. On one condition—that the new, generic drug be equivalent to the original.

Now it is not simple to reproduce any product. No one expects two jellybeans coming off the same production line to be exactly alike. Certainly no one should expect drugs produced in different plants to be identical. And no one does. The new generic drug is not required to be indistinguishable from the original. It must be *equivalent*. Another one of those bothersome words.

Regulators evaluate a drug's performance on two dimensions: effectiveness and safety. An effective antibiotic kills bacteria. A safe antibiotic does nothing else. Thus *effectiveness* is the degree to which a medication does what is intended. *Safety* is the degree to which it does not do what is not intended.

Suppose that a generic drug is 84 percent effective and that the original drug is 84.2 percent effective. Most would agree that the medications are equivalent. But suppose the new drug is only 80 percent effective. What then? The situation gets further complicated when we consider safety as well. What happens when the generic drug is safer than the original but somewhat less effective?

Thus regulatory agencies must *quantify* equivalence—they must define the concept in a way that can be communicated clearly. Statistical thinking translates terms like *equivalence* into values such as "84 percent." In pharmaceuticals this is critical. As we shall see, translating garden-variety thinking into precise language is useful in other areas as well.

DEHYDRATING THE PRIMORDIAL SOUP

My friend, if there is no intuition there is nothing.

S. Y. AGNON[2]

Those of you who have gotten this far have formed an early impression of this book. If asked about this impression, you might say, "Well, it's . . . it's, you know, a book about statistics. I mean, what can you expect." Another may say, "It's fine so far. Ask me again after I've read a few more chapters." Still another might say, "I can understand it. Not bad for statistics."

If pressed, each person will explain how her impression was formed. But the explanation will be lacking because such impressions arise from a kind of primordial soup of fact, fiction, mood, and a whole host of other factors. Some of these are vague. Others are even more vague. We call this *intuition*.

There is in our brain a murky mixture that continually begets feeling, behavior, and comprehension. Many people have investigated this murk, attempting to unfold its onionlike structure. They have found that peeling one layer merely leads to the peeling of another.

Now there are those who spend time designing research to show how inaccurate our decisions can be when we engage in "primordial soup" thinking. In one typical example, individuals were presented with the following description of Tom. They were then asked to conjecture whether Tom is a computer science major or a student of humanities:

> Tom W. is of high intelligence, although lacking in true creativity. He has a
> need for order and clarity and for neat and tidy systems in which every detail
> finds its appropriate place. His writing is rather dull and mechanical, occa-
> sionally enlivened by somewhat corny puns and by flashes of imagination of
> the sci-fi type. He has a strong drive for competence. He seems to have lit-
> tle feeling and little sympathy for other people and does not enjoy interact-
> ing with others. Self-centered, he nonetheless has a deep moral sense.[3]

Ninety-five percent of those asked placed Tom in computer science. In the second part of the study, the participants were told that Tom is 1 of 100 students taking a course and that 80 of the students are humanities majors. They were again asked to guess Tom's major. Virtually none changed their answer. But the answers *should* have changed. After all, they now knew that anyone chosen from the class has an 80 percent chance of being a humanities major. And yet most ignored the new information. This study, and others like it, suggest that there is something deficient in our use of information. Alas, the primordial soup is imperfect.

The study just described is clever. It had to be. Only trickery of the kind we rarely encounter every day can demonstrate our inadequacy. This is so because on the whole we do just fine. Most of us have little trouble getting our left shoe on our left foot on the first try. More people than not get to work and back every day with little effort. In between, their work gets done with a fair degree of competence. Apparently, we do well even without the continual application of analytic reasoning. So if we are not as foolish as we seem, why complicate matters with statistical thinking? Surely not for the fun of it.

Indeed, the statistical reasoning presented in this book is not intended as an alternative to our primordial soup. At the same time, it *is* another mode of thinking—an additional apparatus for comprehending our world.

Some marketing executives will admit that they make most of their decisions intuitively rather than analytically. In truth, analytic approaches are often ineffectual when confronting problems in marketing. For example, it may never really be known why a salesperson succeeds with one customer and fails with another. It just happens. Similarly, it is often impossible to explain why some people freely experiment with new products and others need convincing. Of course, we can always ask people to tell us why they do what they do. But here again we are faced with having to rely on what cannot very well be described. At best, we shall obtain incomplete information. At worst, the information will be inaccurate as well. Nevertheless, applying analytic reasoning to marketing problems can also yield interesting results.

One central issue in marketing is customer loyalty. Simply put, loyal customers make for good business. Jones and Sasser[4] explored this issue at Xerox. They wrote: "Xerox's intense interest in measuring customer satisfaction sprang from a set of beliefs that we share. High-quality products and associated services . . . will create high levels of customer satisfaction. This high level of satisfaction will lead to greatly increased customer loyalty."

The authors felt intuitively that satisfied customers become loyal customers. This is a reasonable assumption—so reasonable in fact that one would question the need to analyze it at all. Yet this assumption gives rise to other questions worthy of answer. For example, to what extent does customer satisfaction lead to loyalty? Suppose that improving the quality of a product merely leads to a marginal increase in satisfaction while substantially increasing costs. Might not the benefit of increased loyalty be outweighed by the cost of customers leaving due to price?

In the question just raised, I used such terms as *extent* and *cost*. As such, the question demands a quantitative answer. Jones and Sasser continue: "One discovery [at Xerox] shattered conventional wisdom: Its totally satisfied customers were six times more likely to repurchase Xerox products over the next 18 months than its [merely] satisfied customers."

Our market researchers had asked Xerox customers to rate their satisfaction on a scale of 1 to 5, 5 being the highest score. They found that those answering "5" were much more likely to repurchase Xerox products than those answering "4." While the authors' hunch had proved correct, not even they had imagined the actual magnitude of the satisfaction-loyalty relationship—at Xerox.

They then asked whether this was true in other industries as well. Figure 1-1 provides the answer. The answer is, "It depends." In cars, for example, customer satisfaction has a strong impact on loyalty. Those satisfied at a level of 5 are much more loyal—much more likely to buy the same make next time around—than those satisfied at level 4. Yet this is not the case for consumers of local telephone services. Here, dissatisfied customers are just as loyal as satisfied ones. This is not surprising when you consider that, typically, local telephone companies are monopolies. Whether you like a monopoly or not, you buy from it. There is, after all, no one else.

The airline industry is not a monopoly. At the same time, competition in the industry is not as prevalent as in many others. For example, each airline flies to a limited number of destinations. If you regularly visit your grandmother in Phoenix, you may have few choices. Airline mileage programs further limit your choice. If you want to accumulate miles, you must use the same airline or those associated with it. Thus many dissatisfied customers will use the same airline again and again regardless. In other words, the semimonopolistic nature of the airline industry leads customer satisfaction to have a relatively small impact on loyalty.

Based on these results, Jones and Sasser made a generalization: The more competitive an industry, the greater is the impact of customer satisfaction

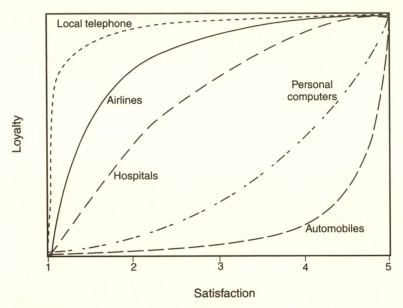

FIGURE 1-1 Relationship between customer satisfaction and loyalty in different industries.

on loyalty. Unhappy customers can spell doom for a business in a competitive environment. Not so where competition is scarce.

Let us take a look at the process just described. The authors began with the intuition that customer satisfaction leads to loyalty. But they did not stop there—they collected data to confirm their hunch. The results surprised them, so they asked another question: Is this true in other industries as well? The question required a quantitative answer, so they collected more data. Finally, they generalized their findings.

There is a certain discipline to the process of analytic reasoning that is foreign to the way we think everyday. It takes more effort, comes less naturally. It is a kind of dehydration of the primordial soup but is not intended to replace it. Indeed, it is a sensible person who knows when to use it and when not.

SEEKING TRUTH

Statistics presents pictures of *reality*. In using this word, I do not mean that statistics is meant to convey deep truths. Our task is much more down to earth. We simply want to present particular states of affairs as accurately as possible.

It takes little effort to assert that late-model cars are more reliable than those produced years ago. To show this, however, we must systematically compare the two. We might, for example, look at the ratio of breakdowns to miles driven between the two. We also could compare the number of electrical failures in each over the period of a year. Alternatively, we might wish to examine the production process itself by assessing how well it conforms to design specifications. For example, we can measure the diameter of an engine's pistons to see just how well it conforms to what the engineers have specified. Presumably, an engine whose pistons are produced precisely will be more reliable than one whose pistons are not.

Over the years, statisticians have developed elaborate methods to get at the truth. Choosing the appropriate method is part and parcel of the statistical process. Whatever the method chosen, however, demanding an accurate picture of reality requires a certain amount of integrity. In statistics this means *reaching conclusions based on data*. This is the statistical equivalent of seeking the truth.

CHAPTER II

What *Is* Statistics

A HEIGHT OF SCIENCE

In 1884, Sir Francis Galton did some simple science. He collected data on the heights of parents and their children and plotted his results on paper. The following year Galton presented his findings to the British Association for the Advancement of Science. They looked something like Figure 2-1.

Each point on Galton's graph represented a pair of numbers—the average height of two parents and the height of their child. Galton's findings did not surprise him. He found that, on average, tall parents had tall children and short parents had short ones. But nature is not mathematics and the relationship is not perfect. Some short parents have tall children. A few of the tall parents have short children. This being the case, Galton knew that he could not perfectly predict a child's height just by knowing the parents' heights. Judging from his results, however, he could do pretty well.

Now Galton had collected the heights of 952 parent-child pairs, which yielded him 1904 numbers. A great deal. He looked for a way to simplify the data and came up with something like Figure 2-2.

Galton constructed his line by specifying different ranges for the height of parents. In each range he computed

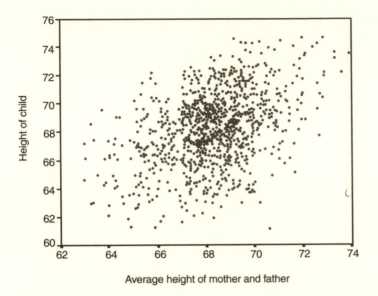

FIGURE 2-1 Galton's original data: the heights of parents and their children.

1. The average height of the parents in the range.

2. The average height of the children of the parents in each range.

In Figure 2-2, I specified nine ranges and obtained nine pairs of averages. Like Galton, I then drew the straight line that best describes the relationship between these pairs. As you can see, my averages fall almost perfectly on the line.

Of course, most of the original (individual) points in Galton's study were off the line. Yet, on average, the line pretty well described the relationship between the heights of parents and children. An interesting result but not surprising. Still, something about the line was completely unexpected. Galton believed that he had discovered a phenomenon of nature.

CHANGING TIMES

Sir Francis Galton was a scientist in simpler times. Although by the nineteenth century people had been doing science for thousands of years, the amount of knowledge that had accumulated was relatively small. A gifted man like Galton could know most of what had ever been discovered in his

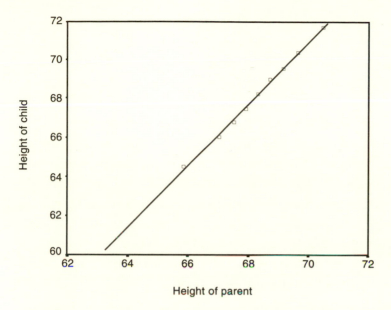

FIGURE 2-2 The relationship between the heights of parents and their children in Galton's data.

areas of interest. And these were many. During his lifetime, Galton made scientific contributions in fields as varied as meteorology, anthropology, and geography. However, his major interest was heredity. More specifically, he was fascinated by the idea that human intelligence, like physical characteristics, might be inherited.

Galton was born in 1822 to a Quaker father and an Anglican mother. His father converted to the Church of England, which made Francis eligible for admittance to Oxford and Cambridge. In those days, Oxbridge was still closed to non-Anglicans.

Galton's father was ambitious for his son. Early on he took the boy on a tour of medical facilities on the Continent, hoping the boy would take to medicine. While the trip did not whet young Galton's appetite for medicine, it convinced him that he wanted to travel.

Galton's childhood was happy, and he credited much of his later success to those early years. Judging by the difficult lives of great men such as Isaac Newton, though, happiness never seemed a prerequisite for good science.

Be that as it may, Galton did not take up medicine. In his twenties, he traveled up the Nile and crossed the desert to Khartoum. He traveled to

Jerusalem and lived for a time in Syria. Later, he would explore distant parts of southern Africa. In between, he studied mathematics at Cambridge.

The times, scientifically speaking, were turbulent. Darwin had just written his *Origin of Species,* and the scientific community was reeling. Heredity had long been accepted as a central force of nature, but Darwin went far beyond convention. He claimed that nature has no master plan. Species evolved as they did because of local conditions. When local conditions changed for whatever reason, so did species. For many, this was unacceptable—scientifically or religiously. Not so for Galton.

Galton's chief interest was individual differences in humans. He felt that Darwin's theory of evolution provided an explanation for both the origin and the value of these differences. Darwin had written: "These individual differences are of the highest importance for us, for they are often inherited . . . and they thus afford materials for natural selection to act on and accumulate."[1]

Charles Darwin maintained that organisms differed because their ancestors did. But only those differences which were advantageous endured. These, in turn, provided the raw material for future selection, thus contributing to the survival of species. About his cousin Darwin's discovery, Galton said that it had driven away "the constraint of my old superstition as if it had been a nightmare."[2]

Galton was particularly interested in differences in human intelligence. Specifically, he was mesmerized by genius and wrote: "It is difficult to understand why statisticians commonly limit their inquiries to Averages. . . . Their souls seem as dull to the charm of variety as that of the native of our flat English counties, whose retrospect of Switzerland was that, if its mountains could be thrown into its lakes, two nuisances would be got rid of at once."[3]

Galton felt that studying an unusual phenomenon such as genius was far more interesting than dabbling in averages. He began with informal observations and then moved on to scientific study. Of his observations on genius Galton wrote: "I began by thinking over the dispositions and achievements of my contemporaries at school, at college, and in after life, and was surprised to find how frequently ability seemed to go by descent."[4]

Over the years, he collected data on human intelligence and concluded that ". . . the results were such, in my own opinion, as to completely establish the theory that genius was hereditary."[5] Galton claimed that mental faculties were no different from physical ones. Like height and eye color, they were inherited. This led him to the field of eugenics, which represented an attempt to improve humanity through selective breeding. The best in society, he claimed, should have many children. The worst, none at all. Clearly, Galton would not have been a popular man these days. And rightly.

NATURE'S WILL TO MEDIOCRITY

Let us return to height. Galton decided to use the line he had drawn for predicting a child's height from that of his parents'. For each location on the horizontal axis—a parent's height—there is a corresponding point on the line. The point's projection onto the vertical axis represented Galton's prediction for the child's height. As expected, his prediction for a tall parent was a tall child; his prediction for a short parent, a short child.

However, by using this procedure, Galton also found something curious. His line predicted that tall parents would have children who, on average, were shorter than their parents. The line also predicted that short parents would have children who, on average, were taller than they. In other words, parents at the extreme ends of the height scale—tall or short—had children nearer to the average than they. Galton termed this phenomenon "regression toward the mean." In 1885 he published his results in a paper entitled, "Regression Towards Mediocrity in Hereditary Stature."

Galton discovered this phenomenon in another area as well. Studying seeds, he observed that small seeds gave rise to seeds that, on average, were larger than they. He also found that large seeds begot seeds that were smaller than they.

A student of Galton's, Karl Pearson, developed the following formula to predict a son's height from that of his father. It was based on data from 1078 father-son pairs.

$$\text{Height of son} = 35 + 0.5 \times \text{height of father}$$

In Pearson's data, the average height of fathers was 68 inches and that of sons 69 inches. Galton's "regression toward the mean" phenomenon can be seen clearly from this formula. For example, let us take a father whose height is 72 inches—4 inches above the average of fathers. Using the formula, Pearson's prediction for the son's height is 71 inches. This is shorter than the father and 2 inches above the mean for sons. Let us now take a father whose height is 62 inches. The formula predicts that his son's height will be 66 inches. This is still below the average of sons but taller than the father by 4 inches.

When we think about it, our world would be a peculiar place if this were otherwise. Suppose, for instance, that tall parents had children who were as tall as they were and that short parents had children who were as short as they were. Since tall women tend to marry tall men, and short women, short men, the world would become an inconvenient place indeed. Over time, there would be two groups of people—very tall and very short. Few would be in between. If this were actually the case, each building would need two sets of stairs. We would need to produce two sets of cars and design two sizes of chairs.

Galton was convinced that he had discovered a phenomenon of nature. Others claim that what he found was no more than a statistical artifact—a mathematical quirk that has nothing to do with the way nature operates. The argument is technical, and here is not the place to get into it. My point is different.

In discovering regression toward the mean, Galton did *statistics*. His research is a fine example of how statistical reasoning works. It goes like this:

1. *Ask a question.* In Galton's case, he asked whether there existed a relationship between the heights of children and their parents.

2. *Design a study and specify its measures.* Choose a method of research that will answer the question. For Galton this was simple—measure height in inches of parents and their children. As you shall see, choosing the appropriate measure is not always so easy.

3. *Collect data and describe them.* Galton obtained many measurements and plotted them on paper.

4. *Simplify the data.* Figure 2-2 shows how Galton turned his 1904 numbers into a single line.

5. *Interpret the data.* The relationship, Galton found, exists. Furthermore, he discovered that it is well described by a straight line. In statistical terms, the relationship he discovered is *linear*.

6. *Generalize the findings.* Galton explored whether what he had found was a more general phenomenon. His study of seeds suggested that it applied to other areas as well.

We have now answered our question, "What *is* statistics? Statistics is what statisticians do—what Galton did.

CHAPTER III

Names and Numbers

TELLING A STORY

In the middle of the summer of 1891 the most extraordinary things began happening in a small Norwegian coastal town. . . . It all started at six one evening when a steamer landed at the dock and three passengers appeared on deck. One of them was a man wearing a loud yellow suit and an outsized corduroy cap.

KNUT HAMSUN[1]

Here, at the very outset of *Mysteries,* Knut Hamsun sets the stage for incidents that will come to pass. "The most extraordinary things," he writes, will happen "in a small Norwegian coastal town." He provides us with the first glimpse of the stranger who will disturb the peaceful souls of the town. A man "wearing a loud yellow suit and an outsized corduroy cap." An eccentric.

With very few words Hamsun paints an elaborate picture. We know we are in Norway, not Denmark, and that the story takes place in a town—not a village or city. We know that the stranger is a man and that he is a bit odd. Yet Hamsun leaves out much more than he has included. We do not know whether the waters of the fjord were calm or turbulent that day. In fact, we do not yet know that the town lies on a fjord. Hamsun does not say whether the steamer's arrival was a rare occurrence or a common one. We have no idea whether the sky was cloudy or clear.

For all that is missing, the picture is ample. So it is with all good writing—fiction or fact. When telling a story, one must choose the essential elements, those which best convey what needs to be known. If the storyteller has done a good job, he has told a great deal with very little.

Statisticians tell stories. Alas, their tales are simpler and less textured. They are less stirring. But they are stories nevertheless. Statisticians recount whether populations have increased or remained stable and whether the market has retreated or advanced. They describe the ages of trees so that we may know whether a forest is ancient or young. Yet the same holds true for both statistics and novels: *Keep to the essence.*

A statistician must select his descriptions carefully. Too much, and the picture is muddled. Too little, and it is incomplete. Thus it is nary impossible to know whether the market has gone up or down by looking at several pages of stock quotes. On the other hand, too little information—say, reporting only that GM stock has advanced—may tell us next to nothing about the market at large.

The statistician's first task, then, is to choose those measures that will best tell his story. More often than not, the possibilities are endless. Suppose that you would like to tell your audience how the market has fared on a particular day. Here are but a few possibilities:

1. The Dow advanced 0.56 percent.

2. The market was bullish today.

3. The broad market moved up.

4. Despite the muggy weather most traders ended the day with a smile.

5. The Nasdaq advanced 15 points.

6. Taking its cue from New York, the Tokyo Nikkei Index moved up 104 points.

Each of these descriptions conveys information. Some of it seems more appropriate to our tale and some less. But this is not the case. Each tells a slightly different story, and each is suitable in its place. If a child wants to know what her trader mother's mood will be at dinner, a report that "most traders ended the day with a smile" tells her more than "the Nasdaq advanced 15 points." For someone wanting to know how world markets fared, the report about the Nikkei is more useful than the others.

Being a formal discipline, statistics has developed a classification system for information. In the term *0.56 percent* we have a numerical description— a point along a scale that ranges from 0 to 100. In the word *smile* we have another sort of description. Yet here too we can speak of a scale. Thus *smile* can be seen as a value on a measuring stick consisting of the values *frown, neutral,* and *smile.*

In statistics, the classification system for different types of information is called *scales of measurement.* We will get there soon. But before we do, we must deal with the elusive concept of the *variable.*

VARIABLES

A time to keep and a time to throw away;
A time to tear and a time to mend;
A time for silence and a time for speech;
A time for war and a time for peace.

ECCLESIASTES

A *variable* is a person, place, or thing that can take on more than one value. Time is a variable—there is 8:00 and 8:30 and 12:27. Hair color is a variable that takes on values, say, of black or blond or ginger. A place can be very large or very small or all points between. A person can be short or tall.

Variables are the building blocks of statistics. Each can take on different values. Simply put, variables vary. To understand the concept in statistics, it is best to examine what statisticians actually do with *variability.*

On the first day of a particular experiment,[2] rats ate 8 grams of food. On the second they ate 10 grams, and on the seventeenth day they ate 12 grams. In this experiment, the variable is Food Intake. The researcher can describe Food Intake over the 40 days of the study in several ways. For example, he can chart the rat's behavior over time on a graph, as shown in Figure 3-1.

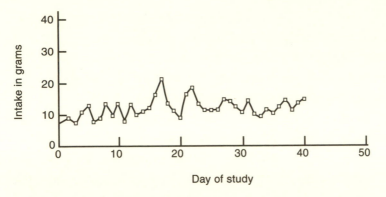

FIGURE 3-1 The daily Food Intake of normal rats.

If he chooses, the researcher also can use a single number to describe the outcome of his study—the *average* daily Food Intake of the rats over the 40 days. The researcher has other options as well. For instance, he may want to report how much the animals ate on the day their intake was greatest.

You have now seen one of the two things that a statistician does with variability—he describes it. This is the principal pastime of statisticians. Its methods are specified in the area of *descriptive statistics*. We will get there. Here I only wish to demonstrate the statistician's basic attitude toward variability: Describe it.

To summarize, a researcher has identified a variable that interests him— Food Intake. He collects data and observes that it varies over time. He then tells his tale in a manner that best illustrates the point he wishes to make. Now, it would be a dull researcher who only wished to describe the eating habits of unsavory animals in a cage. Our scientist, on the other hand, wanted to know *why* rats eat as they do. In fact, his question was even more specific.

Inside the central core of our brain there is structure called the *hypothal-amus*. About 150 years ago a pathologist examining brains noticed that individuals who had damage to their hypothalamus tended to have stomach ulcers. In the years that followed, additional evidence emerged of a connection between this tiny structure and eating and drinking. Evidence also emerged of an association between the hypothalamus and other life-giving functions such as sexual behavior, response to stress, and internal temperature regulation. These are quite a few functions for a structure the size of the tip of an index finger. The scientist wanted to identify the specific sub-structure of the hypothalamus associated with eating.

The scientist's experiment dealt with a part of the hypothalamus known as the *ventromedial nucleus*. He took several rats and simply put them in cages and took others and made lesions in their ventromedial nucleus and put them in similar cages. The scientist then recorded the amount of food eaten by both groups over 40 days. The findings are shown in Figure 3-2.

As can be seen, the animals with lesions turned into fat rats. The researcher had identified the ventromedial nucleus as the substructure of the hypothalamus responsible for Food Intake. Our erstwhile scientist had engaged in the second major activity of statistics. He *explained* variation.

In Chapter 1, I mentioned that a central function of analytic thinking is to present a picture of reality. One way of doing this is to show the picture as it is. To tell the tale. Yet often we seek to do more—to understand why the picture turned out as it did. I have now shown what it means to understand in statistics. It is to *explain variation*.

To get a better handle on what this means, let us take a look at what our scientist did from another angle. The scientist treated two groups of rats differently and then defined a variable Treatment and constructed a two-point scale to measure it. One group of rats had a scale value of "lesion—yes" and the other "lesion—no." The scientist then related the two-point Treatment variable to Food Intake, which he quantified in grams. In other words, the scientist associated variation on one variable with variation on

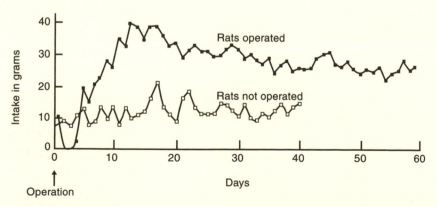

FIGURE 3-2 Daily Food Intake of normal rats and those with lesions in the ventromedial nucleus of the hypothalamus.

another. He found that rats whose value on Treatment was "yes" had higher values on Food Intake than those whose value was "no." This is the nature of statistical explanation—*showing that changes in one variable are associated with changes in another.*

Recall Sir Francis Galton. He also measured two variables. One was the Height of Parents and the other was the Height of Children. He showed that variability in Height of Parents was associated with variability in Height of Children. Galton had provided one explanation for the reason children vary in height.

The examples presented are relatively simple. In each, one variable is related to another, single variable. Our world being complex, most problems involve relationships between large numbers of variables. Thus, in attempting to understand the behavior of stock markets, an economist might choose to explore multiple factors, for example, interest rates, industrial output, election results, and even the weather.

Statisticians have developed *multivariate* methods to deal with more complex problems. Yet, be the problem simple or complex, the statistical path to understanding is always the same: Explore relationships between variables. In other words, determine whether changes in specific measures are associated in a lawful way with changes in others.

On the Unfinished Nature of Statistical Stories

In the preceding section I showed how one scientist described and explained the regulation of Food Intake. The scientist's research demonstrated a relationship between a substructure of the hypothalamus called the ventromedial nucleus and the amount of food that rats eat. In the realm of scientific research, where numerous experiments are conducted and few reach definitive conclusions, this was a successful study.

Suppose, however, that our scientist had conducted the same experiment with slight changes. The scientist could have used larger cages or have kept the rats in a cooler room. He may have fed the animals cake instead of the pellets such rats typically must endure. Would the scientist have obtained the same results? Well, maybe.

These speculations may seem like nit picking, and to a degree they are. But they illustrate an important point. Our determined scientist did not investigate all the factors that might influence eating—not even close. As a result, the explanation was incomplete. Of course, you cannot blame the scientist. When you think of the multitude of factors that could have been explored, you realize that the situation was hopeless. Neither the scientist nor anyone else can ever completely explain why rats eat as they do.

The situation in humans is, if possible, even more hopeless. The number of calories one person ingests may depend on the number of times a week he walks by a doughnut shop. Or it may depend on the degree to which he is partial to beer. For a child, it might be the size of her allowance or whether the school she attends serves lunch. And the list goes on.

Galton's study was no different. Why, for example, is it that two sets of parents whose heights are identical have children whose heights differ? Why, for that matter, do the same parents have children whose heights are not identical? The answer is simple. The height of parents is not the only variable that determines the height of a child. There are many others we know about and likely more that we do not.

I have now described a basic characteristic of statistical explanations. They are incomplete. As panoramic as our statistical canvas is, it will forever show but a portion of the picture. This breaking up of things into parts is the essence of analysis. It is the way of science and, for that matter, any formal research. Statistics, as a tool for researchers, reflects this.

Let us return to Hamsun's Norwegian town with our newly gained wisdom. I had said that novelists tell tales and so do statisticians. And this is true. But the nature of these tales is vastly different. The novelist appeals to our primordial soup. The scientist dries it up.

Hamsun described only a few elements of a picture. He asked that we construct from them a whole. We know how to do this well. If a writer has written as she should, we do not ask whether the waters were turbulent that day or calm. We have no *need* to know whether the sky was cloudy. The picture is complete.

For a scientist, however, the picture is always lacking. It could be one piece of the puzzle, or it could be another. It makes no difference. Analytic thinking condemns its practitioners to a mere part of the whole. The analytic thinker may begin with the complete picture but quickly breaks it up, analyzing each element in its turn. The primordial soup works the other way around. It takes the puzzle's pieces and puts them together.

Now, all of us strive for the complete picture. It is our basic nature, and the analytic thinker is no different. She cannot help it. But she will never get there. She trudges on and on and, if fortunate, will add more parts as she goes along. In time, she will see more and more. But that is all she will see.

CHAPTER IV

Scales of
Measurement

DICHOTOMOUS VARIABLES

DEWEY DEFEATS TRUMAN

CHICAGO DAILY TRIBUNE HEADLINE, 1948

Thomas Dewey was born in Owosso, Michigan, in 1902, his father a local newspaper publisher. He studied law at Columbia and graduated in 1925. Twelve years later he became district attorney of New York County. In 1942 he was elected governor of the state.

Dewey ran New York's finances efficiently. He also introduced the first state-level legislation on antidiscrimination in employment in the United States. Sufficiently liberal on social issues and a fiscal conservative, Dewey kept Democrats off balance and conservative Republicans at bay. He believed he had what it took to be president.

In 1944, Dewey won the Republican nomination for highest office. He ran against Franklin Roosevelt and lost. In 1948, Dewey won the nomination again. This second time around, opinion polls gave Dewey a wide lead over Truman. Dewey was confident, and he was not alone. Daily newspapers stood eight to one in his favor, and the final Gallup poll put him ahead by 5 percent. Certain of the outcome, the *Chicago Daily Tribune* printed its headline before the result was known. Dewey lost by the margin by which he had been predicted to win.

For a statistician, there is something nightmarish about elections. First, she is asked to predict the outcome. Then her prediction is held up to scrutiny. Now, most predictions are not taken very seriously. A coach predicts his team to win, and no one holds him to it. Pundits parade their prophecies in newspapers and on television and are seldom challenged with hindsight. After all, no one reads yesterday's papers. Fewer watch news-show reruns.

While we might expect more from analytic techniques, even here we excuse inaccuracy. We are not terribly upset when the meteorologist misses by a few degrees, and we forgive her when her forecast of rain is off by a few hours. Elections are different. They are measured on two-point scales with no points between. A candidate can receive anywhere between 0 and 100 percent of the popular vote on the "election scale." The actual results may be 32, 47, or 53 percent—all on the continuum. Yet the midpoint of the continuum is critical. Garner above and you win; below, and you go home.

Thus, while the popular vote is measured on a continuous scale, we determine the outcome on a dichotomy. Still, we allow a survey statistician to err as long as she is far from the middle. In 1996, the final CBS/*New York Times* poll erred more than Gallup did in 1948. However, it predicted the winner.

The variable Election Outcome is one example of what statisticians term a *dichotomous scale*. It has two values—win and lose. Others examples include Gender (boy/girl), Cholesterol Level (high/low), and British Citizenship (yes/no). You may have noticed, however, that we have confused apples with oranges here. While we labeled all these scales dichotomous, there are essential differences between them. In elections, the values "win" and "lose" are a result of an arbitrary split. Such is the case with Cholesterol Level as well. One can specify a cutoff of 220 mg/dL or choose 200 mg/dL. Each has been used. Gender, on the other hand, is a natural dichotomy. Biologically speaking, there is nothing arbitrary about it.

This splitting of continuums is an accepted practice in statistics. Sometimes it is appropriate and sometimes not. Here we would like to address another distinction between scales of measurement—ranking. A low level of cholesterol is superior to high, and winning is generally recognized as preferable to losing. In other words, the values on the dichotomous Election Outcome and Cholesterol Level scales can be ranked. Not so with Gender. Boys and girls are simply different. While they represent a natural dichotomy, they do not indicate order. They are *categories*.

CATEGORICAL SCALES

THE TELEPHONE BOOK

734–2739	955–3120	861–3419	495–7375
842–1282	513–7702	678–0482	860–1084
760–6345	482–6745	739–8531	869–8539
488–0758	824–1210	942–6220	498–3231

The first arithmetic operation most of us learned is addition. Using this operation on the digits of the first telephone number above gives us

$$7 + 3 + 4 + 2 + 7 + 3 + 9 = 35$$

Later, we learned subtraction. Taking the first three digits of the first telephone number from those of the second, we have

$$842 - 734 = 108$$

A more sophisticated child wanting to show his numerical prowess might decide to take the average of these two numbers. If he does it right, he will get something like this:

$$(734 + 842) \div 2 = 788$$

Statisticians often find themselves in situations where it is appropriate to add, subtract, or compute an average. Clearly, this is not one of them.

The operations just executed make no sense because telephone "numbers" are numbers in name only. They lack the basic characteristic of numbers—they do not represent quantities. In statistical terms, Telephone Number is a *categorical variable*. Each value simply represents a category—my home phone, Jack's office, Jill's Hardware.

Now you might suppose that statisticians can do little with categorical variables. Not so. Witness Table 4–1. In this table, Game is a variable that

TABLE 4-1 SALES OF GAMES OVER A 6-MONTH PERIOD

GAME	NUMBER SOLD	PERCENT SOLD
Monopoly	435	36.4
Chess	134	11.2
Scrabble	628	52.4
Total	1197	100.0

takes on three values: Monopoly, Chess, and Scrabble. Each represents a distinct category, and there is no obvious way to rank them. What statisticians do best with categories is *count* them. These particular data describe counts of sales on the variable Game. In statistical terminology, the table shows the distribution of sales on the variable Game.

In counting sales, we have attached honest-to-goodness numbers to non-quantifiable categories. We are now in a position to make such statements as

1. Scrabble was the most popular game.

2. Chess was the least popular.

3. Total sales of the three games was 1197.

So far we have remained in the realm of description. We have presented a snapshot of reality and made no effort to understand why it is so.

TABLE 4-2 SALES OF GAMES OVER A 6-MONTH PERIOD ACCORDING TO GENDER

GAME	GENDER		TOTAL
	GIRLS	BOYS	
Monopoly	219	216	435
Chess	18	116	134
Scrabble	327	301	628
Total	564	633	1197

Suppose we want to get a better handle on our data—we wish to explain it. We already know that statistical explanation means relating variables to one another (see Chapter 3). Since our data are for one variable only, we need at least one more. Table 4-2 presents sales for each game by a second categorical variable, Gender. This table shows the *joint distribution* of Game and Gender. Recall that we began with the data in the rightmost column. Hoping to understand the data better, we looked inside the numbers and separated sales to boys from those to girls.

Our goal here is to explain variation in sales on Game by variation in Gender. There are many other options as well. Thus retailers will tell you that the three variables best predicting Sales are Location, Location, and Location. One could, if one wished, tabulate Game Sales by Location. For example, we might specify sale counts for our games in suburban malls, downtown shopping centers, and neighborhood stores. For the sake of simplicity, let us keep to Gender.

Returning to the data, we see that they lead us some way along the path to explaining sales. For instance, the joint distribution of Game and Gender tells us that boys and girls prefer Monopoly about equally. One also might conclude that

4. Overall, boys buy more of these three games than girls do.

5. The difference in the total sales to boys and girls—633 versus 564—is primarily a result of boys' greater preference for Chess.

Now these statements hide at least one assumption that has yet to be proven. When we conclude that the preference for Chess among boys is greater than that among girls, we assume that 116 is larger than 18. Given our knowledge of the number system, this is not such a risky assumption. In reality, however, our conclusion is based on more than just the fact that the two numbers differ. It is also based on the *magnitude* of the difference. Recall that earlier we claimed that girls and boys prefer Monopoly about equally. We made this claim despite the fact that girls purchased three more Monopoly games than boys (219 versus 216). What, then, would we have decided had boys bought 116 Chess sets and girls 102? Some would view this as proof of the relative fondness of boys for Chess. Others would not.

In making decisions based on numbers, we are faced with determining what is a "sufficient magnitude"—a magnitude large enough to reflect a *true* difference. This is a strange statement. After all, what is untrue about the difference of three games found between boys and girls in Monopoly? Certainly we are not implying that the number 3 is less honest than, say, 33. Well, in a way we are.

In this example, intuition led us to conclude that the difference between 116 and 18 is sufficiently large to indicate a preference among boys for Chess. Being a product of our "primordial soup," it is not clear how we reached this conclusion. But neither is it our concern. In formal reasoning we need a *rule* to tell us "how large is large" or, if you will, "how large is true." Statistics, in its peculiar way, will solve this problem for us. But not for a while.

It seems that as hard we try to stay our course, we are forever getting ahead of our statistical game. Let us restrain ourselves and get on with scales.

ORDINAL SCALES

The rise of the Soviet school to the summit of world chess is a logical result of socialist cultural development. . . . [What characterizes] the Soviet school [is] the influence of the traits of the Soviet man of the socialist era, an ardent patriot and tireless seeker of the new. . . .

KOTOV AND YUDOVICH[1]

In their classic book *The Soviet School of Chess*, Kotov and Yudovich present a history of the game in the U.S.S.R. In it they also write about the great soviet players of their day. Along the way, they enlighten us about the reasons for Soviet superiority in chess.

In the U.S.S.R., the era of socialism has passed for now. So has the U.S.S.R. Yet former Soviets still dominate world chess. The top 2 players in the world are Russian, and half the top 20 players are from the Commonwealth of Independent States.

Early chapters of the *Soviet School of Chess* recount the lives and outstanding games of grand masters. Later chapters deal with prominent masters. The authors also distinguish between those players who were formally recognized internationally and those who were not. We can now construct the following four-category ranking scheme for top chess players:

1. International Grand Master

2. Grand Master

3. International Master

4. Master

We have just combined two terms that have been kept separate until now: category and rank. Yet here they are rightly combined. In Chess Ranking, we have an *ordinal variable*—a variable encapsulating information on both category *and* order. Thus, while Master and Grand Master are different classes of player, unlike Gender, they also provide information on relative standing.

In *The Soviet School of Chess*, Mikhail Tal is mentioned among the International Grand Masters, and Pyotor Dubinin is mentioned among the International Masters. Using our ordinal Chess Ranking scale, we would predict that in a game between the two, Tal would win. Suppose that Tal and Dubinin had played 10 games and that the former scored 6½ points to the latter's 3½ points. Would we expect 10 games between another Grand Master and International Master to yield the same result? Not necessarily. This is so because ordinal variables do not provide information on *distance*. The distance between the same ranks in different instances is seldom equal. Furthermore, we cannot say that the difference between International Grand Master and Grand Master is equal to that between International Master and Master. While we can make statements about who is better, we cannot say by *how much*.

Let us take another example from competition. Those placing in the top three spots in the Olympics are awarded medals. Using our now familiar terminology, we say that Medal is an ordinal variable that takes on the values of "gold," "silver," and "bronze." While we know that "gold" is higher than "silver," we cannot state by how much.[*] A marathoner may have missed the gold by 0.05 second or by 8 minutes. It makes no matter. It is only the fact that she placed behind the winner and in front of third that

---

[*] Unless, of course, we are told the difference on a Time scale. But then our information is from a different type of scale—a kind that will be discussed in the next section.

earned her the silver. So far we have progressed from categorical scales to ordinal. We now take the next logical step.

INTERVAL SCALES

A body temperature of 37°C (98.6°F) in humans is considered normal. Below this, there is no fever, and above it, there is. Thus Fever is a dichotomous variable, whereas Temperature is *continuous*. Our dichotomous scale is ordinal and so encapsulates less information than the Temperature scale from which it was derived. However, the latter not only provides greater resolution than ordinal scales, but it also provides qualitatively different information—it indicates *distance*.

We can use ordinal scales to rank things. At the same time, there is never a single value for the distance between two ranks. The difference between win and lose can be 2 percent or 22 percent. The difference between Fever and no Fever can take on different values as well. For example:

$$38.4 - 37.0 = 1.4$$

and

$$39.2 - 36.7 = 2.5$$

In both cases we have computed the distance between the same two points on the categorical Fever scale—Fever and no Fever. Yet in each case we obtained a different value on our Temperature scale. Temperature is different in that it yields a single distance between any two points. Measures that can provide this kind of information are called *interval scales*.

Interval scales yield categorical information as well. For instance, we can specify the class of individuals whose Temperature is 38°C or assign a person to the category of individuals whose Temperature is 37.5°C. Thus the higher-level interval scale, or any higher-level scale, embodies all the information in lower-level scales and then some—by definition.

A note: Our example of Temperature is a continuous scale, one in which there always exists a third value between any two values on it. Interval scales can be *discrete* as well, for example, Number of Children in families.

We have come a long way from our meager categorical scale. Yet even the interval scale has its limitations. When measuring in Centigrade, 0° is specified as the Temperature at which water turns to ice. This is arbitrary. We could just as easily have chosen the point at which the King of Prussia sneezes. This lack of absolute zero limits the kind of arithmetic done with Temperature.

The absolute zero point—the temperature at which molecules in all matter cease to move—is −273°C. This is a true zero in the sense that it signifies complete absence of heat. It is also the point where all motion stops. Temperature can go no lower. Suppose that we now specify −273°C as the zero point. Using our new scale, 40°C becomes 313° (273° + 40°) and 20°C become 293°. Normally, we would say that 40 is twice 20. Yet we would certainly not claim that 313 is twice 293. When the value 0 on a scale is not the true zero point, computing ratios with it is wrong.

Another example: A teacher devises a test to gauge Arithmetic Ability. A child answering all 10 items correctly earns a score of 10; one getting all items wrong scores 0. Yet 0 does not indicate an absence of Arithmetic Ability. It simply means that no problems have been solved correctly on this particular test. On an easier test, the child might have scored higher. This easier test also measures Arithmetic Ability, but its scale values mean something different.

Suppose that one child scored 10 and another scored 5. Clearly, the first child's score was twice that of the second. But we cannot say that the child scoring 10 is twice as able as the other. The ratio 10/5 is fairly meaningless with regard to Arithmetic Ability. Had our examination been easier or more difficult, or had it included more items, the result would have been different. But changing tests does not change Arithmetic Ability. It is simply the zero point that has moved and with it all other values. There is still, it would seem, another level up.

RATIO SCALES

[Jean Martin] Charcot was, in his time, both highly respected and chastised as a third-rate show-off. Charcot's scientific career was a continuous mixture of rigorous clinical neurology . . . and uncontrolled, controversial and sometimes even theatrical experiments in the field of hysteria.[2]

In 1868, Jean Martin Charcot examined a woman whose bodily tremors, slurred speech, and abnormal eye movements baffled him. After the woman died, he found in her brain scars that today we call *plaques*.

Many know Charcot as Sigmund Freud's teacher. Having heard of Charcot's work on hysteria, Freud made the pilgrimage from Vienna to Paris to study with him. Other prominent researchers, such as Alfred Binet and Pierre Janet, did the same. But in medical circles Charcot is known for much more than his experiments with hysterical women. To many, he is the founder of modern neurology.

Charcot was a complex character. In his laboratory and at home he ruled with an iron hand. At the hospital he hypnotized patients to recreate hysteria for students, which earned him the title "the Napoleon of the neuroses." Those in Charcot's inner circle also saw an agreeable man with a sense of humor and a man who also took special interest in wine and good food.

Charcot was a professor at the University of Paris for 33 years. In 1862 he began his long association with Salpetrière, an asylum in Paris. Twenty years later he established there a neurologic clinic that was unique. His great talent was observation, and he used it to classify disease. Charcot's sharp eye took note of unique symptom constellations, thus identifying specific conditions. Some of these had hitherto been unknown.

Charcot was the first to identify multiple sclerosis (MS), the disease contracted by the woman he saw in 1868. Years later, other physicians confirmed his findings. By the end of the nineteenth century, most everything that could be known about MS from observation alone was already discovered. Yet observation can only go so far. It was only with advances in medical instrumentation that scientists began to understand how the disease operates. And they are still not sure what triggers it.

MS is a disease of the central nervous system. This system, which includes the brain, consists of millions of nerve cells. Within each cell, signals are electrical. In humans, the signals travel efficiently because our brain cells are wrapped in an insulating material called *myelin*. In MS, the myelin gets damaged, and signal transmission deteriorates. This leads to perceptual and motor difficulties that can be severe.

MS is also an immune disorder. Our immune system produces T cells, whose function is to attack foreign agents such as bacteria and viruses that enter the body. If the cells are successful, they have rid the body of potential danger. In MS, the T cells misidentify myelin as a foreign agent and attack it. In MS, the body attacks itself.

Myelin is made up of different proteins. Scientists have been trying for years to figure out which of these proteins induces the T-cell attack. In a typical experiment, a researcher takes blood from an MS patient and places it in two test tubes. One of the test tubes contains the blood only, whereas the other contains a myelin protein as well. After a time, the scientist counts the T cells in the tubes and computes the following ratio:

$$\text{Stimulus Index} = \frac{\text{T-Cell Count in test tube with protein}}{\text{T-Cell Count in test tube without protein}}$$

If the Stimulus Index is large enough, the researcher concludes that the particular protein induces the erroneous T-cell response. In other words, it is a "candidate trigger" for the disease.

Now recall that ratios make sense only where there is an absolute zero point. In T cells, this is simple—0 indicates that the cells are absent. Thus 80 T cells are twice 40, and 20 T cells are twice 10 (which is not the case for 60°C and 30°C). In other words, the Stimulus Index is a meaningful ratio because T-Cell Count has a true zero point. Measures that have this quality are called *ratio scales*.

Up to now, a number of different proteins have been found to induce the proliferation of T cells—in test tubes. Scientists believe that this will lead to a better understanding of the mechanism of MS. And this, they hope, will lead to a cure.

SUMMARIZING AND A BIT MORE

This chapter has presented a classification scheme for scales. We began with dichotomies, illustrating their two types—categorical and ordinal. We then moved on to the more informative interval and ratio scales.

You may justifiably ask why statisticians need such a scheme at all. The obvious answer is that classification is an instinctive activity of analytic thinkers. They just do it. But the party line is equally valid.

Consider subtracting a silver medal from a gold medal or computing the average Gender of a group of employees. These operations are as meaning-ful as taking the square root of a telephone number. While statisticians often subtract and compute averages, they also find it necessary to apply more complex procedures. When dealing with simple arithmetic operations, it is clear what is permitted with particular scales and what is not. When the operations are more complex, this is less clear. Only by knowing the kind of scale we are dealing with can we know the operations that are appropriate with it.

There is another reason for classifying scales. Recall that the aim of statistics is to describe and explain phenomena using data. In statistics, we *extract information from data*. This point is critical. Data by themselves do not provide information—the numbers must be made to talk, to tell their story.

A good statistical procedure maximizes the information extracted from a collection of data. *But statistical procedures are only as powerful as the data on which they are based*. Classifying scales allows you to assess the amount of information each scale provides. For example, we now know that an ordinal variable provides information on rank but not distance. Such knowledge enables us to make wise choices between variables. Here, knowledge is indeed power. And higher-level scales provide more of it. A physician who knows that her patient has a temperature of 39°C has more information than one who only knows that her patient has a fever. Consequently, the former is in a more powerful position to provide the necessary treatment.

It should come as no surprise that, as a rule, one ought to choose the highest-level scale possible for any particular problem. But the rule has many exceptions. For example, reporting that a candidate garnered 50.04 percent of the vote is usually less informative than simply saying that he won. While the former is a ratio scale and the latter ordinal, the term *won* provides the necessary information more directly. Thus the choice of scale depends only partly on the amount of information it provides. The most important consideration in selecting a scale is whether it will serve our purpose. Before an election, we typically want to know the distance between two candidates—information provided by the ratio "percent scale." After the election, we are usually only interested in whether or not the candidate won—a value on an ordinal scale.

The moral of the story is simple: Statistics can go only part way in deciding on which scale to choose. We must also use our heads. At all times we must be aware of our *goals* in measuring. These, more than any technical issue, must determine how and what we measure.

In future chapters we shall discuss how to go about selecting suitable scales of measurement. But before we do we must take a closer look at what the measurement process itself gives us—and equally important, what it does not.

CHAPTER V

Error

WHAT WE SEEK AND WHAT WE GET

I got my feet off the desk, stood up and looked out. There she was. And nobody ever looked less like Lady Macbeth. She was a small, neat, rather prissy-looking girl with primly smooth brown hair and rimless glasses. . . . She had no makeup, no lipstick and no jewelry. The rimless glasses gave her that librarian's look.

RAYMOND CHANDLER[1]

The "Little Sister" would not give her name. Nor was she sincere about her reason for seeking Marlowe's services. It makes for a good detective story. And it makes for bad measurement. Outward appearance, we seem to think, reflects the inner. The "Little Sister" knows this and puts on her best Kansas look in Marlowe's seedy L.A. office. Detective stories being what they are, she is ultimately revealed. Sometimes we are less fortunate.

We have now entered the realm of that slippery relationship between what is seen and what is not. In Outward Appearance—"prissy looking, no makeup"—we have what statisticians term an *observed variable*. In Inner Person we have a *latent variable*.

Marlowe is concerned with what lies underneath. His world is inhabited by shady characters, and his life may depend on discerning what is beneath the surface. But trying to discern the concealed from the revealed invites perilous error. Statisticians' lives being more staid, they have learned to live with error—so much so that they have developed theories about it.

We once suggested that statistical reasoning is often similar to the kind of thinking we do every day. The difference, at times, lies in form only. Such is the case here, where Marlowe engages intuitively in what we termed "explaining variability."

People vary in Outward Appearance. They are tall and short, brown haired and blond. The Inner Person varies too. Some are honest, and some deceitful; some are restless, and others have inner peace. Both detective and statistician are constrained to measuring the outer when looking for the inner. Only where there is a lawful relationship between the two is this a gainful activity. In the case of the "Little Sister," there was little affinity between the observed and the latent. And while the contrast is rarely so great, the relation between the two is often tenuous.

Let us examine a simpler relationship—that between Age and Health. Younger people tend to be healthier than older people. It is reasonable therefore for insurance companies to ask a person's Age before fixing the price of his policy. But insurance companies have no interest in Age per se. They want to know Health and measure what they can. In the variables Health and Age we have an association that is less tenuous than before. Still, it is far from perfect. Let us try a more straightforward relationship.

Recall Galton. He measured Height. What he really wanted to measure was . . . Height. Yet even here we are compelled to make the distinction between the seen and unseen. Every person has a *true* Height. It may be 5 feet 6 inches, 6 feet 2 inches, or 5 feet 11 inches. But even in measuring something so obviously observed we can expect *error*. One tape measure yields a more accurate reading than another; some people measure more carefully, others less. Indeed, the same person measuring Height on different occasions may obtain slightly different readings. While we wish to know true Height, we have only the reading on our tape measure.

Many factors influence the accuracy of measurement. Two were just mentioned—the *instrument* used and the *person* using it. There is also the *object* being appraised and the *circumstance* of its appraisal. Thus we will measure an adult on land more precisely than a fidgeting child on a sailboat. Be that as it may, even tangible variables such as Height, Weight, and Blood Count cannot be perfectly appraised.

We have made a distinction between what we seek—the truth—and what we get. At times, the disparity is great. At other times, it is small. Nevertheless, the disparity is always there and must be accounted for. If not, we might start believing what we see. And this, for the detectives among us, can be a dangerous habit indeed.

Getting Answers to Questions

The Associated Physicians Health Maintenance Organization (AP-HMO) was losing clients and losing money. It had several choices. One of these was to try to hold on to its existing members. Another, was to attract new members.

Associated Physicians is an old institution, and most of its members are no longer youngsters. Management decided to focus on attracting younger, more profitable clientele. Telephone interviews with those who had left indicated that the HMO's services needed improvement. Yet management correctly reasoned that telephone interviewing was not the best method for getting at the truth. People's memories being imperfect, it would do better to conduct a survey at the clinics themselves.

The survey commissioned revealed a number of problems. Among these were long waiting times during the morning hours and difficulties in obtaining appointments with cardiologists. Management corrected the problems, and within months, the rate of attrition fell dramatically. Notwithstanding, the rate of new membership remained the same.

The managers of Associated Physicians had made a basic mistake. They asked one question but answered another. Their question was, "How do we encourage new membership?" Their survey answered the question, "What can we do to keep our existing members happy?"

Let us translate what happened into the language we just learned. What management really wanted to know was how to improve the HMO's service to attract younger clientele. The latent variable of interest was Service to Potential Members. What management actually measured was Service to Existing Members. But most younger members, unlike many older ones, go to work in the morning. While they would certainly prefer shorter waiting times during morning hours, it is not their major concern. Neither is the availability of cardiologists.

In the preceding section we cited several sources of measurement error. All were associated with the process of measurement itself. Here, we have another kind of error—one that resulted from choosing the wrong variable. In both cases, however, the result is the same. The information we really need is assessed inaccurately.

Now that we know more about statisticians, we can expect that they have developed a classification system for error. And they have. We will discuss this in the next section. Here, we deal with the early phases of research: the initial phase in which the question is formulated and the second phase in which the research design is specified.

Answers, like cucumbers, do not grow on trees. One should not expect the act of measuring by itself to provide adequate answers. The goal of analysis is to obtain solutions to *specific* problems, and this requires formulating specific questions. If Associated Physicians had stated their question more clearly and related it to appropriate measures, they would not have made the mistake they did.

This point is so basic and the errors associated with it so common that it deserves to be reiterated. The first step in any research is to ask a question. We know how to do this well. One has only to get stuck in an elevator with a 4-year-old to discover that we begin this early on. Yet in everyday life we seldom formulate questions precisely—there is little need. Research is different, however. Let us look at a few more examples:

1. *Personnel selection.* Pacific Cellnet, a cellular telephone service provider, was having difficulties holding on to its customer service representatives (CSRs). Personnel was unhappy because it was spending a great deal of time and money on training. Customers complained that inexperienced CSRs were providing inadequate solutions. Finally, two managers quit because they could no longer cope with the high rate of attrition in their department. As a result, Pacific decided to implement a new personnel selection program.

After 2 months, Pacific Cellnet evaluated the new program by interviewing its service managers. The feedback was reasonable, but the real test would come after 12 months—the date set for a formal evaluation. When the time came, Pacific Cellnet was faced with choosing which variable to assess. The most obvious seemed to be Employee Retention, in months—a continuous measure. However, the vice president for personnel had long maintained that, from her point of view, a CSR must remain with the company for at least 10 months before personnel could claim success. Thus the appropriate measure should be dichotomous—Ten-Month Retention (yes/no). And what about measuring Customer Complaints? After all, the new program was implemented in the hope of improving service as well. Clearly, without formulating the question precisely, Pacific Cellnet will not select the appropriate measure. If this happens, the company has little chance of getting the answer it needs.

2. *Pharmaceuticals.* We mentioned in an earlier chapter that a pharmaceutical company must demonstrate that its product is effective before placing it on the market. Asking whether a drug is effective, however, is not good enough. One must define the meaning of *Effectiveness.* If the question is, "Does it kill bacteria?" one must count Bacteria. If the question is, "Does the drug make people feel better?" one had better measure people's Feelings rather than their microbes.

3. *Advertising.* Illinois Compuware manufactures modems. In launching its new line of microproducts, the company advertised extensively in computer publications. A month passed, and Compuware wanted to evaluate the campaign's impact. But how should it do this—should it count Sales or Profits? If no dramatic change in sales was expected in the short term, it might consider measuring the change in Product Awareness instead.

4. *Traffic.* A particular stretch of California highway has been problematic. As a result, the California Highway Patrol (CHP) decided to increase enforcement on the stretch. In evaluating success, CHP can choose to measure change in average Speed, number of Fatalities, or serious Accidents. However, many other options are available, each appropriate depending on the question.

In all these examples, framing the question correctly was critical. Therefore, before we go on to worry about measurement error, we had better make sure we are measuring the right thing. Once this is done, statistics will help us get where we want to go. But not before.

Systematic and Random Errors

We noted previously that statisticians have developed a classification system for error. In the Associated Physicians example, we had what is termed *systematic error*—error that is always in the same direction. In choosing the wrong people to survey, Associated Physicians obtained data that describe the needs of existing clients better than they do those of younger potential members. Regardless of the number of times Associated Physicians conducts such surveys, the results they obtain will be *biased* in one direction. The results will provide information on one type of client only.

Polling by phone on Friday night presents a similar problem. People who are at home on Friday night may differ from those who are not. Maybe they are older, perhaps less affluent. No matter. Polling on a Friday night will always be biased in one direction, which is the reason that some survey organizations will not conduct surveys on Friday nights. A tape measure that is off by an inch on the plus side also will yield systematic error. Here too the data will regularly be biased in one direction; anyone measured will appear taller than he really is.

The second type of error statisticians distinguish is *random error*—error that can go either way with no consistent pattern. For example, measuring the height of a fidgeting child on a sailboat is difficult. At times this difficulty will cause the child to appear taller than he really is and at other times shorter. In this situation, there is no consistent pattern to the error.

Let us take a somewhat more involved example. Suppose that we have two sprinters who are equally fast—both run the 100-meter dash in 10.2 seconds *on average*. We shall say about each of these sprinters that his *true* speed is 10.2 seconds. Yet in any given competition we can expect one to win and the other to place second.

Statistically speaking, we can view our two-man race as a form of measurement—an appraisal of who is faster. When applying this measurement a number of times, we can expect different results with no consistent pattern. If our world were perfect and sprinters always ran at their true speed, all races between these two would end in ties. But they do not.

Slyly, we have slipped in the term *on average*. This is not such a simple term in this context. Recall that we stated that a sprinter's true speed is his average speed. But is this really the *truth*? Well, one can argue this way or that, but in statistics it is true. You see, because we can never truly know the latent—because all measurement is imperfect—we have no choice but to base our concept of reality on faulty measurement. It is a sad state of affairs, but this is the way it is.

Yet the idea is not without justification. The concept is more easily explained with our tried and true Height variable. Let us agree that there is such a thing as true Height and that our man, Alfred, is 6 feet tall exactly. An accurate tape measure would yield Alfred's true height if it were not for the human factor. Alfred does not always stand perfectly straight, and Regina, who measures, is not perfect either. The readings Regina obtains are sometimes above 6 feet by a tenth of an inch and sometimes below by about the same. In any event, if Regina is generally careful, her error on repeated measurements will be in both directions. It will be random.

By definition, random error varies inconsistently. Thus, if Alfred were measured several times and his measurements were averaged, the errors would cancel each other out. In the long run, averaging Alfred's results will yield the true value—6 feet. But only in the long run. This is true because even random error does not necessarily cancel out after a few measurements. Suppose that the first time Alfred was measured Regina's error was +0.06 inch and the second time it was −0.10 inch. Averaging these results will yield a result nearer the truth than either measurement by itself, but it will not be perfect. However, if Regina keeps trying, we expect that, ultimately, her *average error* will be 0 and that only the truth will remain. We say that

$$X_{observed} = X_{true} + \text{error}$$

The formula suggests that any observed measurement X contains two elements: One is the truth, and the other is the error. If the error is random, by definition, it will be about equally positive and negative. Thus, in the long run, the error will average to 0, and we shall obtain the true measurement.

Now it seems that we have gotten very statistical here. And we have. Yet we are still knee deep in everyday thinking. What this formula and the accompanying assumption about random error indicate is this: The more we measure, the nearer we approach the true value. This is something that we accept intuitively. For example, we are more willing to label someone a good student if she has scored high on several tests than if she has scored high on only one test. Similarly, we deem a poll more credible when it is conducted on 500 people than on 50.

In fact, there are countless examples that demonstrate our acceptance of the assumption that many measurements yield more accurate results than fewer measurements. For example, a fourth-grade arithmetic test typically will include a number of problems. If a teacher could measure Arithmetic Ability using only one item, he would certainly do it. But he knows that the result on a single item is likely farther from the truth than the result on many items. Similarly, when we are not sure of ourselves, we "look twice." In other words, we appraise the situation again to confirm what we see. Indeed, the very word *confirm* would not exist if one measurement were enough.

Yet again we have shown that statistical thinking mirrors something we already know. Why statistics, then? Well, one may intuit that multiple measurements lead to more accurate results. Intuition alone, however, will not tell us by *how much*. We do not say that we are twice as sure that someone is a good student when she did well on two tests as opposed to one. And how much more certain are we that team A is superior to team B if the former defeated the latter three times in a row as opposed to two?

This is not a mere technical issue. In our effort to know the truth, we measure. And if we know that our appraisals are always inaccurate, we must have an indication of the degree. More important, one needs to know how many times to "look" in order to be confident of what one sees. Only in this way can we determine how many people to survey to achieve reasonable accuracy. And only thus can we specify the number of widgets to examine to assess whether the production process in general yields quality widgets. This is the crux of the area of statistics called *estimation*.

Thus random error has its advantages. But it also can cause havoc. Thus a sprinter whose average time is 10.4 seconds will sometimes defeat a sprinter whose time is 10.2 seconds. Over many races we can expect the faster sprinter to win more than he will lose. But here again we seek redemption in the elusive long run.

Obviously, this makes for an interesting world. Indeed, we often take particular pleasure in seeing the underdog win. But while it makes for an interesting world, it also makes for inaccurate measurement. Occasionally, however, the statistician's headache is our pleasure.

CHAPTER VI

Central Tendency

WHAT WE DO

In the United States, they call him Joe. His height is average, and the color of his hair is the kind most frequently seen on Main Street. Half the people earn more than he does and half less. Pundits discuss his politics endlessly but have never discussed politics with him, let alone seen him. Still, he is not quite fiction.

He is a stereotype—Joe Average—an agglomeration of all that is most common. While stereotypes may have earned a bad reputation, we could not function without them.

At every moment our senses are bombarded with stimuli. We see colors and shapes, hear sounds, and feel textures. By themselves, these stimuli mean nothing. Only when processed in some meaningful way do they make sense. Thus, when we observe a four-legged creature that has a tail, barks, and soils our driveway, we classify it as a dog. Indeed, even if the unfortunate animal were to have three legs, it would still be classified thus. Despite its peculiarity, we stereotype it a dog.

In Chapter 3 we suggested that both statisticians and novelists had best keep to the essence. In telling their tales, they ought to select those elements which best describe what they want to describe, omitting all others.

Well, each and every one of us does this all the time. At this very moment you are reading a book. Looking at the page, you see a great many shapes that by themselves mean nothing. Only when recognized as letters, and their combinations as words, are they coherent. Even if the font were different, you would still recognize the words. A *dog* is a dog, despite the difference in form.

While all this processing is going on, you are also doing something more subtle—tuning out extraneous stimuli. You do not truly hear the sounds that surround you, nor are you aware of the surface you are sitting on. In focusing on this page, you may not even be aware of where you are.

Let us agree, therefore, that the process of understanding involves at least two activities. The first is focusing on stimuli, and the second involves filtering other stimuli out. Now, separating these two activities is artificial. After all, the very act of pinpointing light on a particular object involves dimming the light around it. Still, the distinction is useful, and we shall keep it.

When we see an object that has a trunk, branches, and leaves, we say that it is a tree. This is useful. Once we have classed the object as a tree, we know what to expect from it. We know that it needs water and will provide us with shade in summer; we also know that if it is of a certain type, it will cause a great deal of yard work in the fall. Yet even two trees of the same type are not identical. Thus, among trees that share the name *oak,* there is variation. Some are larger than others, some are old, and some are young. Still, the similarity among oaks is such that we disregard their differences and give them all the same name.

Stereotyping an object as an oak necessitates the two activities mentioned above. First, we must focus on those features which make it what it is—its "oakness." Second, we must differentiate it from other objects such as redwoods. This is done intuitively. As we have already seen, statistics often takes intuition and formalizes it. So it is here.

A brief detour is warranted. Note that our classing the object as an oak was done by choice. We could just as easily have categorized it as a tree as opposed to, say, a rock. Sometimes it is sufficient to name an object a tree. Other times it must be defined more precisely. Thus it is enough to know that the thing is a tree to conclude that one had better not try to drive through it. Yet only when we class it as an oak, as opposed to a redwood, do we know that it sheds leaves in fall. The choice is ours. However, we have no choice but to select specific features while neglecting others. Most of what we see is simply too complex for us to note all its idiosyncrasies. Therefore, if we could not stereotype—focus on similarity and disregard singularity—we could not survive.

We have described three properties that are intrinsic to every object:

1. Similarity to other objects in its own group

2. Uniqueness—divergence from objects in its own group

3. Divergence from objects not in its group

Descriptive statistics is an area of study that provides methods for describing these properties. In this chapter we are concerned with the first. More specifically, we are concerned with describing what statisticians term the *central tendency* of a group of objects—its character. Even more specifically, we aim to describe the central tendency of particular variables on which a group is measured.

An individual can be measured on a large number of variables, including Height. When describing the central tendency of the variable Height in a group of individuals, we strive for a single number that best describes the characteristic Height of the group. Now, this number, say, the average, is in some sense fictitious. In fact, there may be no single person in the group whose height is exactly average. Measures of central tendency relate to the group rather than to the individual and, as such, are stereotypes.

To this point we have sung the praises of stereotypes. They are compact and simple to comprehend. Thus the Dow Jones Industrial Average is easily understood, whereas four pages of stock quotes are just so many numbers. But there is a reason for stereotypes having earned a bad name. To the extent that they reduce complexity, they obliterate uniqueness. Our price for using measures of central tendency is *loss of information*.

Every time we summarize a set of data—represent it by something less than the complete set—we end up with less than we started out with. It is impossible otherwise. By definition, the whole of the information is embodied in the complete set, and anything less is simply that. The trick is to retain the essence and keep the loss to a minimum. Good statisticians know how to do this.

THE MEAN

Lambert Adolphe Jacques Quetelet was born in Belgium in 1796. He studied mathematics in Ghent and astronomy in Paris, and he measured anything and everything. Quetelet collected statistics on mortality, crime, and drunkenness; he measured propensity to marry and the daily temperatures between the end of the previous frost and the blooming of the common lilac. During his long life, Quetelet made contributions to disparate scientific fields. He is best known, however, for introducing the concept of the "average man." Every characteristic of man, he claimed, consists of two parts: the average of the characteristic in the group and the man's deviation from the average—the norm.

Recall that in Chapter 5 we said that any observation contains both truth and error. For example, when measuring Height we obtain a reading that, hopefully, has a large kernel of truth to it—its *essence*. But we can expect inaccuracy as well.

Quetelet conceptualized an individual's characteristics with regard to her group in a similar manner. Thus a woman's Height consists of two components:

1. The average Height of her group

2. Her peculiarity—her deviation from the average

For Quetelet, the essence of the woman's Height is the average—the *mean*—of her group. Thus, if the mean Height of Italian women is 5 feet 7 inches, the essence of every Italian woman's Height is exactly that. Uniqueness—the woman's deviation from the norm—is viewed as error and, as such, uninteresting.

Quetelet's idea was that both physical and behavioral attributes of individuals generally conform to the norm, with minor deviations only. A salient characteristic of individuals, according to Quetelet, is that they have little individuality. This assertion of regularity in both physical and behavioral human attributes caused a great deal of controversy. After all, suggesting that the essence of a person's behavior is the average of her group's behavior implies she has little free will. And this was Quetelet's point precisely.

While controversial, Quetelet's approach was typical of his times, when many people believed in a natural order—a "great clockwork." Even years later there were those who were still convinced that regularity in the affairs of the world was akin to a law of nature. The Austrian diplomat Clemens von Metternich, who worked tirelessly to maintain the old European order, would write in 1880:

> Society has its laws just as nature and man. It is with old institutions as with old men, they can never be young again. . . . This is the way of the social order and it cannot be different because it is the law of nature.[1]

It was Galton who focused on the unusual rather than the norm, who was the exception.

Our times are more confused. When we accept Quetelet's approach, we risk treading on divine individuality. If we take up Galton and focus on genius, retardation, or any other abnormality, we find ourselves more than halfway to discrimination. Be that as it may, statisticians find calculating means helpful, so we shall risk computing them ourselves. We simply add our values and divide the sum by the number of values.

$$\text{Mean of } (3, 6, 4, 5, 2) = \frac{3 + 6 + 4 + 5 + 2}{5} = 4$$

The mean is by far the most commonly used measure of central tendency. There are others, however. It would seem, though, that since the mean is simple to compute and understand, there would be no need for additional measures. Still, it has a number of limitations. Observe the following set of numbers:

$$3, 6, 4, 5, 2, 93, 97$$

Computing the mean, we obtain 30.

Technically speaking, the number 30 is a measure of central tendency. But really, it does not represent the data's tendency very well. Neither the small values, which range from 2 to 6, nor the large ones, 93 and 97, are near the mean. This example demonstrates a basic weakness of the mean: It is sensitive to *extreme values*. In statistical terms, it is not *robust*.

A possible solution is to specify two numbers to describe these data—the mean of the small values and the mean of the large values. This is a good solution. In fact, this procedure is the workhorse of a number of powerful statistical techniques that we shall discuss in later chapters. This is not the only solution, however. In the next section we will show how, if we are willing to lower our expectations, one number can still do the job.

Another limitation of the mean is that its application is limited to variables that have an interval scale or ratio scale of measurement (see Chapter 4). Recall that interval scales provide information on distance, whereas lower-level measures do not. Thus we cannot compute the mean for Hair Color, a categorical variable. Similarly, it does not make sense to say that a chess player who has been a grand master for 2 years and a master for 4 years has a mean rank in the last 6 years of a master-and-a-third. The mean is only suitable for measures that provide information on distance. Consequently, in describing the central tendency of ordinal and categorical variables, we will have to find alternatives.

Finally, the mean has a limitation common to any statistic we compute. It is only appropriate where it is appropriate. If it cannot provide a good answer, it should not be used—even if the scale of measurement allows it.

Suppose that a particular basketball team, which has a very tall center, is preparing for a game. Now tall players tend to be slower than shorter ones, and this center's abilities conform to those of his group—very tall basketball players. In making his game plan, the coach must obtain information on the height of the opposing team. Here the mean is fairly useless. Knowing that the average height of the opposition is, say, 6 feet 6 inches tells the coach little about the other team's ability to challenge his center. In this context he needs a more informative statistic. For example, it might be helpful to know how many players over 7 feet tall are on the opposing team.

Statistics can tell us which measures are technically correct. It cannot tell us which are *meaningful*. Having formulated our question, we need to choose those measures which have the potential for providing the solution we seek. To do this, we must have additional alternatives.

THE MEDIAN

Following are three sets of data:

Set *A:*	5, 5, 5, 5, 5
Set *B:*	3, 4, 5, 6, 7
Set *C:*	1, 1, 2, 4, 17

Let us summarize them as concisely as possible—tell their tale as best we can.

The mean seems as good a place to start as any. In statistics, we use the Greek letter μ (pronounced "mew") to designate the mean. Having computed μ, we find the same value in the three data sets. But the sets are different in obvious ways—by reporting only μ we have conveyed but a portion of the information inherent in each. By itself, this should not concern us. Our very use of central tendency indicates that we have reconciled to the loss of information. We no longer ask whether we have described *everything*. Rather, we ask whether we have captured the *essence*. Well have we?

Here is some of what we can say about the differences between these three distributions:

1. In set *A*, all the numbers are the same. This is not the case in sets *B* and *C*, where the numbers vary.

2. The variation in set *B* is symmetrical about the mean. In set *C*, it is not.

3. In set *C*, one number is very different from the others. While the first four numbers cluster in the range between 1 and 4, the fifth, 17, is further away. This is not the case in set *B*, where the numbers are nearer one another. It is even less so in set *A*, where the numbers are all the same.

These differences suggest something about the suitability of the mean to represent each of the sets. While μ perfectly describes set *A*, it provides a less accurate picture of sets *B* and *C*.

Let us introduce a new concept with which to evaluate whether we have described data well: *symmetry*. In set *B*, the values are distributed symmetrically about the mean. In set *C*, they are not. Specifying this criterion for evaluating central tendency, we conclude that the mean is an appropriate summary statistic for set *B*. For set *C*, it is not. When data are symmetrical, the mean's lack of robustness is not an issue—it is not pulled in any one direction.

A caution: We have said that the mean provides a suitable description of set *B* because its values are symmetrically distributed around it. Yet we can think of countless examples where this criterion is not enough. For example, in the distribution 0, 1, 11, 12, the values are spread symmetrically about a μ of 6, but none resemble it. The *distance* of the numbers from 6 suggests that the mean is not a good summary statistic for this distribution. Here we have introduced an additional criterion for suitability: *distance*. Later we will have something to say about this. For now, we shall remain with symmetry. Using this criterion alone, μ is an appropriate descriptor for set *B* but not for set *C*.

To this point we have only mentioned numerical descriptors. Yet we have an alternative that does away with central tendency altogether. Look at Figures 6-1 through 6-3. These figures present the whole of the data—they convey all the information contained in the original distributions. While this is no mean feat, it has its drawbacks. First, graphs cannot be manipulated arithmetically. For example, one cannot subtract Figure 6-1 from 6-2, an essential operation for comparing two distributions. Second, the figures just presented were simple to construct because of the small number of points involved. Presenting large data sets in graphs is more complex. While statisticians have developed graphic techniques to display large amounts of data, the first problem remains.

Note that in each of the figures we placed a fulcrum at the mean. If we treat our data points as weights corresponding to their numerical size, we

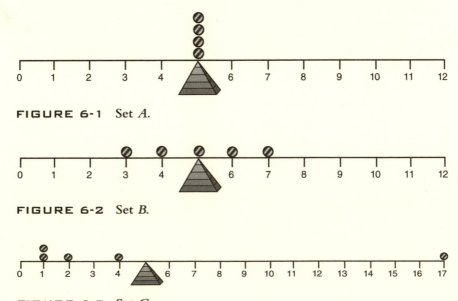

FIGURE 6-1   Set *A*.

FIGURE 6-2   Set *B*.

FIGURE 6-3   Set *C*.

find that the scale is balanced at the mean. In this sense, the mean is the "physical center" of a distribution. Interesting as this is, it still does not tell us whether it is also suitable for describing a particular set of data.

After all this, we are still left with finding an appropriate measure of central tendency for set C. Recall that our problem was the mean's lack of robustness—its sensitivity to the extreme value 17; while most of the values in set C clustered between 1 and 4, this single value pulled μ upward. Clearly, a more robust measure is called for. Such is the *median*.

The *median* is defined as the middle value in a set of data when the numbers are arranged in order of magnitude. That is, in any distribution, equal proportions of the numbers are below the median and above it. In set C, the median is 2, which summarizes the distribution tolerably well because it ignores the magnitude of the value 17. While it recognizes 17 as the largest value, it ignores its great distance from the other values. We have compromised. Having realized that there is no single number that can describe both the smaller values and the large one, we chose a statistic that describes *most* of the values in the distribution.

Figure 6-4 displays set C, indicating both its mean and median. If we were to replace the number 17 with, say, 120, the mean would increase from 5 to 25.6—an even less appropriate descriptor of the distribution. The median, however, would not change.

Examining Figure 6-4, we find that the median is smaller than the mean. This is always the case when the extreme values in a distribution are at the higher end of the scale. However, extreme values also can be small. In the distribution −8, 12, 14, 15, 17, the mean is 10, whereas the median is 14. Where extreme values are small, the mean is smaller than the median. In distributions that are perfectly symmetrical, the mean and median are identical.

Having specified both mean and median, we learn something about the *shape* of a distribution—its *spread*. The further the two are apart, the more

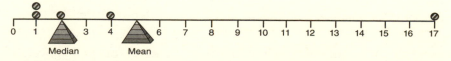

FIGURE 6-4 The median and mean in set C.

skewed is the distribution (and the less suitable is the mean). When the extreme values in a distribution are on the left—in the negative direction— the mean is smaller than the median. This is so because the mean is pulled in the negative direction, whereas the median is insensitive to these extreme values. In this case we say that the distribution is *negatively skewed*—it "trails off" to the left. When a distribution's tail is on the right—when it trails off in the positive direction—the mean is larger than the median, and the distribution is *positively skewed*.

It is now time to summarize our efforts to describe set *C*. We began with the mean and found that we had not only lost information but also had misrepresented the essence of the data. We then computed the median and found that it did a decent job of describing most of the data. But the median's strength—its robustness—caused us to ignore the magnitude of one of the values in the set. Adding the mean to our description, we gained back some of the information we had lost.

In examining the disparity between the mean and the median, we have gone beyond central tendency—we have learned something about spread as well. Central tendency provides us with a single, typical score—a particular location to which the values "aspire." While central tendency provides information on what the points have in common, spread tells us something about how they differ. Karl Pearson, Galton's student, quantified *skewness*— described shape—based on the difference between these two measures of central tendency.

The median is particularly useful when summarizing distributions that are bounded at one end of the scale but not at the other. Yearly Income, for example, can be very high but is typically not less than 0. Most people's incomes cluster at one end of the scale, whereas a few have incomes that are very high. Consequently, a typical income distribution is positively skewed, indicating use of the median. For example, in 1992 the median income for male lawyers and judges in the United States was $78,052.[2] The mean was $94,757. Thus a relatively small number of very highly paid professionals "pulled" the mean more than 20 percent above the median.

Another example is Reaction Time, that is, for example, the time it takes a driver to initiate evasive action after perceiving an obstacle on the road. The fastest times typically are around three-tenths of a second, but the slowest times can be much higher. Here again, the median does a better job describing the distribution than the mean.

We now have two alternatives for describing central tendency. In the next section we will show that in some situations neither tells our tale as we would like. Let us then proceed to our last statistical adjective for central tendency.

THE MODE

In 1972, José Ferdinand Xatral Lopez, a citizen of the Philippines, made a pilgrimage to the Holy Land. José's ancestors were Spanish, and in the Holy Land he felt a closeness to them that he had not felt before. He spent a week in Jerusalem and made the short trip to Bethlehem. He climbed Mt. Tabor and walked the steep streets of Nazareth. But it was a forgotten castle in the upper reaches of the Galilee that moved him most. Staring at the ruins, he felt nostalgia for the age of Christian soldiers. It was there that he conceived the idea of recreating times past—times, according to family tradition, in which a Lopez ancestor had fought and died in the Holy Land.

In the year 1096, Christian knights and members of medieval hosts commenced their eastward trek from France and the Low Countries. A year later they crossed the Bosphorus into Asia and made their way to Constantinople. It was the first of three major crusades—the start of a tormented time when Europeans set out to seize the Holy Land for Christianity.

Headed by nobles such as the Duke of Lorraine and brothers to the kings of England and France, the European armies fought their way southward to the Holy Land. In June of 1099, they conquered Jerusalem. On their way they passed the port city of Acre. It was through this very city that crusaders of a later generation would flee after their defeat at the hands of Saladin at Hittin—a battle that was to spell the beginning of the end of the third and last great crusade.

On his pilgrimage, José Lopez spent an afternoon in Acre and decided that it was there that he would build his monument to the past. He envisioned a restored castle inhabited by locals dressed in eleventh-century garb and engaged in the everyday activities of the times. He could almost see pilgrim visitors praying in the chapel and listening to medieval minstrels in the courtyard on summer nights.

The project meant a great deal to José, but it could only succeed if enough modern-day pilgrims found it worth the modest entrance fee.

Being a realistic man and an entrepreneur in the bargain, José commissioned a market study.

The pilgrims participating in the study were presented with the concept of Castle Crusade. They viewed sketches of the planned site and listened to a description of Lopez's vision. Each pilgrim was then asked to complete a questionnaire that included an item on his or her likelihood of visiting Castle Crusade. The answers to the item were given on a scale of 1 to 10, where 1 meant "not at all likely" and 10 meant "very likely." We shall call this variable Intent to Visit. Figure 6-5 presents the results obtained from a sample of 284 pilgrims.

In these data the mean is 6.1, and the median is 6.0. The two statistics are sufficiently similar to suggest that either could describe the data well. For José Lopez, the results were discouraging. Yet, in examining the graph, he could see that the tale was more complex than suggested by either measure of central tendency.

We noted earlier that in symmetrical distributions the mean and the median are identical; in "almost" symmetrical distributions we would expect them to be similar. And they are. However, while all more or less

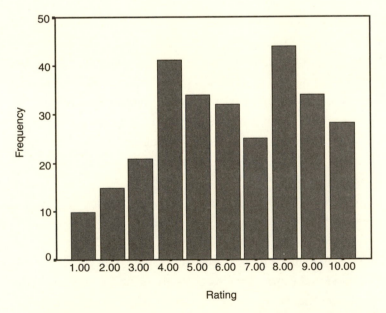

FIGURE 6-5 Distribution of Intent to Visit ratings for Castle Crusade.

symmetrical data sets yield means and medians that are similar, the reverse is not the case; not every set in which they are similar is symmetrical.

Examining the graph, we can see that the distribution of ratings appears negatively skewed—its tail stretches to the left. But the data also have a characteristic that we have yet to encounter. In the figure there are two "humps"—one at the value 4 and the other at 8. Indeed, 30 percent of all respondents gave one of these two answers. In other words, among the pilgrims, the values 4 and 8 were especially *frequent*.

For these data, neither the mean nor the median is appropriate. The former misleads because of the lack of symmetry. The latter misses the essence of the data because it says nothing about the relative popularity of the responses 4 and 8.

A statistician looking at this figure will guess immediately the reason for the humps. We shall get there soon. At this point let us just introduce a third measure of central tendency: the *mode*. The *mode* is defined as the most frequent, or popular, value in a set of data. Among José Lopez's pilgrims, the mode was 8, which was the rating given by 16 percent of the sample. However, the answer 4 also was relatively popular; 14 percent of those interviewed gave it. Because our data have two relatively popular values, the distribution is said to be *bimodal*. That is, it has two modes. Thus a reasonable way to summarize this distribution is to provide the values of the two most frequent responses—4 and 8.

A statistician looking at this distribution would conclude that these data were obtained from two different groups of individuals. To understand why this is so, let us present two examples that show this more intuitively:

1. *Income.* In many cities, wealthy neighborhoods border on poor ones. If we were to measure income in an area that includes both a wealthy neighborhood and a slum, the resulting distribution would be bimodal. Many in our sample would congregate around some lower value of income, whereas a large number would cluster around a much higher value. Although the area in which we surveyed was contiguous, those measured belong to different income groups.

2. *Height.* Suppose that we measure the height of 300 individuals visiting a mall on a Sunday afternoon. If our sample includes both males and females, we can expect a bimodal distribution. Women's average

height being somewhat lower than men's, the females in our sample would cluster around a relatively low value, whereas the males would cluster around a higher value.

In each of these examples we obtained a bimodal distribution because the sample was not *homogeneous*—it included two groups, each with a different mode (and mean).

José Lopez wanted to understand his data better. As you may recall, in statistics we understand by relating variables to one another. One of the variables measured in the market study was Country of Origin. In José Lopez's sample the variable was dichotomous, taking on values of "American" and "German." It is from these countries that the largest numbers of people make pilgrimages to the Holy Land. Graphing the distribution of Intent to Visit for each nationality separately, Lopez obtained the results shown in Figures 6-6 and 6-7.

In graphing the groups separately, we obtained two distributions, each with a single mode. Thus, by restricting our descriptions to a relatively homogeneous group of individuals, we have eliminated bimodality.

The two figures clearly show that attitudes toward Castle Crusade differ

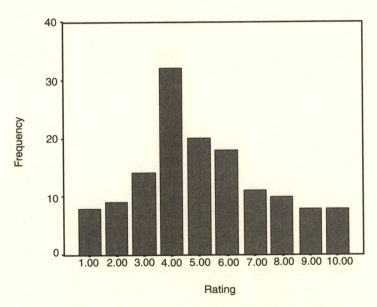

FIGURE 6-6 Distribution of Intent to Visit ratings of German pilgrims.

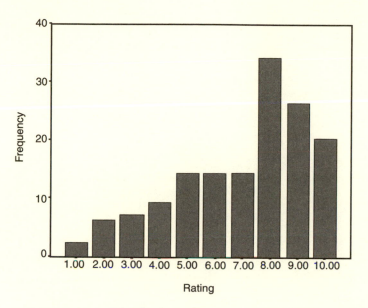

FIGURE 6-7 Distribution of Intent to Visit ratings of American pilgrims.

between the two nationalities. Whereas most German pilgrims show little interest in the site, many Americans state that they are likely to pay it a visit.

José Lopez decided to delve deeper into his data to discover why this is so. Statistically, this meant relating Intent to Visit to yet another variable. In an earlier part of the survey pilgrims had been asked about their hopes for the pilgrimage. Lopez found that Germans primarily are interested in seeing sites associated with events described in the Bible. For Germans, authenticity is crucial. Being inauthentic, a reconstructed castle is also uninteresting. Americans, on the other hand, are most interested in "experiencing" the atmosphere of the Holy Land. Any site that enhances their religious experience—be it authentic or not—is of interest.

Based on these data, José Lopez concluded that Castle Crusade has a good chance of attracting large numbers of American pilgrims and little chance of attracting German pilgrims. To obtain a specific projection for the number of visitors to Castle Crusade, Lopez summarized the data for American pilgrims as in Table 6-1. The table displays the frequency of pilgrims in each rating category. It also shows the relative percent of pilgrims in each rating. For example, 14 American pilgrims responded 7, which represents 9.6 percent of all Americans. In the rightmost column we have the

TABLE 6-1 FREQUENCY DISTRIBUTION OF INTENT TO VISIT RATINGS OF AMERICAN PILGRIMS

		FREQUENCY	PERCENT	CUMULATIVE PERCENT
Rating	10	20	13.7	13.7
	9	26	17.8	31.5
	8	34	23.3	54.8
	7	14	9.6	64.4
	6	14	9.6	74.0
	5	14	9.6	83.6
	4	9	6.2	89.7
	3	7	4.8	94.5
	2	6	4.1	98.6
	1	2	1.4	100.0
Total		146	100.0	

cumulative distribution of the ratings.* Each number in this column indicates the sum of percentage values for all the ratings from 10 down to the particular rating. For example, at 7 we have a cumulative distribution of 64.4 percent; that is, 64.4 percent of the sample gave a rating between 7 and 10. Figure 6-8 presents this cumulative distribution graphically.

The distribution shown in Figure 6-8 indicates that 55 percent of Americans gave a rating of 8 or higher. Since over 200,000 American pilgrims visit Israel every year, and since Lopez could expect at least some visitors from other countries as well, he concluded that Castle Crusade would attract at least 100,000 pilgrims yearly. His accountant had calculated that at least 70,000 visitors were needed to make the site financially viable. Based on this, José Lopez decided to proceed with his vision.

---

*Cumulative distributions typically are presented in ascending order (e.g., from 1 to 10) rather than, as here, in descending order. Since Lopez was most interested in the higher values, it was more convenient for him to use a descending cumulative distribution.

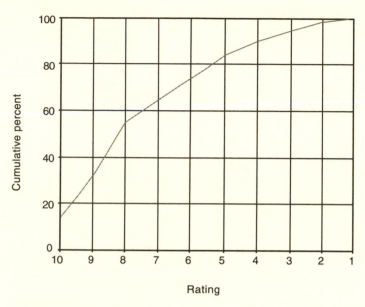

Rating

FIGURE 6-8 Cumulative percent of Intent to Visit ratings of American pilgrims.

In presenting José Lopez's market study we have demonstrated that not all numerical data can be described adequately by the mean or the median. To remedy this, we introduced the mode. The mode, however, is also particularly useful in describing the central tendency of categorical variables. Recall that in an earlier chapter we said that it makes no sense to manipulate categorical scale data numerically. Since categorical scales are nonnumerical by nature, neither mean nor median can describe them. In Chapter 4 we used as an example the sales of three games over a 6-month period (see Table 4-1). In this example, Game is a categorical variable that takes on three values: "Monopoly," "Chess," and "Scrabble." These three values cannot be placed on the kind of continuum that is used for ratio data such as Height or interval data such as Grade. While 6 feet 0 inches is greater than 5 feet 9 inches and 94 is greater than 92, Monopoly is neither larger nor smaller than Chess. It is simply different. Thus, computing the mean and median for Height and Grade is appropriate, whereas for Game it is not.

We *can,* however, state that Scrabble was the most frequently purchased game—that it was the most popular. In other words, the mode of our data is Scrabble. Figure 6-9 presents the data graphically. As you can see, Scrab-

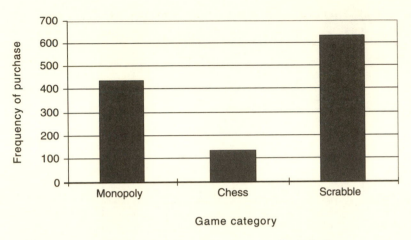

FIGURE 6-9 Sales of games over a 6-month period.

ble provides the largest bar. It is the central tendency of the distribution in the sense that more people "tend to it" than any other game.

To summarize, the mode is useful in at least two instances. For data that are at least interval, it describes the relative popularity of specific values. It is particularly helpful in describing measurements that were taken from more than one group of individuals. For categorical data, the mode is the *only* appropriate measure of central tendency.

ORDINAL SCALES AND CENTRAL TENDENCY

In this chapter we presented three measures of central tendency, all of which can be computed for interval and ratio data. We also demonstrated that the mode is an appropriate measure for summarizing categorical data. Yet all along we have avoided making mention of ordinal scales. Table 6-2 should help explain the reason.

The variable Grade is measured on an interval scale and has a mean of 86. Since the number of students is even, there is no precise middle point. In such cases the median typically is computed as the mean of the two middle values. In this case the middle values are 85 and 86, so the median is specified as 85.5.

For data such as these, it is often useful to *transform* the interval scale into an ordinal one, that is, to change the actual grades into rankings. Doing this

TABLE 6-2 GRADE AND RANK OF STUDENTS ON AN ENGLISH TEST

STUDENT	GRADE	RANK
Linda	98	1st
James	95	2d
Jeffery	91	3d
Colette	88	4th
Randy	86	5th
Abby	85	6th
Carrie	83	7th
Susan	81	8th
Alphonse	78	9th
Henry	75	10th

gives the relative rank of each student in her class, which is provided in the rightmost column. In specifying ranks, we have eliminated all information on distance. For example, based on rank alone, we no longer know that the distance between Linda and James is smaller than that between James and Jeffery. Since any other distribution of 10 grades would have yielded the same ranking scheme, neither the mean nor the mode is useful here. Finally, since each student's rank is unique,* the mode is also useless.

VOLUME DISCOUNTS

Let us return for the moment to José Lopez's market study. When presenting his conclusions, we spoke of Americans and Germans in general; we did not limit our conclusions to the specific group of pilgrims who had participated in the study. In doing this we *generalized* from a small group of indi-

---

*In cases where students earn the same grade, they are given the same rank. Thus it is technically possible for there to be a mode for ranks. In any event, it is of little use.

viduals to all German and American pilgrims. More often than not, this is the aim data collection—to learn about a large group from a subset of its members. In statistical terms, our objective is to discover something about the *population* from a *sample*. Here Lopez wished to learn about the population of all pilgrims from a sample of 284.

José Lopez had engaged in the typical human activity of looking for a discount. Having realized that to survey all pilgrims is prohibitive, he chose to measure a few instead. Now, whenever one buys at a discount, one risks a defective product. Whereas Mr. Lopez hoped that his sample would provide a good estimate of Intent to Visit among all pilgrims, he could not be sure. Statistically speaking, *estimation* of a population from a sample involves *uncertainty*.

In Chapter 5 we encountered a concept closely related to uncertainty. We called it *error*. It was noted there that any measurement contains inaccuracy. We also mentioned that statisticians distinguish two types of error—random and systematic. In selecting a sample for estimating the population, we expose ourselves to *sampling error*—a type of random error that happens when a sample does not represent the population well. If a sample markedly differs from the population it is intended to represent—if the sampling error is large—the central tendency computed will differ markedly from its true value in the population.

The issue of sampling and sampling error deserves its own chapter. It will get it. Here, we simply wish to make two points: (1) that the concepts of sample and population are central—that they account for a great deal of what we do in statistics—and (2) that in sampling we have little interest in the objects we actually measure—instead, our goal is to extrapolate from these to the population at large. For instance, when surveying the voting preferences of 500 individuals, the goal is to predict Election Outcome. This limited sample is only interesting to the extent that it provides information about the population—all those who will vote on Election Day.

A Final Word

Early on we said that a statistician's task is to tell tales. Her raw material is data, and her tools include summary statistics such as the mean, median, and mode. She also has graphic methods at her disposal.

In presenting our measures of central tendency, we showed that particular measures are sometimes technically incorrect. But we also pointed out that even when a particular statistic is technically correct, it may not necessarily be useful. Thus, while we are already knee deep in rules and regulations, we must apply common sense as well. What we have is a menu of tools from which to choose. What we do not have is a cookbook.

We also mentioned that measures of central tendency stereotype and so lead to loss of information. In particular, any specific measure of central tendency tells us nothing about the variation of the data—its spread.

Historically, this approach of focusing on stereotypes is identified with Quetelet. But there is also Galton, who focused on uniqueness—deviation from the norm. Fortunately, we need not choose between them.

CHAPTER VII

Variation

FROM SPECIFICS TO GENERALITIES AND BACK

The environment provides us with more stimuli than we can deal with, so we stereotype—extract the essence from a myriad of detail. Yet, when we do this, we necessarily disregard some information.

There is, in our brain, a constant tension between the general and specific that we are continually compelled to resolve. Thus we must decide whether to call a dwelling a "hut," a "hut with a thatched roof," or a "small, four-windowed hut with a raggedly thatched roof and red door." This "psychological back and forth" between generality and detail has its physiologic correlate. Apparently, the left side of our brain focuses on detail, whereas the right side focuses on abstraction. In everyday life, we engage in this process intuitively, almost automatically. In statistics, the procedure is formal.

One way in which we move away from specifics is by computing measures of central tendency. Yet, having computed them, we have gone to the other extreme and ignored differences altogether. Typically, we would like to retrieve some of the information lost. But not all of it. After all, focus on each and every difference and you are back at square one.

Thus our challenge becomes to find a method for summarizing differences—to compute a kind of "central tendency of differences," a single number that will represent the stereotypical *variation* in a set of data. And it will be based on distance.

DISTANCE

Very deep is the well of the past. Should we not call it bottomless?

THOMAS MANN[1]

A young boy sits at the edge of a well and contemplates his people. He looks back to his father and grandfather. He looks beyond to their forefathers. As far back as he goes, there is always farther. At a certain point he stops. Not because he has met a barrier—there is none. But because he must stop somewhere. Henceforth, time-distance will originate from this point.

The boy has placed himself at one end of a timeline. As boys do, he sees the events from the beginning of time leading up to him. But in so doing, he encounters the infinite and finds it beyond him. So he chooses an arbitrary origin. Now he is able to contemplate distance.

The boy, for whom the passage of time is marked by events, places the origin in the "days of Set." Thomas Mann writes

"From the days of Set"—young Joseph relished the phrase and I share his enjoyment. . . . Wherever I look I think of the words: and the origin of all things, when I come to search for it, pales away into the days of Set.

But in seeing only the beginning and end, one loses sight of all that is between. Not so the boy:

. . . in times long gone by—Joseph was never quite clear how far back they lay—a brooding and inwardly unquiet man, with his wife . . . had departed to do as the moon did . . . to wander and rove.

"In times long gone by," thinks the boy. But really it is not as far as all that. The brooding and inwardly unquiet man is his great grandfather—much nearer to him than Set. The man who left his home and settled in the land where years and events later Joseph is born.

Thus the young boy, who contemplates distance from the days of Set, also contemplates lesser distances. He measures all from himself, who is at the center—if not of time, then of the universe. And because he relates all points to his own, short lifetime, even the days of his great grandfather are in "times long gone by."

We have, in the boy's thoughts, three elements of distance:

1. *The greatest distance.* That between the nearest and farthest. In the collection of time events that the boy contemplates, this is the distance between himself and the days of Set.

2. *Lesser distances.* That between any point, not necessarily the nearest or farthest, and the central point. One of these is the time between the journey of the brooding man and the central point of Joseph's lifetime. Now the event of the boy's life is not the center in the sense of middle. It is the center because he *chooses* it to be. Recall, we too determine the center in various locations depending on our needs— for us there are the mean, median, and mode. All this to show that we can fix any point we wish and call it "center." Regardless, to measure distance, we must fix a point.

3. *The meaning of distance.* By itself, distance is neither great nor small. To comprehend its size, one must place it in context. When contemplating the brooding man, the young boy thinks of "times long gone by"—a great distance. However, it is only great when considered in the span of a young boy's life. When placed in another context—say, the age of the universe—the same distance is a fraction of nothing.

In our familiar prosaic language we will need to formalize these elements of distance—to measure them. Yet, before we go on to do this, we must examine reference points, without which we could not measure distance in the first place.

REFERENCES

The locating of objects in space requires *reference points*. For example, placing an object in relation to the mean puts it in a specific group, which is represented by the mean. The point in Figure 7-1 represents the mean size

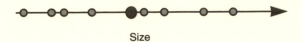

Size

FIGURE 7-1   Distribution of car sizes with one mean specified.

of eight car sizes. The sizes described in the figure share the same mean and so belong to the same group. That is, by specifying a single mean for all these numbers, we have determined that they all belong to the same group and can be represented by a single number (despite their differences). Our decision to compute a single mean for all the cars was arbitrary. But having made the decision, we assign all cars to this group, which is represented by one number—the mean.*

Uniqueness is the flip side. In it we focus on how *far* an element is from the typical point of the group. None of the points in Figure 7-1 are at the mean exactly. They are all in some sense unique. It is just that some are more unique than others. Now that we have a central point, we are able to specify a quantity for each car's distance from the mean. In addressing uniqueness, nothing has changed. We have the same distribution and the same mean; the cars are still in the same group. It is only our focus that has shifted. Instead of noting what is common to the cars—their single mean— we focus on their distance from it.

Discussing the distance *between* groups is a different story. No element can be said to be in or out of a group based on a single reference point. To most of us, an orangutan seems distant from birds, but this alone does not place it in another group. The group of All Breathing Things includes both. To place objects in different groups, we must have at least two points, for example, Things That Fly and Things That Climb. An orangutan belongs to the latter because it is nearer to it than to Things That Fly.

We shall now return to our previous example, but this time specify two points (Figure 7-2). In computing two points of central tendency, we assert that our cars do not all belong to a single class. We have created another arbitrary grouping. The triangle represents a car that is distant from both

---

*Statisticians have developed methods for determining a point's central tendency in ways that are far from arbitrary. We will get there. But we must cover a number of concepts first.

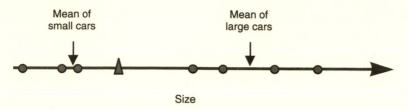

FIGURE 7-2 Distribution of car sizes with two means specified.

means. Yet because it is nearer to that of Small Cars, we say that the car is one of them. It was not the absolute distance from a single reference point that determined group membership. It was its distance from one point *relative* to its distance from another.

The real world is rarely so simple. Cars can be measured on many variables, including Color, Cost, Acceleration, and Size. Rocks can be measured on Type, Hardness, and Weight. Take any object and you will find that you can measure it on multiple dimensions. Let us then complicate matters a bit and add Acceleration to our current example (Figure 7-3). Here, too, we determine group membership based on relative distance from central tendency, designated in the figure by the larger points. But this time each central point represents two variables and is fixed at the mean of Acceleration and Size of its respective group.

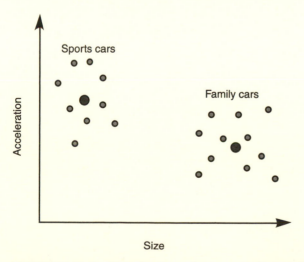

FIGURE 7-3 Distribution of cars according to Size and Acceleration.

Of course, we can define as many dimensions as suit our purpose. Yet the principle remains the same. When there is only a single point, we can measure distance, but it is always within a group. Where there are more, we can classify into separate groups.

To *interpret* distance—to give *meaning* to its size—we need something different. By itself, absolute distance is neither great nor small and must be placed in *context*. For example, the distance between Edinburgh and London is 640 kilometers. This is neither great nor small. If our mode of travel is flying—if the context within which we measure distance is flight—this is not such a great distance. If our context is driving, it is.

In the next chapter we shall present a formal procedure for creating contexts with which to evaluate distance—contexts that are based on *variation*.

Measures of Variation

Measures of central tendency are also called *measures of location*—statistics that summarize the *position* of a distribution on some scale of interest (e.g., inches, kilometers). As noted, a measure of central tendency can be viewed as what the data have in common—the "location to which they tend." In the following sections we show how to summarize *variation*, which indicates the degree to which the elements in a distribution differ—in a sense, how their locations differ.

The Range

The *range* is the distance between the largest and smallest measurements in a set of numbers. The following is a distribution of Height in centimeters:

$$172, 177, 184, 189, 192$$

Here, the range is $192 - 172 = 20$. However, in the following distribution, which is very different, the range is also 20:

$$172, 172, 172, 172, 192$$

Thus the best that can be said about the range is that it is a "quick and dirty" measure of distance. It is of limited use because in focusing only on the largest and smallest values, it ignores all that is between.

The Standard Deviation

Hans Schnier is a mime who has lost his Marie. He takes to drink and his life falls apart. He tells us[2]

> For the past three weeks I had been drunk most of the time and had gone on stage with a deceptive air of confidence, the consequences showed up faster than with a slacker in school who still retains illusions about himself right up until he gets his report; six months is a long time to dream. After three weeks there were already no more flowers in my room, by the middle of the second month I no longer had a room with bath, and by the beginning of the third month the distance from the station was already seven marks, while my fee had shrunk to a third.

As Hans drinks more and more, he is paid for his performances less and less. He can no longer stay at respectable hotels. There are no more flowers in his room. What is more, as time and drink progress, his hotel is farther from the train station: "There is a way of calculating the distance from station to hotel, from hotel to station—by taxi meter. Two marks, three marks, four marks fifty from the station." In his pain, Hans Schnier contemplates distance and measures it by the digits on a taxi's meter.

Recording the variable Taxi Fare for the third month after Hans has taken to drink, we obtain the following in deutschemarks:

$$4.9, 5.8, 6.1, 6.4, 6.3, 5.8, 5.3, 6.8, 5.3, 7.3$$

On average, his Taxi Fare is 6.0 deutschemarks. Because the data are more or less symmetrical, and because there are no extreme values, the mean is an appropriate measure of central tendency for this distribution. At the same time, in reporting only the mean, we no longer have information on how the numbers are spread out. To get a better handle on this, we construct Figure 7-4. This graph is a *histogram*, which is a commonly used method for displaying interval and ratio data. It is constructed by dividing the range of the distribution into intervals* and counting the frequency of values in each. The intervals are labeled by their respective midpoints. The height of each bar represents the *frequency* of values in each interval range.

---

*Here, as in most histograms, the intervals are of equal size.

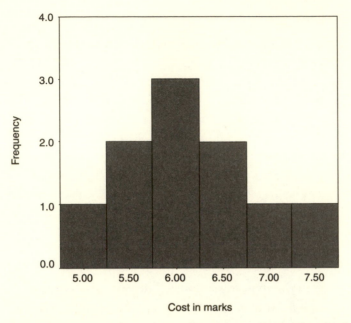

FIGURE 7-4 Histogram of Taxi Fare during the third month after the start of the binge.

For example, in the interval 5.75 to 6.25, the midpoint is 6.0 and the frequency is 3. Since there were three fares in this range, this is also the height of the bar above this interval. In Table 7-1 we arrange the data in the manner typically used for constructing a histogram.

The histogram provides a great deal of information about the distribution. Looking at it we immediately gain some information on central tendency. This results from identifying the tallest bars, which are placed on the intervals that include the largest number of values. The histogram also provides us with an estimate of the range, and finally, it describes the shape of the distribution—its spread.

Note the following:

1. As is always the case when summarizing data, the histogram leads to loss of information. For example, we know that there were three values between 5.75 and 6.25, but we do not know their values. Based on the figure alone, we do not even know their mean. Instead, we regard them all as 6.0, which is the midpoint of the interval. Yet none of the values in the interval are at the midpoint exactly.

TABLE 7-1 CLASSIFIED TAXI FARE DATA

INTERVAL	MIDPOINT	VALUES	FREQUENCY	PERCENT
4.75–5.25	5.0	4.9	1	10
5.25–5.75	5.5	5.3, 5.3	2	20
5.75–6.25	6.0	5.8, 6.1, 5.8	3	30
6.25–6.75	6.5	6.4, 6.3	2	20
6.75–7.25	7.0	6.8	1	10
7.25–7.75	7.5	7.3	1	10

2. Because the interval 5.75 to 6.25 contains the largest number of values, we say that it is the mode. This does not conform to our original definition of the mode, which is the most frequent value in a distribution. After all, the values in the interval—5.8, 6.1, and 5.8—are not all the same. As we shall see, this definition of the mode turns out to be very useful. Sometimes, it is the only one possible.

Thus the histogram provides us with just about all the (summarized) information we need. But graphs are of limited use in that they cannot be manipulated mathematically. Having already presented numerical descriptions for central tendency, we must now devise quantitative ones to summarize variation. We already mentioned one—the range. But the range is of limited use.

Recall that distance can only be measured after we have fixed a point. Nothing is more natural than measuring distance from the central point. In the distribution of taxi fares, we measure distance from the mean. More generally,

$$\text{Distance} = \text{individual observation} - \text{mean} = x - \mu$$

where μ represents the mean, and x is a specific observation in a distribution.

Conceptually, it is natural to view a specific element's uniqueness as its distance from the single value that represents its group. In any collection of numbers there are as many distances from the mean as there are numbers.

An obvious measure of dispersion—of variation—is the mean of these distances, which is expressed as follows:

$$\text{Mean of distances} = \frac{\text{sum of individual distances from the mean}}{\text{number of distances}}$$

In our distribution of taxi fares, we have

$$\text{Mean of distances} = \frac{(4.9 - 6) + (5.8 - 6) + \cdots + (7.3 - 6)}{10}$$

$$= \frac{-1.1 + (-0.2) + \cdots + (1.3)}{10} = 0$$

We have a problem. In any distribution the sum of distances from the mean is always 0. As a result, the average distance from the mean will always be 0 as well. This is a mathematical characteristic of the mean. While an interesting attribute, it is also troublesome. The obvious solution is to ignore the sign of each individual distance and take its absolute value. That is, to always take the positive distance. Doing this here we obtain:

$$\text{Mean of absolute distances} = \frac{|4.96 - 6| + |5.8 - 6| + \cdots + |7.3 - 6|}{10}$$

$$= \frac{1.1 + 0.2 + \cdots + 1.3}{10} = \frac{5.8}{10} = 0.58$$

It would seem, then, that we have developed a straightforward method for summarizing variation in a distribution. Yet there remains a difficulty. Statisticians find it cumbersome to manipulate absolute values mathematically and avoid it when they can. The alternative they choose is to square the distances rather than to take their absolute values. This also ensures that the numbers are always positive. Substituting squared distances into our preceding formula, we obtain the *variance*:

$$\text{Variance} = \sigma^2 = \frac{(4.9 - 6)^2 + \cdots + (7.3 - 6)^2}{10} = \frac{1.1^2 + \cdots + 1.3^2}{10} = 0.49$$

In (not so plain) English, the *variance* is the average of squared deviations from the mean.

The variance has a drawback, however. In computing it, we square distances and so lose our original metric. To remedy this, we take the square root of our result and so retrieve the original scale:

Standard Deviation = σ

More formally:

$$\sigma = \sqrt{\frac{\Sigma(x-\mu)^2}{n}} = \sqrt{\frac{(4.9-6)^2 + \cdots + (7.3-6)^2}{10}} = \sqrt{\frac{1.1^2 + \cdots + 1.3^2}{10}} = 0.70$$

The symbol Σ indicates that we are summing. Here we are asked to sum the squared distance from the mean of the individual values in a distribution.

This formula nicely expresses what we want to achieve, which is to summarize variation in a distribution. Using it, we compute each value's deviation from the mean—its uniqueness. Then, taking the average, we produce a measure of "average uniqueness." Finally, taking the square root returns us to the units with which we began.

We are well aware that the term *average uniqueness* is a bit awkward. After all, *average* refers to the norm, and *uniqueness* refers to the opposite. At the same time, this term expresses well what σ describes. For example, in the distribution 4, 4, 4, the mean is 4 and the standard deviation, the average squared distance of the values from the mean, is 0. In the distribution 1, 4, 7, the mean is again 4, but σ is 2.45.[*] The uniqueness in the second distribution is, on average, larger than in the first. Thus, in computing σ, we have produced a measure of "average uniqueness." Once again we encounter a mean. But this time it is not a mean of points but a *mean of distances.*[†]

An additional note: The standard deviation is computed by averaging distance from the mean. Alternatively, we could have chosen to measure distance from any other point. What makes the mean special is that it minimizes the sum of squared distances from the mean. In other words, using in our formula any value other than μ will always yield a larger average distance.

For each distribution we can now specify two numbers:

1. The mean, which describes location "in general"

2. The standard deviation, which summarizes the degree to which the numbers in the distribution differ from the mean

---

[*] Here, the variance is $2.45^2 = 6.0$. Note that 6.0 is greater than any single distance from the mean in the distribution. This example shows plainly why the variance is not intuitively meaningful, which is why we typically take its square root when describing variation.

[†] Actually, it is a mean of squared distances, which is different from the mean of absolute differences. With your permission, and for conceptual convenience, we shall call it the mean of distances nevertheless.

Having done this, we have provided a partial solution for the information lost when specifying central tendency alone.

This is a typical statistical comprise. On the one hand, we concede that we cannot deal with distributions at the level of its individual elements. On the other, we say that summarizing a distribution using a single number—central tendency alone—is far too simplistic. Therefore, we specify another, single number for variation as well.

CHAPTER VIII

Putting Distance in Context

RELATIVE DISTANCE

My how time flies.

A LADY IN KENT

We previously asked whether the 640 kilometers between London and Edinburgh is a great distance and answered that it is impossible to know. To evaluate distance—to give it *meaning*—requires more than mere points on a map. So we pointed out that 640 kilometers is more for driving than it is for flying. In saying this, we left our map and entered Mode of Travel. Of course, we might have chosen other contexts. Thus 640 kilometers is a greater distance for laying railway tracks than for laying power lines. And it is nothing for communicating by phone and something else again for sending a message by carrier pigeon. Be that as it may, to evaluate the relative magnitude of distance, we must have a context.

Hans Schnier, of mime and drinking fame, writes[1]

> Of course I could continue to make the rounds of the cheap music halls at the thirty to fifty mark level. . . . I didn't really mind, in those low-class places the audience is really nicer than in the vaudeville theaters. But thirty to fifty marks a day is simply not enough, the hotel rooms are too small, you

keep bumping into tables and chairs while you are practicing, and I don't feel . . . that, when you travel with five suitcases, a taxi is an extravagance.

In comparing the cost of a taxi to Pay, Hans places Taxi Fare in a context outside of it. We learn that 14 deutschemarks for a round trip is substantial—a third, sometimes half of his Pay. There is little left over for schnapps and cigarettes, not to mention luxuries.

This is one approach to rendering distance meaningful and, for the statistician, inconvenient. First, he must seek out additional variables—by itself, distance in kilometers will not do. Second, by invoking concepts outside his distribution, he concedes that there is no single criterion for evaluating distance.

Recall that in computing a reference point for distance, we had no such problem. There we used the mean, which was based on the data at hand. Once computed, all distances were measured from it. In the same way, it would be convenient to give meaning to distance while remaining within our numbers. Well, this is not very difficult.

Hans also tells us

There is a way of calculating the distance from station to hotel, from hotel to station—by the taxi meter. Two marks, three marks, four marks fifty from the station. . . . by the beginning of the third month the distance from the station was already seven marks.[a]

"Already seven marks"—a great deal—substantial when compared with the two and three deutschemarks he had been paying. Here Hans compares the numbers within his distribution to one another and so remains within a single context—Taxi Fare.

Alas, everything is relative. In one context a Taxi Fare of seven deutschemarks is significant relative to Pay. In another, it is substantial compared with other fares. Either way, the word *relative* is one of those terms we will need to define more precisely.

THE STANDARD SCORE

Consider the familiar distance

$$\text{Distance} = \text{uniqueness} = x - \mu \tag{8.1}$$

We have said often enough that by itself this absolute distance is of limited use. A natural yardstick for assessing relative magnitude is the average distance in the group. For us this means contrasting a specific distance with that typical in its distribution. We have

$$\text{Relative distance} = \text{relative uniqueness} = \frac{(\text{absolute distance})}{(\text{average distance})} \quad (8.2)$$

The formula has two elements, both of which we know to compute. *Absolute distance* is obtained by subtracting the mean [Equation (8.1)]; *average* distance is the standard deviation (σ; see Chapter 7). Substituting into Equation (8.2), we have

$$\text{Standard score} = z = \frac{\text{individual observation} - \mu}{\sigma} = \frac{x - \mu}{\sigma} \quad (8.3)$$

Here, we compute the ratio of a specific distance to the average distance in a distribution. When z is 0, an object is perfectly typical—it is at the mean. When z is 1, the object is of "typical uniqueness"; it differs from central tendency neither more nor less than is average.[*] The greater z, the more unique is the object.

Standard scores express distance in units of σ. For example, a z of 1.5 tells us that an observation is one and one-half standard deviations above the mean; a z of -0.33 tells us that it is one-third of a σ below.

Observe the following distribution of heights in centimeters:

$$174, 169, 183, 181, 176, 199, 178, 177$$

Here:

$$\mu = 179.6$$
$$\sigma = 8.9$$

Computing a standard score for the person nearest the mean we have:

$$z = \frac{178 - 179.6}{8.9} = -0.2$$

Computing it for the tallest person we have:

---

[*]That is, average as defined by the formula for σ.

$$z = \frac{199 - 179.6}{8.9} = 2.2$$

As you can see, the person nearest μ has a score near 0, whereas the tallest has a score more than twice 1. In fact, we can say that the tallest person is about 10 times farther from the mean in average distance terms than the one nearest.[*] We can say this because standard scores are measured on a ratio scale (see Chapter 4). This is so because they possess the following two characteristics:

1. Similar distances have similar meanings. For example, the difference between a z of 2 and a z of 3 is equal to that between 3 and 4—both indicate a distance of one standard deviation.

2. z has an absolute zero. When $z = 0$, there is, in fact, "no distance"—the particular number is at the mean.

In computing z we *transform* raw data points into standard scores. More generally, transformations convert numbers into other numbers using specific rules.

To summarize, standard scores specify *relative distance* from the mean within a distribution—relative, that is, to other distances in the distribution. It is important to understand that σ *is just another unit of measurement.* To date, we have measured in miles, pints, pounds, and gallons. We can now add another unit to our list.

A note: The z score is also called a *standard score* because it standardizes distributions—transforms them to look the same in the sense that

1. All values have the same mathematical meaning—they are distances expressed in σ.

2. The mean of z values is always 0.

This first characteristic of transforming different measurements onto a common scale is something that we do all the time. For example, we might say that a 6-year-old dog is about as old as 37-year-old human because both

---

[*]We have ignored the sign because what we wish to assess is relative uniqueness—difference from the mean regardless of direction. In these terms, a score of −0.2 is equally unique (or typical) as +0.2. Both indicated an identical distance from the mean.

have lived about half their expected life span. In dividing "dog years" and "human years" by Life Expectancy, we placed them on a common metric of "years lived relative to life expectancy" and can compare them. The second characteristic noted relates to an attribute of the mean mentioned in Chapter 7—that the sum of distances from the mean is always 0.

Thus, by standardizing distributions, we also allow for comparisons between them. For example, in the United States, final high-school grades are usually given on a scale of 1 to 4. In many other countries, the scale is 1 to 100. Suppose that at Robert E. Lee High School

$$\mu = 3.2 \quad \text{and} \quad \sigma = 0.2$$

and at Charles De Gaulle High School

$$\mu = 76 \quad \text{and} \quad \sigma = 7$$

Based on this, we say that a grade of 3.6 at Robert E. Lee is equivalent to 90 at De Gaulle. In both cases, $z = 2$. That is, students earning these grades are equally above the mean in their respective schools.

So it seems that we have devised a method for giving meaning to distance. And we have. What is more, the method enables comparisons between values measured in different units. But we are not out of the woods yet. A moment ago we claimed that z allows for making definitive statements about a number's relation to its distribution. Well, we have slightly overdone it.

A FLY IN THE OINTMENT

Table 8-1 presents two distributions consisting of 11 numbers each. A quick glance at the values in distributions A and B shows an obvious difference between them. These can be seen clearly from Figures 8-1 and 8-2.

In distribution B, the numbers are clustered in the intervals between 4.5 and 9.5. Also, there is one relatively large value. In distribution A, there are many observations in the interval 8.5 to 9.5. In addition, another interval contains two data points, whereas all the others include one observation at most. In other words, the *density* patterns of the two distributions differ. Still, distributions A and B have similar means and standard deviations so that comparable values from them will yield comparable z scores. In distribution A,

TABLE 8-1 TWO DISTRIBUTIONS

DISTRIBUTION	VALUES IN THE DISTRIBUTION	N^a	μ	σ
A	9.14, 8.14, 8.74, 8.77, 9.26, 8.10, 6.10, 3.10, 9.13, 7.26, 4.74	11	7.5	1.93
B	7.46, 6.77, 12.74, 7.11, 7.81, 8.84, 6.10, 5.39, 8.15, 6.42, 5.73	11	7.5	1.93

[a]The symbol N typically is meant to represent the number of elements or observations in a distribution. In this case, each of the distributions consisted of 11 observations.

Source: Adapted slightly from Anscombe, F. 1973. Graphs in statistical analysis. *The American Statistician,* 27:17–21.

$$z_{6.10} = \frac{6.10 - 7.5}{1.93} = -0.73$$

which is the same z yielded by the value 6.10 in distribution B.

Based on z, we say that the data point 6.10 has the same meaning in both distributions. Looking at the histograms, however, we get a different picture. In distribution B, 6.10 is in the "mainstream"—it resides in the area

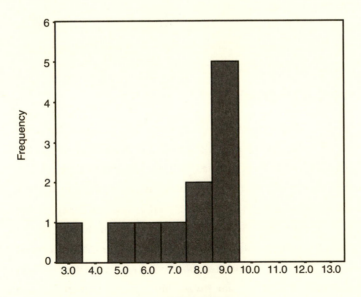

Distribution A

FIGURE 8-1 Histogram of distribution A.

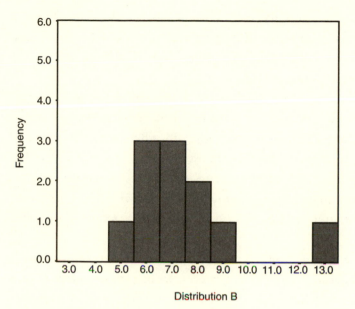

Distribution B

FIGURE 8-2 Histogram of distribution B.

of greatest density and so can be considered typical. In distribution A, this same value "stands alone." There is no other value in its interval, and it is surrounded by intervals containing one value only.

To understand what happened here, let us recall a characteristic of the mean already noted (see Chapter 6). The mean is not *robust*—it is sensitive to extreme values. For example, the distribution

$$2, 2, 3, 3, 3, 3, 4, 4, 6, 100$$

has a mean of 13, much larger than most of the values in it. More generally, the mean is greatly influenced by the *shape* of a distribution. It should be no surprise that being a kind of mean (of distances) itself, σ is not robust either—it too is sensitive to shape. Consequently, distributions that differ in one or a few outlying values only may yield very different standard deviations.

In a sense, σ is even less robust than the arithmetic mean. Remember that all distances used to compute it are squared and so are positive. As a result, outlying values will produce large distances that do not, as in the case of the arithmetic mean, "balance out." Here, this lack of robustness was used to achieve an opposite result. Shapes were chosen such as to equalize mean and σ values despite apparent differences. Either way, the implication is clear: Standard deviations of different distributions can have different meanings. It follows that z values that place numbers in the context of σ can have different meanings as well.

Another way of looking at these data is by examining the *mode*. Recall that the mode is that part of the distribution containing the greatest number of observations—the most popular value. In other words, the mode is that area of the distribution with the greatest density. Distributions A and B have different modes. Consequently, the relation of z to the mode also differs between them. In distribution B, the observation 6.10 is near the mode of 6.5.* In distribution A, this value is relatively distant from the mode, which is 9.

All this implies that without knowing shape, the meaning of z is equivocal. We shall vindicate z soon. First, however, we need to introduce a concept that for you is old hat.

PERCENTILES

Liberal Arts University only accepts students who finished in the top 10 percent of their class. Conservative University takes them where it can get them. Shirley finished in the 95th percentile at Robert E. Lee High School and has a good chance of attending Liberal Arts University. By definition, 94 percent of the students at Robert E. Lee High School achieved grades that were lower than Shirley, and only 5 percent achieved higher grades.

To obtain *percentile*, we arrange all observations in order of magnitude. For any particular observation, the *percentile* is defined as the proportion of observations below it. Thus, if 94 percent of students at Robert E. Lee High School scored below 3.6, anyone achieving this grade is at the 95th percentile. Similarly, if 94 percent of Charles De Gaulle High School students scored below 90, the grade is at the 95th percentile.

In computing percentile, we have again transformed the data. And, as in z, we have made the distributions comparable. Thus, while the values 3.6 and 90 are very different, their percentile score suggests an equivalent meaning.

---

* Here, as in the preceding chapter, the *mode* is defined as the interval containing the largest number of values—the one with the tallest bar.

TABLE 8-2 GRADE AND RANK OF STUDENTS ON MIDTERM AND FINAL ENGLISH EXAMINATIONS

STUDENT	MIDTERM		FINAL	
	GRADE	RANK	GRADE	RANK
Linda	98	1st	100	1st
James	95	2d	99	2d
Jeffery	91	3d	98	3d
Colette	88	4th	97	4th
Randy	86	5th	90	5th
Abby	85	6th	87	6th
Carrie	83	7th	86	7th
Susan	81	8th	83	8th
Alphonse	78	9th	82	9th
Henry	75	10th	63	10th

To understand the relation of percentiles to raw scores, look at Table 8-2. The first three columns in this table are identical to a table presented in Chapter 6. But we have also added grades and ranks for a second examination. The students taking these examinations have retained their *relative standing* on the two tests. But while their ranks have remained the same, each student's distance from other students—and from the mean—has definitely changed.

Rank is an ordinal variable and provides no information on distance. What we have, then, are identical percentiles that imply different distances. For example, the 90th percentile on the midterm is farther from the top score than 90th percentile is on the final.

Thus, while percentiles provide a measure of *relative standing,* they do not provide a measure of *relative distance.* By transforming grades into percentiles, we have changed a scale from interval to ordinal. We have lost information.

We now expand our table to include z scores (Table 8-3). As you can see, the students have retained their relative standing but not their z scores—their relative distance from the mean has changed. For example,

TABLE 8-3 GRADE, RANK, AND STANDARD SCORES OF
STUDENTS ON MIDTERM AND FINAL ENGLISH EXAMINA-
TIONS

STUDENT	MIDTERM			FINAL		
	GRADE	Z	RANK	GRADE	Z	RANK
Linda	98	1.65	1st	100	1.02	1st
James	95	1.24	2d	99	0.93	2d
Jeffery	91	0.69	3d	98	0.84	3d
Colette	88	0.28	4th	97	0.76	4th
Randy	86	0.00	5th	90	0.13	5th
Abby	85	−0.14	6th	87	−0.13	6th
Carrie	83	−0.41	7th	86	−0.22	7th
Susan	81	−0.69	8th	83	−0.49	8th
Alphonse	78	−1.10	9th	82	−0.58	9th
Henry	75	−1.52	10th	63	−2.27	10th

Henry, who earned the lowest score on both tests, is farther away from the
mean on the final exam than on the midterm.

To this point we have used histograms to describe the shape of distributions. Let us introduce another graphic technique—the *boxplot* (Figure
8-3). Boxplots provide compact descriptions of distributions. The upper-
most line in each plot—the upper *hinge*—represents the value of greatest
magnitude in the distribution; that is, the value at the 100th percentile. The
lower hinge represents the smallest value.

The upper and lower frames of the box indicated the 75th and 25th percentiles, respectively. In other words, the box represents that area of the distribution that includes the middle half of the observations. The thick line
within the box is the median, or 50th percentile.

Here are some of the things we can say by simply examining the boxplots:

1. The distribution of the midterm grade is relatively symmetrical. The
   distance between the lower and upper hinges and the median is sim-

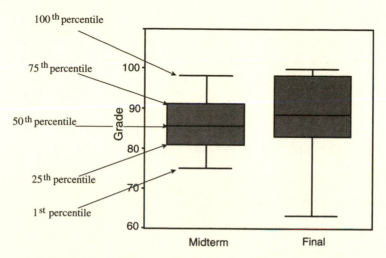

FIGURE 8-3 Boxplots of midterm and final examination grades.

ilar; the distances between the lower and upper frames of the box and the median are similar as well.

2. The distribution of the final grade is clearly asymmetrical. The distance between median and upper frame of the box is much greater than that between the median and lower frame. Also, the maximum score is much nearer the middle than is the minimum.

3. The range on the final grade is greater than the range on the midterm grade.

All this to say that only when we know shape can we know the meaning of *z in terms of relative standing*. In other words, different distances can imply identical percentiles. The converse is true as well. It follows that *comparing z scores from different distributions is appropriate only when the distributions are similarly shaped*.

Now grades typically are distributed in the same manner regardless of school. Most students are near some middle value, and a few are distant on either side. Assuming similar shapes, our comparison between Robert E. Lee High School and Charles De Gaulle High School is appropriate. But this is only an assumption. To know this for a fact, we would need to compare shapes formally. As you might expect, statisticians have developed methods for doing this. But this is getting ahead of the game. Besides, it is not the issue here.

Now recall our claim that the further z is from 0, the more exceptional the observation. As rules of thumb go, this is not bad. Still, it is far from precise. The fact remains that similar z values can have different meanings in terms of relative standing (percentiles), and our rule of thumb is lacking.

RELATIVE STANDING AND RELATIVE DISTANCE

You can't always get what you want.

TWENTIETH-CENTURY FOLK SONG

After all this, you may ask why we bother with z at all. We began with a problem—the equivocal nature of distance. This led to a need to go beyond mere absolute distance and give it meaning as well. At first, it seemed that appealing to contexts outside our distribution could only do this. We did not like this. It meant that in every instance we must seek a specific context that makes sense. Thus we asked whether this could be done using the numbers available only. We answered that, "Yes, it can." More specifically, we computed the ratio of absolute distance to average distance in the distribution. This yielded z—the distance of an observation from its mean in units of σ.

We were content. Now, all data points were expressed in similar units—units of standard deviation. Being standard units, these also enabled comparisons between values measured in completely different units. For example, grades at Robert E. Lee High School could now be compared with those at Charles De Gaulle High School.

Yet our bliss was short-lived. We went on to show that z's meaning is inconsistent—that it depends on the shape of a distribution. Put another way, the same *relative distance* can represent different *relative standing*. We showed this by relating standard scores to percentiles.

Still, hope was not lost. After all, when a distribution's shape *is* known, z is meaningful. What is more, when two distributions have similar shapes, we can use standard scores to compare between them. Thus, while we had not gotten all that we had wanted, we had gotten something.

All this implies that in the future we must limit our z comparisons to similarly shaped distributions. Now this is not as bad as it seems. As it turns out, many distributions are similarly shaped. For example, many conform to what we call the *normal distribution*. All normal distributions look the same. But again, we have strayed.

Getting back to the issue at hand, we say that relative distance (z) and relative standing (percentile) are equivalent in specific circumstances. Let us then use relative distance only in such circumstances. But this seems foolish. After all, why not use percentile only and ignore the issue of shape altogether. Unlike standard scores, percentiles *always* have the same meaning. For example, in all distributions, 57 percent of data points are smaller than the observation at the 58th percentile. If we stick to rank, there is no need to worry about shape.

The truth is, we have already answered this question in the preceding section. We wrote

> Thus, while percentiles provide a measure of relative standing, they do not provide a measure of relative distance. By transforming grades into percentiles, we have changed a scale from interval to ordinal. We have lost information.

Where possible, we would like to get what we want. In this case we wish to have

1. Measures of distance that are meaningful

2. Meanings that are invariant across distributions, that is, measures that have clear implications for relative standing

3. Meanings that can be computed using numbers at hand—that do not require external contexts

It seems that while *we* may be reasonable, our demands are not. Using z, we have relative distance on a ratio scale. But we do not have invariant meaning in terms of relative standing. Using percentiles, we have invariant meaning on relative standing but not relative distance.

We are now faced with choosing between two solutions, each with its advantages and disadvantages. However, there is also a third: Use z, and where shape is known, relative standing is known as well.

A Peek Ahead

In statistics we describe numbers. Yet often we wish to compare between them as well. For example, one might wish to know whether a particular variety of cow yields more milk than another. Another person may want to assess the relative effectiveness of two medications measured on a quantitative parameter such as Fever Reduction. All such comparisons require measuring distance. And all distances must be placed in context.

We now know that our statistician has at her disposal two methods for giving meaning to distance while remaining in her distribution: standard scores and percentiles. We also know her preference. She would like to use a measure that yields accurate information on both relative distance and relative standing, that is, z.

Where the shapes of distributions are known and are known to be similar, our statistician will have her wish. Otherwise, she will have to do with less. In statistics, comparative procedures that use information on distance are called *parametric* techniques. They are so named because they assume that the distributions compared have known parameters that relate to shape and that these parameters are similar. *Nonparametric* techniques do not assume this.

For our statistician, parametric and nonparametric tests are diagnostic tools. They enable her to detect differences between phenomena. Using more information, parametric techniques generally are more powerful than their nonparametric brethren.

Since we have yet to introduce comparative procedures, this may all sound a bit vague. The principle, however, should be clear regardless. As early as Chapter 4 we distinguished between scales based on the amount of information they provide. In the same chapter we wrote that, in general, one ought to choose the most informative scale available. It follows that statistical procedures based on interval and ratio scales generally are more useful than those based on ordinal or categorical scales. Still, there is information and there is information.

A Robust Measure of Spread

Suppose that a sprinter had never run the 100-meter dash in more than 11 seconds in official competition. However, in a recent race he sprained an ankle and was clocked at 16.3 seconds. Clearly, such information is worse than no information at all. In computing his typical speed—the central tendency of the sprinter's speed—we would do well to ignore this very slow time.

It is for cases such as this that we introduced the median—a robust measure of central tendency. By definition, the median is the 50th percentile. Using it, we ignore distance and, in this case, provide a more accurate picture of that which is typical in the distribution. The median's apparent weakness—its disregard of information on distance—can, in some situations, also be its strength.

So it turns out that in some instances it is better to use less information than more. For central tendency, the median fits this bill. Being the 50th percentile, the median is an ordinal measure of central tendency and so is unaffected by extreme values. Well, it would be nice to have a robust measure of variation as well. This is so for cases where we would like to describe variation in a distribution that includes extreme values. Recall that σ, like μ, is sensitive to extreme values.

Earlier in the chapter we presented boxplots (see Figure 8-3). In essence, the boxplot is an "ordinal graph"; its major elements—its hinges and box frames—represent percentiles. Yet the boxplot also provides information on distance between quartiles. For example, using the boxplot, we can measure the distance between the 25th and 50th percentiles, that is, the range between the lower quartile and the median.

By definition, the values in the middle quartiles in any distribution are not extreme. They are the "heart" of the distribution. Being ordinal measures, quartiles are not sensitive to extreme values. For example, the smallest 10 percent of observations can be relatively large in magnitude or relatively small, but this will in no way affect the spread of the middle 50 percent of values.

It follows that the *interquartile range*—the range described by the box— is a robust measure of spread. It tells us the range within which the middle 50 percent of observations reside and is not influenced by extreme values.

In the interquartile range we have a robust alternative to σ. The interquartile range is to variation as the median is to central tendency. Both statistics ignore some of the information in a distribution in favor of presenting a total picture that may be more realistic.

Now, wherever we can we would like to use the σ. After all, it is measured on a ratio scale and so provides information on distance. The interquartile range, on the other hand, is an ordinal measure. It tells us nothing about what is happening inside the middle 50 percent. In an extreme example, one value in the interquartile range is large, another is small, and all others are at the median exactly. Here, the interquartile range is determined by two values that do not represent the others very well. Still, when a distribution "looks weird," σ can be very misleading. In later chapters we will explain what we mean by the term *weird* in the context of the shape of distributions.

In introducing the interquartile range we have detoured. Our main concern in this chapter is to give meaning to distance. In doing this, we showed ways to compare observations within and between distributions. In this section, however, we tackled another issue—that of finding a robust alternative to the σ. Yet the two topics are very much related. Thus it is the standard deviation's lack of robustness that causes distance to be problematic, and it is this very same characteristic that required us to find an alternative for it.

In the next chapter we shall summarize what we have learned so far. Also, we will clear our desk of a number of essential concepts that are critical for moving forward. So let us move forward.

CHAPTER IX

Descriptive Statistics: A Review and More

WHY WE DO IT

1. I think it's going to rain.

2. Satisfied customers are loyal.

3. A new generic drug must be equivalent to the original it aims to reproduce.

These statements are taken from Chapter 2. In the first, a woman discusses the weather with herself, contemplating an umbrella on her way out. She has looked out her window and seen clouds. In the second, a market researcher relates his thoughts on customer satisfaction. In the third, a regulatory agency specifies its requirements for the approval of a generic drug.

None of these statements is precise. The woman attaches no specific probability to her prediction of rain, whereas the market researcher has defined neither *satisfaction* nor *loyalty*. The regulator demands *equivalence* but has yet to specify what this means.

In Chapter 2 we noted that everyday communication is rarely very accurate. We seem to get along fine as is. Yet there are circumstances that require precision. It is for this reason, in part, that we do statistics.[*]

---

[*] Of course, there are other disciplines that can help us communicate more precisely. However, *this* book is about statistics.

Using statistics, we attach quantities to statements. "Thinking" it will rain becomes "80 percent chance of showers" and "satisfied" becomes a value on a scale of 1 to 5. At Xerox, "more loyal" translates into "six times more likely to buy a Xerox product in the coming 18 months." For a regulator, "equivalence" might mean "within 5 percent of each other."

Thus we do statistics to communicate more precisely. However, there is also the question of integrity. At times we are asked to put our version of reality on the line—to test it. This is a kind of "putting our numbers where our thoughts are." For example, when a good market researcher claims that Customer Satisfaction leads to Brand Loyalty, he demands proof of himself. He goes out and collects data and analyzes them. Based on his results, he discovers whether or not the statement he has made is correct.

How We Do It: Dealing with Error

In our efforts to be precise, we measure. Even when measuring, however, we are not perfectly precise. More formally:

$$x = \text{truth} + \text{error}$$

We say that any measurement x contains an element of truth and an element of error. In statistics, we distinguish two types of error: *random* and *systematic*. Random error, we believe, displays no particular pattern—at times it will cause our results to be overestimates and at times underestimates. Averaging multiple measurements will "cancel out" random error. Where there is only random error, the more we measure, the nearer the truth we get, on average.

But there is also systematic error, or *bias*. Bias is always in one direction and cannot be eliminated by multiple measurements. We deal with this kind of error by using our heads. First, we need to articulate our research questions clearly. For example, when conducting an election poll, we must define precisely what it is we wish to know. In the case of a poll, this is straightforward—we wish to predict an election's outcome. Having formulated our question well, we now know that (1) we ought to survey only those who plan to vote and (2) our question must relate directly to voting. For example, we should ask, "Who will you vote for?" rather than, say, "Who do you like?"

Usually it is not so simple. For instance, when measuring Mathematics Ability, we need to make certain that this is all we measure. If, for example, a teacher includes "word questions" on her examination, she may obtain information on English Ability as well as Mathematics Ability. In other words, her grades will be biased by something she had not meant to measure. Thus a student may know mathematics well but do badly on the test because he does not know English. Only by defining the research question clearly can the teacher eliminate bias on her test.

Research yields data. More often than not, research yields a great deal of data—much more than is easily comprehended by the naked eye. To remedy this, we summarize the data using descriptive statistics.

How We Do It: Descriptive Statistics

In summarizing data, we simplify. Simplifying, or stereotyping, a large number of measurements allows our limited faculties to grasp them. But simplification leads to loss of information. It is a necessary price. A statistician's challenge is to extract the *essence* of data—the fundamental story line so to speak. This must be done while keeping information loss to a minimum.

In statistics we describe essence with the aid of *location* and *variation*. For the former we have *measures of central tendency,* and for the latter we have *measures of variability*. Once central tendency is computed, all elements in a group are represented by a single value. Throughout we have dealt mostly with the *mean*. It is the most frequently used measure of central tendency, and for the most part, we shall remain with it. The mean is simple to compute and to understand. But it is not *robust*—it is heavily influenced by extreme values. Where extreme values occur, specifying the *median* or *mode* instead often remedies the problem.

Describing variation involves focusing on the *uniqueness* of measurements. In statistics we conceptualize uniqueness as distance, or deviation, from the mean. Based on all these distances, we compute the *standard deviation* (σ), which is a kind of "average uniqueness" in a distribution—a measure of variation.

Being a summary statistic, σ does not provide information on the uniqueness of individual observations. However, it does give a general sense of the similarity of the measurements in a distribution to their mean and so to one another. Where σ is small, the distribution is homogeneous—the observations are generally similar. Where it is large, the distribution is heterogeneous.

The standard deviation must be approached with caution. First, we have yet to say what constitutes a large σ or a small one. Second, and related to the first, σ is not robust. Like the mean, it is sensitive to extreme values. But σ can yield information regardless. For example, analytic chemists often examine the size of σ relative to the mean. For example, when σ = 1 and the mean is 2, the variation can be said to be greater than when the mean is 10. In the former, σ is 50 percent of the mean, and in the latter, 10 percent. Expressing variation as a percentage of the mean yields the *coefficient of variation*.

The standard deviation is also useful when looking at distributions with the same mean. In such cases, the distribution with the smaller σ is usually the one whose elements are more similar to one another. Usually, but not always. This is true because one extreme value can make a distribution look more heterogeneous than it "really" is. That is, the standard deviation is not robust.

The standard deviation's lack of robustness led us to devise a robust measure of spread: the *interquartile range*. The interquartile range describes the area of a distribution containing the middle 50 percent of observations. This statistic tells us something about the "heart" of the distribution; as such, it is not affected by outlying values.

We already mentioned uniqueness. When we wish to focus on this aspect of an observation, we compute its distance from the mean. But distance alone is fairly meaningless. For example, 2 seconds are very little in the context of a lifetime. Yet, in the Olympics, they can spell the difference between winning and losing. Hence identical distances can have completely different meanings.

We say that distance makes sense only when placed in context; we must assess it "relative to something." A convenient yardstick for evaluating the relative distance of a specific value is the average distance in the distribution. Following this reasoning, we compute the *standard score z*. Computing it, we divided an observation's absolute distance from the mean by the "average distance" from the mean of all the observations. The larger *z*, the more unique is the observation.

To this point our formulas have dealt with one group only. In real life there are usually more, each with its own central tendency. Introducing other groups into our statistical story leads to a "negative" description of objects. Now each measurement is defined by the group that it does *not* belong to as well. Again, we compute distance, but this time it is between an object and a mean of a group that is not its own. An object belongs to one group rather than to another if its distance from the mean of the first is smaller than that from the other. For example, let us say that in our data the mean weight of small cars is 1200 kilograms and that of large cars is 1650 kilograms. A car weighing 1300 kilograms will be classed "small" rather than "large." This is so because its weight is nearer that of small cars relative to its distance from large cars.

Finally, we compare differences *between* groups by examining the distance between their means. In later chapters we shall make extensive use of such comparisons in the context of *inferential statistics*.

As you may have already guessed, this absolute distance between groups also will need to be placed in context. That is, we shall have to divide it by a kind of standard deviation that represents both groups.

THE ABSTRACT NATURE OF STATISTICAL DESCRIPTION

Analytic thinking has led us down a curious path. We set out to capture the essence of things and in the process removed ourselves from them. We began with something we can touch—an object, a thing that can be measured directly. By calculating the mean, we lost the individual object in a crowd. Thus, when computing central tendency, we *created an abstraction*. After that, all distances were measured from this abstraction. We then took the mean of these distances. Finally, we lost the individual item altogether by comparing distances between means—points that are fictitious in that there may be no single element exactly there.

A major difficulty in survey research is that the people questioned often approach events and objects very differently from the statistician. Let us examine the following question: "On a scale of 1 to 5, where 1 means 'very little' and 5 means 'very much,' do you like to go to parties?" This particular survey item aims to measure a person's Extroversion—the degree to which he or she is outgoing. Asking the question outside a survey will likely lead to the answer, "It depends." This is so because people do not usually approach parties in the abstract. Most relate the question to specific parties, each characterized along many dimensions. For example, a party can be characterized by the types of

1. Participants: young, old, aliens, journalists, etc.

2. Drinks served: beer, scotch, Ripple, etc.

3. Locations: my house, your house, the White House, etc.

And the list goes on.

Asking a person whether he likes to attend parties may conjure up memories of last year's class reunion or last week's cocktail party. In this case, however, the statistician is interested in neither. She aims to measure the person's attitude "on average"—in the abstract. What she really asks is, "Relative to other people, and taking into account the kind of parties that people like you generally go to, do you, on average, like to attend parties?"

If your answer is based on last Thursday's affair, you have given the statistician only a portion of the information she wants. From her point of view, you may have provided a great deal more error than truth. The kind of thinking we usually do—that based on specifics rather than abstractions—is, for the statistician, error.

In some research this problem is more acute than in others. For example, professionals such as physicians tend to focus on the individual. When treating a patient, the physician sees in front of him a unique person: one with a distinct history, a singular set of symptoms, and a specific tolerance for pain. His approach is "clinical" rather than statistical. Asking him whether a particular medication for hypertension is effective simply may remind him of a patient he saw this morning. As a result, asking physicians general questions often elicits the "It depends" type of answer.

The physician's difficulty in dealing with generalities mirrors the challenge inherent in medical research. While the researcher aims to discover general laws, she often falters precisely because individuals vary greatly; the same treatment can lead to very different outcomes depending on the individual. Notwithstanding, it is the medical researcher's task to derive general rules. The researcher begins with individuals and ends up with abstractions—generalities. The physician, on the other hand, focuses on the individual. In medical school he learned the rules, but for him this is only the beginning. Applying the rules in everyday practice, he finds that they do not always work. So he ends up designing specific treatments for individual patients.

In other areas there is also variation, but it is limited and simpler to deal with. For example, a voter "treats" a ballot box in one of a number of finite and predetermined ways. As a result, the question "For whom would you vote if the election were held today?" is usually easier to answer than "How would you treat hypertension?"

We have pointed here to another crucial difference between the kind of thinking we do every day and statistical thinking. For us, the essence of a particular object is usually the object itself. For the statistician, it is the mean. When we extract the essence in statistics, we abstract. In life we tend to be more concrete.

This book deals with *applied* statistics. At some stage we will need to descend from abstractions to terra firma. This is our challenge: to use abstractions as a tool to describe and understand the real world better.

CHAPTER X

The Significance of Variation

VARIATION EXISTS

The behavioristic moral—and we must have morals—is: Women do not like to work (neither do men). There is no natural "instinct" to work. Biologically speaking the hungry animal reaches up and pulls down a banana, reaches out and grasps his female (or vice versa); his hunger adjusted, he rests and sleeps. Work habits are the result of civilization and competition. *If you want your children to have careers, be they boys or girls, teach them from infancy habits of manipulation, skillful technique, endurance.*

J. B. WATSON[1]

We have all of us, said J. B. Watson, the same inborn fondness for industry—none. Among lower animals and higher, there is no natural variation in inborn Inclination to Work. But Watson had a problem. Observing the world, he noticed that there is a modicum of variation in this characteristic of living things. His solution was typical of the school of behaviorism he founded. He maintained that while there is no inborn inclination toward industry, there is one toward learning. Our natural disposition, he claimed, is to learn from the environment and to respond to it. This, rather than our genes, compels us to toil. And since there is variation in people's environments, there are disparities in their Inclination to Work.

For the past 200 years much of humanity has been greatly disturbed by the fact that individuals differ from one another. Some are able and some are less able, some are industrious, others lazy. Some are simply lucky. And of course, some are rich and some are poor. There are those who have proposed to solve inequality by ignoring ability and rewarding by need. Others suggest that all individuals be given the same opportunities—that they be placed at the same starting line and released to run the race as best they can. Rewards will follow speed. Still others believe that it is always "each man for himself."

Whether you place your faith in one school or another, variation among individuals is a fact of life—a fact that makes existence alternately interesting and disconcerting.

Indeed, variation is sufficiently conspicuous in our existence that terms associated with it have become cliches. We say that there are "different strokes for different folks" and that "birds of feather flock together"; we say, "variety is the spice of life." In previous chapters we have presented methods for quantifying variation. Here we begin to examine where this gets us.

Variation as Uncertainty

Kawa Sweeg is an island located about 420 miles south-southwest of Java. Today there is no one there. In 1973, a team of Chinese anthropologists sailed to Kawa Sweeg in search of evidence that humans had once inhabited the island. After 5 weeks of digging, the team uncovered a site containing fish bones and crude tools. During the following month, the team discovered two more sites. In one they found an artifact that resembled a needle. Apparently the inhabitants of Kawa Sweeg—or perhaps they had only been passing through—could tailor clothing. Based on these artifacts, the scientists concluded that humans had been to the island about 13,000 years before.

The Chinese returned to the Kawa Sweeg the following year and discovered several more sites. Toward the end of their stay, they came upon three human skeletons that had been elaborately buried. The characteristics of two matched those of Austronesian people known to have sailed the waters of Polynesia more than 10,000 years ago. They were short of stature and had high skulls and almond shaped eyes. The third skeleton—that of a woman in her early thirties—was different. She had been much taller, and the shape of her eyes was similar to those of skeletons found in Madagascar.

Returning to the island the following year, the anthropologists resumed their excavations. Still, they could find no explanation for how or why the woman had gotten there. Most of the scientists' discoveries had pointed to a particular age of human history and a particular people. But the one woman remained a mystery. Because of her, the scientists could not conclude with certainty who had inhabited the island and when. The Chinese did not return to Kawa Sweeg, and no expedition has been there since. The variation in the skeletons they found baffles still.

There are circumstances in which variation is a nuisance—situations in which we wish for consistency so that life were simpler. Let us take a look at another, more commonplace example of "variation as uncertainty." The label on the box says "Aspirin 50 mg." Inside the box are two dozen pills, all produced at Rothbart's La Grange plant in Illinois. The factory produces about 30,000 pills daily. Every hour of every day a pill is randomly selected, and the Amount of Active Ingredient in it measured.

The Quality Assurance Department at Rothbart charts the measurements obtained over time. Figure 10-1 shows these quantities for October 21, 1997. According to standards set by the regulator, the active ingredient in each pill must be between 49.5 and 50.5 mg. As can be seen from the figure, on October 21, 1997, all went well until 12:00 A.M.— every pill that had been sampled yielded a quantity within the allowable limits. The pill sampled at noon, however, yielded 50.6 mg. Immediately following this discovery the production process was stopped, and 30 additional pills were sampled. All yielded quantities of active ingredient within the specified limits. For almost 3 hours production remained at a standstill while systems were checked and rechecked. All was found to be in order. At 14:52 production was resumed. No other irregularities emerged that day.

The chart presented in Figure 10-1 is similar to the kind used to keep track of production processes in many industries.* Thus one may graph the width of surgical blades over time, the diameter of jellybeans, or the weight of pasta packages. Measuring critical product attributes over time is an important tool for keeping tabs on the quality of products coming off production lines.

---

* Actually, the limits on the chart, which are specified by dotted lines, typically are computed a bit differently.

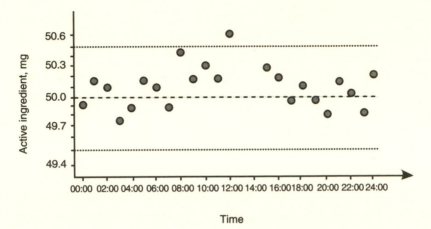

FIGURE 10-1 Amount of Active Ingredient: October 21, 1997.

In industrial production, variation is unwanted. But it is a fact of life. While regulators would like there to be no variation at all, they accept it within tolerable limits.

In accepting variation, both regulators and engineers implicitly admit that they cannot understand why it happens. If they could, they would initiate corrective actions to eliminate it. At Rothbart, living with variation means accepting a degree of uncertainty in the production process. Despite the best of intentions and the greatest of efforts, all pills cannot be made identical.

There are times, however, when the amount of variation encountered is unacceptable. When this happens, Quality Assurance wants to understand the reason. Statistically speaking, the engineers seek to *explain variation*. In so doing, they wish to reduce uncertainty, thus enabling the production process to be adjusted appropriately.

Both the Chinese anthropologists and Rothbart's engineers approached variation in the same manner. At Kawa Sweeg, three skeletons were found. Two were identified as Austronesian. While they were not identical—while they varied—they were sufficiently similar to be classified as belonging to the same race. The scientists accepted this variation and did not attempt to explain it. However, the third skeleton was different enough to require an explanation. At Rothbart, most of the pills were sufficiently alike to be classified into the same "acceptable" category. Although the pills varied, Rothbart engineers made no attempt to understand the reason. Yet one pill was different enough to require an explanation.

For both the anthropologists and the engineers some of the variation encountered spelled uncertainty. Had it not been there, they would have been more confident of their conclusions. The anthropologists would have been more certain that humans had inhabited the island 13,000 years before, and the engineers would have been confident that the pills coming off the production line would comply with regulation.

VARIATION AS INFORMATION

Angela Stuart is an eighth grade mathematics teacher who constructs graphs such as the one shown in Figure 10-2. This figure describes the relationship between True Ability in Mathematics and the likelihood of solving a particular problem correctly.* Ms Stuart studies such relationships to devise tests that enable her students to demonstrate their relative abilities. She hopes that by constructing tests in this way, her examinations will be fair.

Now Angela Stuart is generous in nature. Deep down she would like every student to solve all the problems on her examination correctly. How–

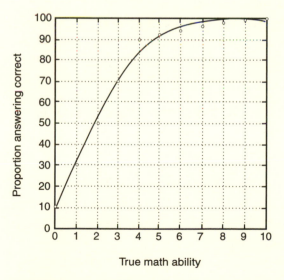

FIGURE 10-2 Observed performance on a simple problem as a function of True Mathematics Ability.

*There is indeed a way to measure and graph the relationship between the observed (e.g., score on an item) and the latent (e.g., true ability), but this is well beyond the scope of this book, and we shall take it as a given.

ever, if all Ms Stuart's students achieve a perfect grade, she will have defeated the purpose of the test. After all, examinations are designed to provide information on the differing abilities of students.

Apparently Ms Stuart is not that generous. If she were, she would administer tests that included only simple items that all her students would solve or difficult ones that none would solve. On such tests, all her students would achieve the same grade—there would be no variation. Being more conscientious than she is charitable, Angela Stuart does the next best thing. She constructs examinations on which the variation in Grade genuinely reflects True Mathematics Ability. In other words, variation in Grade is explained by variation in True Mathematics Ability.

In an environment that rewards ability and punishes the lack of it, Angela Stuart must administer tests that distinguish between more and less able students. Without variation on Grade, this information would not be available. In the context of tests at school, variation on Grade is *information*.

A test of mathematics can be regarded as any other measuring tool. Thus, to measure Ability, one constructs tests, and to measure Health, one uses a thermometer. In the case of both instruments—the test and the thermometer—when there is no variation, there is no information.

In the preceding section we spoke of differences between measurements as uncertainty—differences that are neither wanted nor understood. In this section we have shown the flip side—variation as information.

THE RELATIONSHIP BETWEEN UNCERTAINTY AND INFORMATION

Let us return to Rothbart Pharmaceuticals—but with a difference. In Figure 10-3, the Amount of Active Ingredient for October 21, 1997 is charted as before. In this figure, however, the values are distinguished by the Shift on which they were produced. The results for each of the three 8-hour shifts are indicated by a different shape.

From Figure 10-3 we deduce that the "Circle" and "Parallelogram" shifts produced tablets whose Amount of Active Ingredient was within allowable limits. Furthermore, the variation is these shifts was more or less symmetrical around 50 mg. From an engineering standpoint, the "Circle" and "Parallelogram" shifts have done their job properly.

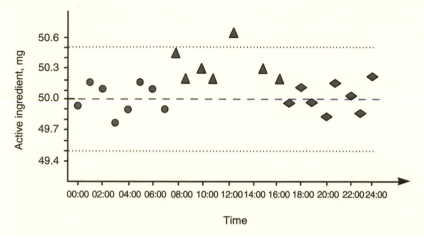

FIGURE 10-3 Amount of Active Ingredient by Three Shifts on October 21, 1997.

During the "Triangle" shift, however, something has gone awry. First, the active ingredient in one of the pills exceeded the allowable limits. Second, the mean of the "Triangle" shift varied around 50.3 mg, not around 50.0 mg. Clearly, something in the production process was not right between 8:00 A.M. and 4:00 P.M.

Amount of Active Ingredient is a continuous variable measured on a ratio scale. Shift is a categorical variable taking on three values. By relating variation in Amount of Active Ingredient to that in Shift, the engineers at Rothbart have explained variation.

Note that with this information alone the Quality Assurance engineers cannot yet correct the problem. They must now further explore the production process during the "Triangle" shift. Only in this way will they obtain information that will enable them to rectify the problem. For instance, the engineers may discover that the manager of the "Triangle" shift is new on the job and does not know how to calibrate her instruments properly. By relating Amount of Active Ingredient to Calibration (rather than to Shift), they will have identified the problem and be in a position to correct it. Statistical explanation by itself—in this case, knowing only that irregularities arise during the "Triangle" shift—does not necessarily solve problems.

As always, one is never exempt from using one's head. Useful information will result only when the appropriate variables have been related to one another. Thus statistical explanation is merely a statement of mathematical relationship. Our task is to translate the mathematics into actionable information. We will only be able to do this if the measures with which we produced our mathematical statement make sense in the particular context.

We have now shown the difference between variation as uncertainty and variation as information. *In statistics, variation that is unexplained is uncertainty. Variation that explains (or is explained) is information.*

Let us conclude with José Lopez, who was confronted with a bimodal distribution on Intent to Visit Castle Crusade (see Chapter 6). By relating Intent to Visit (on a scale of 1 to 10) to Country of Origin (on the dichotomous scale of United States/Germany), he explained variation; he discovered that American pilgrims were more partial to the Castle Crusade than Germans. Here, variation between Country of Origin groups explained Intent to Visit and so provided information.

However, José Lopez could not explain all the variation on Intent to Visit. For example, some Germans gave high Intent to Visit ratings, whereas some Americans gave low ones. Thus Country of Origin explained some of the variation in the data, but there remained unexplained variation within each Country of Origin group. These *within-group* differences remained unexplained and so led to lack of certainty.

Because of within-group variation, José Lopez could not perfectly predict Intent to Visit based on Country of Origin alone. In the following chapter we will show how the concepts of "description" and "prediction" are intimately related.

CHAPTER XI

Uncertainty, Error, and Uniqueness

I am not sure what is bothering me.

A NINETEENTH-CENTURY BUREAUCRAT[1]

STATISTICAL UNCERTAINTY

In Chapter 10 we wrote: "In statistics, variation that is unexplained is uncertainty." Now this is a very general statement. At least in some cases it would seem unjustified. After all, what is uncertain about junior high school students differing in Ability? It is the way it is. Also, the fact that skeletons from the same race differ from one another does not appear to distress many people. Certainly it did not bother our Chinese anthropologists.

Here again, we encounter a difference between statistical reasoning and the kind we use every day. For us, variation sometimes leads to uncertainty and sometimes not. Our attitude toward it *depends on the circumstance*. The statistical view is more consistent.

Most people regard variation in Ability as a fact of life and are not perplexed by it. When giving a test, Angela Stuart merely wants to assess differences between students. In the circumstance of administering an examination, she has no desire to discover the *reason* for variability. Indeed, she uses it to her advantage—she measures Ability with it. On other occasions, Ms Stuart may well want to find out why students differ in the grades they achieve. On these occasions, variation is a kind of "nuisance" that needs explaining. In attempting to understand this variability, Ms Stuart may relate Ability to Attentiveness or Diligence; she also may explore whether test performance is associated with Parents' Education or with Gender.

Similarly, engineers take for granted that variation in production is inevitable. Still, they often make great efforts to increase the quality of a product even when variation is within the limits allowed. On these occasions, variation is seen as a "nuisance to be explained." To discover the explanation, they experiment with different production methods, hoping this will lead to more reliable manufacturing—such that will reduce variation even further.

For both teachers and engineers, variation that at times is considered normal will, at other times, require explaining. But statistics does not distinguish between what we consider natural and what we do not. In statistics, unexplained variation leads to *uncertainty* regardless of our feelings about it.

The difference between statistical and everyday perspectives may seem confusing, but it is only a characteristic of language that makes it so. When using language, we often attach sentiment to words. Reflexively. For most people, the term *uncertainty* has negative connotations. But statisticians, like psychotherapists, are not in the business of passing judgment—statistics has no intrinsic value system. In statistics, the term *uncertainty* denotes neither a negative phenomenon nor a positive one. It simply signifies that variation is unexplained. We must always keep in mind that statistics is merely a tool— a methodology for manipulating numbers. It is up to those who use the tool to attach meaning to the results it yields.

DISTANCE, UNCERTAINTY, AND ERROR

Recall the following formula from Chapter 5:

$$x = \text{truth} + \text{error}$$

You also may remember that in the same chapter we said that, in statistics, the mean is equated with truth. Substituting the mean into the preceding formula, we obtain

$$x = \mu + \text{error}$$

Put another way:

$$\text{Error} = x - \mu$$

But this is also our definition of distance. From Chapter 7, we have

$$\text{Distance} = x - \mu$$

In other words, in statistics, *distance from the mean is error*. Recall that the average distance from the mean is computed as follows:

$$\sigma = \sqrt{\frac{\Sigma \, (x - \mu)^2}{n}}$$

Here then is another definition for the standard deviation. It is a measure of the average error in a distribution.

In the preceding section we learned that, in statistics, variation is also uncertainty. We now have a quantitative measure of the degree of uncertainty in a distribution. It is σ.

PREDICTION

Forecasting is hazardous, especially about the future.

SAMUEL GOLDWIN

Suppose that you are sitting in a room and every few minutes a person enters through the door. Your task is to predict as best you can each person's height. Now, aside from being a fairly useless activity this is also not a simple one. How should you proceed?

For the sake of simplicity, let us imagine that only seven people enter through the door and that the following are their heights in centimeters:

$$167, 168, 169, 170, 171, 172, 173$$

Of course, no one can expect you to predict all these heights perfectly, and neither do we. Rather than striving for perfect prediction, one strategy would aim to *minimize error overall*. For lack of a better approach, let us select a single value and use it for predicting the height of anyone entering the room. We shall then compute our error for each prediction by

$$\text{Error} = \text{observed value} - \text{predicted value}$$

That is, we will subtract from each height we observe our prediction for it. To eliminate negative values, we shall, as we have done before, square the result. Thus

$$\text{Squared error} = (\text{observed value} - \text{predicted value})^2$$

Finally, we shall compute our overall error by summing all the squared distances, or squared errors:

$$\text{Total error} = \Sigma \, (\text{observed value} - \text{predicted value})^2$$

Recall that our strategy is to minimize error overall. Thus we must now find the predicted value that will minimize "total error" (assuming, of course, that such a value exists). Keeping things simple, let us limit our choice of predicted values to the numbers in the distribution itself. The principle we shall derive with this method will apply to any other value we might choose.

For example, if we select 167 centimeters as our best guess for the height of all who enter the room, our total error will be

$$\text{Total error} = (167 - 167)^2 + (168 - 167)^2 + \cdots + (173 - 167)^2$$
$$= 0 + 1 + 4 + 9 + 16 + 25 + 36$$
$$= 91$$

Let us also compute the formula for the standard deviation to compute average error, except that here we shall replace μ with our predicted value. Selecting 167 centimeters as our prediction, we obtain

Average error =

$$\sqrt{\frac{(167 - 167)^2 + (168 - 167)^2 + \cdots + (173 - 167)^2}{7}} = 3.61$$

Table 11-1 shows the results of this computation for each of the values in the distribution. As you can see, the predicted value that yields the smallest total and average errors is 170 centimeters. But this is also the mean height of those who entered the room! *Indeed, in any distribution, it is the mean that minimizes error.*[*] In other words, the sum of squared errors, and that of average error, will always be smallest when choosing μ for our predictor.

---

[*]Squared error, to be precise.

TABLE 11-1 AVERAGE AND TOTAL ERROR WHEN SELECTING EACH VALUE IN A DISTRIBUTION TO PREDICT ALL THE VALUES IN THE DISTRIBUTION

PREDICTION	TOTAL ERROR	AVERAGE ERROR
167	91	3.61
168	56	2.83
169	35	2.24
170	28	2.00
171	35	2.24
172	56	2.83

When predicting the mean, the formula for total error becomes what statisticians define as the *sum of squares*. More formally:

$$\text{Sum of squares} = \Sigma(x - \mu)^2$$

In fact, this is the numerator of the *variance,* the formula for which was presented in Chapter 7.

Let us summarize. We were presented with the task of predicting a set of values. We agreed that rather than aim for perfect prediction, our goal should be to minimize overall error. We then showed that in predicting the mean, we accomplish this.

Now you may say that this reasoning is as useless as it is impressive. After all, we only had the mean *after* we obtained our measurements. Thus, while the mean is a good predictor—or at least the best there is—we cannot use it because we do not have it. Well, often we do, and this will be addressed in future chapters.

We have now learned a basic statistical rule for prediction. In the absence of any other information, predict the mean.* While you may appear foolish doing so, you will likely appear more foolish doing anything else.

---

*The mean minimizes error as defined by the sum of squares. We can, of course, select other criteria for error and strive to minimize those. For example, rather than attempting to minimize overall error, we may wish not to exceed a particular magnitude of error for any given prediction. This will necessarily lead to an "optimal" prediction that is different from the mean. While this is an important issue in many fields, it is beyond the scope of this book ("beyond the scope of this book" being the mode of Reasons given by authors who wish to avoid certain topics).

FROM PREDICTION BACK TO DESCRIPTION

Long ago we said that in using descriptive statistics we aim to extract the essence of a collection of numbers. We do this by abstracting—by specifying a stereotypical number to represent a distribution. Most often this number is μ.

In selecting the mean, we implied that it is a logical value for representing the essence of a distribution. But we also pointed out that in specifying this single number we forgo information on the manner in which individual values differ from one another.

In Chapter 7 we confronted the task of quantifying this information on variability. We wrote then that "Conceptually, it is natural to view a specific element's uniqueness as its distance from the single value that represents its group [which is the mean]." We then went on to show that "average uniqueness" in a distribution is computed by the standard deviation. Therefore, in choosing the mean, we also implied that it is a reasonable reference point for computing uniqueness. We can now say that this choice has a mathematical logic to it as well.

Earlier in this chapter we equated error with distance. Thus, by minimizing error, we also minimize information loss with respect to distance. In other words, by specifying the mean to represent a collection of data, we lose the least amount of information.[*]

Thus the mean is

1. A measure of central tendency.

2. A natural reference point for computing uniqueness.

3. The value that minimizes overall error.

4. The best predictor.

We can now conclude that, both mathematically and conceptually, the mean is the best single descriptor for a distribution.[†]

---

[*]Again, we must point out that we have minimized error—information loss—as defined by the sum of squares. Another criterion for error will lead to another "optimal" value.

[†]There are certainly exceptions to this rule. We mentioned some of these when presenting alternative measures of central tendency. With your permission, and for the sake of simplicity, let us ignore the exceptions for now.

Terminology

In this chapter we have used a large number of terms and related them to one another. We have shown that some are equivalent and that others are intimately related. Now all this may seem a bit confusing. After all, the statistical approach aims to simplify rather than complicate. Why, then, use several terms where one will do? The answer is that one will not do; while many of these terms are computationally equivalent, they are not conceptually equivalent. By understanding their relationships, we gain a deeper understanding of what it is we do when we engage in statistics.

Thus the *distance* of a particular value from central tendency is the degree to which it is *unique*. In statistics, however, distance is also a measure of the *error* that results when we use the mean as a *predictor* for a particular value. In the context of prediction, which is different from description, uniqueness happens to be the *uncertainty* associated with predicting the mean for any value in a set of data.

Finally, when specifying the mean as the single value to represent a set of data, we lose information on uniqueness. Uniqueness, like error, is quantified as distance. In making use of the mean, we minimize the sum of squared distances. In other words, representing a distribution by this single number minimizes our loss of information.

CHAPTER XII

From Description to Inference

MAKING CONNECTIONS

> Charles Gray had not thought for a long time, consciously at least, about Clyde, Massachusetts, and he sometimes wondered later, what caused him to do so one morning in mid-April, 1947.[1]

It is the morning commute. Charles Gray, assistant vice president at the Stuyvesant Bank, is on the subway reading a newspaper. He glances at the headlines and the financial section. Inexplicably, his thoughts turn to the town he had left almost 20 years before.

At the bank that day Charles learns that he must travel to Clyde. A company there needs looking into. He suspects that the directors at Stuyvesant want him out of the way for several days—the time it will take to decide whether he is to become a vice president of the bank. Charles is a good banker, but he is also good-natured. Perhaps he has not been aggressive enough to earn the promotion.

When Charles Gray lived in Clyde, it was a place where the old families kept to tradition and themselves. He himself had been born on the right side of privilege—but only just. As a young man he chose to leave. Opting for the wider world, he left behind childhood memories and said goodbye to the cold Jessica, his boyhood love.

Charles moved to Boston. After a few years, he moved to New York and to Stuyvesant. His advancement was impressive but not spectacular. In between was World War II. Charles volunteered for the war, although he was old enough to have remained at home. Perhaps the fact that his older brother had been killed in World War I had something to do with it. Whatever the reason, Charles's long absence hurt him at the bank. During his time away, a new man had joined Stuyvesant. It was this man he was competing against.

If Charles is promoted, he will pay off the mortgage on his house and send his son to a good school. He will make Nancy happy. Without the promotion. . . well, it will be different. Soon Charles's fate will be sealed. One way or the other.

Back in Clyde, Charles meets Jessica. She has never married. He meets old friends who are friends no longer. He completes his inquiries and travels back to New York. On his return to Stuyvesant, Charles is asked to dinner at the president's house. He is certain that it is there that he will find out.

Dinner is done, and it is time to discuss business. The two men rise from the table. Charles feels that the dinner has not gone well. "It's over," he said to himself as he walked across the hall. "Thank God it's over." It was the first time he had felt really free since he had met Jessica at the firemen's muster [many years before].

They enter the study, and the president takes out a cigar. He offers one to Charles. They exchange pleasantries. The minutes drag on, but Charles is not troubled. He knows now that he will not become vice president. If anything, he is relieved.

The president begins to talk about the bank—his years at the institution, his thoughts about the profession. Then Charles hears that he has got the promotion. He does not feel the exhilaration he might have expected. Instead, "It was like the time at Dartmouth when he had won the half mile at freshman track. He felt dull and very tired."

Charles's fate is sealed. It is a good fate, but it is sealed nonetheless. He has reached the *Point of No Return*—the title of the book. In truth, Charles has long been at this point. Only now, however, does he know it for certain. For Charles, there is a security in staying the course, in keeping to the path he has been on for nearly 20 years. Certainly it is no mean feat to have become vice president, but there is also a kind of dullness that comes with knowing that he will remain where he is.

Charles had always vaguely longed to go beyond. It is what drove him from Clyde as a young man. Yet this longing was more than a simple need to excel on the course he was on. It was an urge to go beyond the limits of his path altogether.

In the realm of thought it is this very "going beyond" that seems to lead to eventful discoveries. Arthur Koestler, in his book the *Act of Creation*, cites Kohler's classic study with chimpanzees. Nueva is a young female chimpanzee who has remained isolated in her cage:

> A little stick is introduced into her cage; she scrapes the ground with it, pushes banana skins together in a heap, and then carelessly drops the stick at a distance of about three-quarter meter from the bars. Ten minutes later, a fruit is placed outside the cage beyond her reach. She grasps at it, vainly of course. . . . about seven minutes later . . . she suddenly casts a look at the stick, ceases her moaning, seizes the stick, stretches it out of the cage, and succeeds, though somewhat clumsily, in drawing the bananas within arm's length. . . . The test is repeated after an hour's interval; on this second occasion, the animal has recourse to the stick much sooner and uses it with more skill; and at a third repetition, the stick is used immediately, as on all subsequent occasions.[2]

On previous occasions the bananas had been placed outside the bars but within reach. The chimpanzee had merely to use her arms. For Nueva, the stick had only existed in the context of play. But at a certain moment—the moment of "going beyond"—all this changes. Koestler writes:

> The moment of truth occurred when Nueva's glance fell on the stick while her attention was set on the banana. At that moment . . . the "stick to play with" became a "rake to reach with."

The chimpanzee used the stick as a tool, something researchers had long believed that animals could not do. Koestler makes the analogy to the domain of scientific discovery:

> I have repeatedly mentioned "shifts of attention" to previous neglected aspects of experience which make familiar phenomena appear in a new, revealing light, seen through spectacles of a different color. At the decisive turning points in the history of science, all the data in the field, unchanged in themselves, may fall into a new pattern, and be given a new interpretation, a new theoretical frame.[3]

Let us return from the heights of discovery to the more mundane. In Chapter 8 we were faced with interpreting the meaning of distance. We asked whether 640 kilometers is a great distance or small. To answer the question, we were required to place the number 640 in context—to compare between this particular value and others. We then went on to describe two types of comparisons.

In one instance we compared 640 with other values in its distribution. We pointed out that it is not a great deal relative to the mean covered by a traveling salesman. In a second instance we associated the continuous variable Distance and the categorical variable Mode of Travel. We pointed out that the meaning of 640 in the context of Flying is quite different from its meaning in Driving.

In relating 640 to other distances in a distribution we described its relative uniqueness. In relating it to Mode of Travel, we engaged in the statistical activity of explanation. This latter type of comparison required of us to go beyond the numbers at hand and into a new context.

Statistical *description* involves characterizing data. We do not seek to understand the reason that they appear as they do. In contrast, statistical *explanation* happens when, to use Koestler's words, "two different matrices" of phenomena are connected. It is the going outside of a particular phenomenon in order to understand it.

Apparently, there is a natural inclination to go beyond. For Charles Gray this meant leaving the path he was on. His promotion, welcome as it was, thwarted the inclination. In the statistical domain, this "going beyond" involves moving from mere description to explanation.

This relating of different contexts to one another is the essence of *inferential statistics*. As the term implies, we make use of this discipline to infer— to understand—why a set of data looks as it does. More specifically, in doing inferential statistics, we ask why our phenomena are not all the same. Thus we ask why the meaning of 640 varies, and answer that this is so because one Mode of Travel is faster than another. Similarly, we ask why it is that some pupils score higher on tests than others and answer that this is so because some have more Ability and others less. *Inferential statistics is the discipline of explaining variation.*

Throughout this book we have provided examples of statistical explanation. Let us now return to several of these with our newly acquired language.

1. José Lopez explained variation in Intent to Visit Castle Crusade by variation on Nationality.

2. Sir Francis Galton explained Height of Child using Height of Parents. In other words, to explain variation in height of children, he entered the new sphere of Height of Parents.

3. A physiologist related variation on Weight to variation in Lesion in a certain part of the brain. By going beyond a mere description of Weight and manipulating the brain, he inferred the relationship between the ventromedial hypothalamus and weight regulation.

Yet inferential statistics cannot *select* connections. This we must do ourselves. Evidently, the inclination to "go beyond" is not enough. If we wish to arrive, we had better know first where it is we want to go—we must, with forethought, select the variables that will show the way.

Still, it is not so simple. Koestler writes:

> But the collecting of data is a discriminating activity, like the picking of flowers, and unlike the action of a lawn-mower; and the selection of flowers considered worth picking, as well as their arrangement into a bouquet, are ultimately matters of personal taste.[4]

So even here there is a role for "personal taste"—for "primordial soup" thinking. It is intuition and not statistics that will determine whether we are to make a discovery of substance or merely demonstrate an obvious connection.

To show the manner in which inexplicable processes are involved in scientific discoveries, Koestler cites Archimedes. Tradition has it that Archimedes discovered the concept of volume in the bath. In entering the bath and displacing water he discovered a way to measure volume. Now we can assume that Archimedes had taken baths before—the phenomenon had been there for the discovering all along. It was not forethought that led to his discovery; it was a "primordial soup" moment of "going beyond." He had related changes in water level to the volume of things placed in the water.

The great physicist Richard Feynman wrote

> To what extent do models help? It is interesting that very often models do help, and most physics teachers try to teach how to use models and get a

good physical feel for how things are going to work out. But it always turns out that the greatest discoveries abstract away from the model and the model never does any good.[5]

In doing statistics we make use of analytic thinking—we collect data and specify models. We use logic. It cannot be otherwise. At the same time, if we forgo our intuition and remain with our standard models only, we are forever destined to discover only trivial connections.

A run-of-the-mill scientist does not expect to make momentous discoveries daily. Indeed, if she makes one during her lifetime, she considers herself fortunate. For the most part, therefore, she plays by the rules. However, if she does *only* this, she will never go much beyond the commonplace.

FROM DESCRIPTION TO EXPLANATION

To this point we have dealt primarily with descriptive statistics; we have computed means and distances, calculated standard deviations, and drawn graphs. It seems that we have not yet shown you how to do inference analytically. But this is not entirely the case.

In Chapter 10 we charted the Amount of Active Ingredient in aspirin tablets over time (see Figure 10-3). In using different shapes, we differentiated between categories of the variable Shift. Looking at the graph, we see that there is a relationship between Shift and Amount of Active Ingredient. In making this observation, we have, apparently, explained variation in production by variation in Shift.

What, then, is the difference between what we have already done and the practice of inferential statistics? Well, there is, in inferential statistics, a dimension we have yet to encounter. Sometimes the aim of statistics is merely to state with precision that which we know intuitively. Consequently, it is not enough to say that we "think" that phenomena are related—that one explains the other. We also must quantify this term *think*. For example, most would agree that there exists a relationship between Traffic and Noise Level. Simply put, Traffic explains Noise Level. But it is not the only factor that affects what we hear. The same "noise" will be heard differently on the first floor and on the ninth—it is explained by Traffic *and* Location. There are many other factors as well. Inferential statistics will *quantify* for us the relative contribution of the different factors explaining Noise Level. Neither a graph nor intuition can provide this kind of information.

THE NATURE OF STATISTICAL EXPLANATION

Statistical explanation involves showing formally that a lawful relationship exists between variables. At the same time, we must distinguish between the statement *lawful relationship* and the term *cause*. Galton indeed concluded that Height of a Parent *causes* the Height of a Child. However, this is certainly not the case in every relationship we demonstrate. In fact, many, if not most, of the relationships we quantify are not causal. For example, on average, the more expensive an automobile, the greater is its acceleration. However, the cost of an automobile does not cause a car to accelerate faster or slower. Similarly, while Shoe Size and Height are related, we do not say that needing larger shoes affects one's height.

Once again, we have encountered the limitation of statistical explanation. Using the discipline, we can demonstrate lawful relationships and quantify them. But determining cause is something we must do for ourselves.

CHAPTER XIII

Reliability and Validity

FROM THE LAB TO LIFE

Perhaps it really does begin with a scientist in a white lab coat bending over her test tubes on a rainy night. Probably not. In any event, the discovery of a new molecule usually begins in the laboratory and stays there for a while. The molecule needs perfecting and testing. Often, other variants of the molecule are developed and must be tested as well.

If the results are promising, research in animals begins. Deciding on the animal to use is not trivial. Frequently, the scientist selects more than one strain. Sometimes, more than one species. If the outcome warrants, the scientist initiates experiments in humans. This is risky business. No one knows whether the molecule is safe for humans and at what dose, and extrapolating from animals is as much an art as a science. Thus phase I of human testing is concerned primarily with determining the drug's safety. But this is not all. The researcher must learn the rate at which the drug enters the body and leaves it. And she must identify the organs in the system it affects.

Phase I is usually done in hospitals. Typically, only a few healthy individuals take part. The conditions are well controlled, and participants are followed closely. The scientist must demonstrate that the drug is safe—that its side effects are tolerable. Showing that the compound works—that it actually alleviates disease—is still in the future.

At some point the researcher knows enough, and phase II begins. Several doses are administered to those for whom the drug is intended. The primary goal is to identify the optimal dose and to begin showing effectiveness. But the researcher is not done with safety yet. In phase I she has provided evidence that the drug is safe in healthy humans. Now she must show the same in sick ones. Then there is the issue of feasibility. The scientist needs to demonstrate that it is practical to use the drug in circumstances that resemble real life, that patients are capable of keeping to schedule, and that the medical care required is practical.

Finally, the pivotal phase III begins. The drug is given to a large number of individuals who have the disease—hundreds, sometimes thousands. Others who have the disease are given a placebo for comparison. The participants are followed for the duration of the trial, which can last for days or years. The research takes place at many sites and, often, in more than one country.

Phase III is done. The data are collected and analyzed. Statisticians determine whether the results are *statistically meaningful*—whether the outcome for those who received the drug is consistently different from that for those who did not. Physicians evaluate the medical implications—whether the drug's effects are also *clinically meaningful*.

On conclusion of phase III, scientists, physicians, and statisticians pool their efforts in a final report. In the United States, the Food and Drug Administration (FDA) evaluates the report. If all has gone well, the new drug is placed on the market.

By now years have passed. Many have invested a goodly portion of their lives and money in the effort. All the while, new drugs for the same disease are being developed elsewhere. Within a short period the new drug will be new no longer. No matter. There will be enough rainy nights to keep our scientist busy.

GETTING IT RIGHT

The process of research in drug development is complex. In it are numerous elements, including human, scientific, and logistical. Along the way, large quantities of data are generated. In previous chapters we focused on the statistical aspects of summarizing and presenting these data. Here we deal with an earlier stage—that at which the elements of research are specified in the first place.

Now the word *element* is very general. Still, we use it with consideration. In specifying the term, we refer to just about anything in the research process—anything, that is, that requires *selection*.

Let us be more concrete. In testing the drug on animals, our scientist might select among rats, chimpanzees, and armadillos. When proceeding to humans, she may decide to study males or females or both. She must specify the ages, race, and health status of those who will participate in her trials.

Our scientist also must select those variables which are relevant for her research. She might choose Body Temperature, Bone Healing, or Level of Pain. She will then measure these variables, which again requires choices. Temperature can be assessed by thermometer or estimated by pulse rate. Bones can be imaged by x-ray or by more sophisticated computer-aided techniques. Pain may be measured with the aid of a questionnaire or by recording the activity of nerve cells. In addition to all these, our scientist must select the sites at which to conduct her research—the laboratories, the hospitals, the countries. And the list goes on.

It is impossible to cover all these "selection possibilities" in this book or in any other. In fact, the number of technical details involved in just a single clinical trial is seemingly endless. The scientist's task would appear to be impossible. Yet this is not so. The *principles* guiding the selection processes in research are relatively few, and we focus on some of these here. In particular, we shall focus on some of the assumptions that scientists make when doing research. Good scientists articulate these assumptions. Articulated or not, when they are incorrect, the research is useless.

WHAT NEEDS ASSUMING

In the preclinical phase, the scientist tested the molecule in a laboratory. Whatever her method, a critical assumption hovered low above all her efforts. She took for granted that what she had obtained in one study was not unique—that other, comparable experiments in her laboratory would yield similar outcomes. Indeed, she assumed that what had transpired in her laboratory could be replicated in other laboratories as well.

Our scientist also has made other assumptions. She believes that what takes place in her test tubes simulates reactions in animals. And she assumes that reactions in animals simulate those of humans. Finally, she hopes that what she has observed in those participating in her trials is what would be observed in those who might take the drug in the future.

These are no idle assumptions. Therefore, before going on, let us articulate some of them more clearly:

1. Comparable experiments in the same laboratory will *replicate*—will yield similar results.

2. Comparable experiments in different laboratories will *replicate*.

3. Reactions in test tubes *predict* those of animals and humans.

4. Reactions of those who participate in trials *predict* the reactions of those using the drug in the future.

Now these statements are related in more ways than one. First, at the practical level, if a scientist cannot replicate results in her own laboratory, she cannot expect them to replicate in others. Furthermore, if her results are inconsistent—if they vary within or across laboratories—it is more than likely that they cannot simulate the reactions of animals or humans. Different members of the same species have similar biologic systems. Thus their reaction to the drug should be similar as well. Certainly a researcher cannot hope to simulate a relatively consistent reaction in large groups of people with a drug that elicits greatly variable results in individuals of the same experimental species.

The ultimate goal of research in drug development is to predict what will happen when the medication reaches the market. This can only happen when the assumptions enumerated hold. Thus our scientist needs to design her study in a way that ensures that her assumptions materialize. She must measure well and measure the right things. She must select the correct objects to study and the appropriate techniques to measure them. She must choose suitable sites.

Clearly, the assumptions enumerated are related at the practical level— they are links in a chain that must remain intact for the research to succeed.

But they are also related conceptually. We shall explore this further later on. For now, we shall remain at the practical level.

RELIABILITY

De Ja vu all over again.

YOGI BERRA

The first assumption in the preceding section stipulates that similar experiments in the same laboratory must yield similar results. The second requires that results from different laboratories are similar as well. Both these statements relate to replication—to obtaining comparable results from comparable experiments. Another way of saying this is that the results must be *consistent*. For us, this idea is old hat.

When similar experiments yield different data, our results are inconsistent, and we have measured with *error*. It may be that we are not technically able to construct experiments that are similar or to measure their outcome well. Perhaps our technicians lack training or our instruments lack accuracy. Whatever the reason, greatly variable results suggest that the data may be too prone to error to be useful. Simply put, a measure that cannot provide consistently accurate results is useless.

In Chapter 12 we mentioned that variability and error can be one and the same. This is evident here. When a researcher observes variability where there ought to be none, she has observed error. The degree to which measurements of identical phenomena yield consistent outcomes is termed *reliability*. In other words, a reliable measure is one that yields similar outcomes when applied to the same phenomena; a reliable experiment yields similar data across replications.[*]

Recall the familiar formula

$$x = \text{truth} + \text{error}$$

This formula states that any observation x contains two components. Using it, we say that the more reliable the measure, the smaller the error component

---

[*]Which can only happen when our instrument is reliable.

is relative to the truth. Another way to state this is as follows: The greater the proportion of truth in *x,* the more reliable is the measure. More formally:*

$$\text{Reliability} = \text{proportion of truth in an observation} = \frac{\text{truth in } x}{x}$$

Back to our scientist, who is now in a quandary. She knows that her research will be useful only if her measures are reliable. So she must assess reliability. But how is she to assess reliability, which is defined as "proportion of truth"? After all, as we have often said, in statistics it is impossible to know the truth. And we stand by this still. Thus it seems that our scientist must do the impossible. Well, not entirely.

Statisticians have developed methods for assessing "proportion of truth" that do not actually require *knowing* the truth. This is a mathematical sleight of hand no doubt and well ahead of our game besides, so let us conclude with the one point we wish to make in this section. Namely, reliable measurement is necessary for research to be any good.

Making a Distinction

We were not as precise as we should have been in the preceding section, and it is time to straighten this out. We wrote: "When similar experiments yield different data, our results are inconsistent, and we have measured with *error.*" This is true. But the reverse is not. That is, when similar experiments yield the same results, our data are not necessarily accurate. In other words, we can have consistency but *also* have error. A simple example is a thermometer that regularly overestimates Temperature by 0.5°C, which makes it both reliable *and* inaccurate.

In Chapter 5 we pointed out two types of error: *random* and *bias.* An instrument whose error is random yields overestimates and underestimates about equally, producing variable results whose mean is the truth. A biased instrument, however, yields error that tends to be in one direction.† Con-

---

* It turns out, however, that defining reliability in this way is not very useful from a computational standpoint. Thus statisticians have developed alternatives for it. Yet for those of us who are only concerned with the concept rather than computation, this will do.

† A measure that is both biased and unreliable will, over many measurements, yield outcomes whose mean is different from the truth by the degree to which it is biased.

sistency by itself does not ensure accuracy. Had we wished, we could have defined reliability to include both consistency and accuracy. But the distinction is important because the solutions for random error and bias are different.

When there is only random error, one solution is to measure more. For example, if a physician wishes to know Temperature by measuring pulse, he would do better to take pulse over 30 seconds than over 10 seconds. In other words, measuring *more* yields more reliable values. A second, obvious solution is to use a more reliable method, such as a thermometer.

Still, there are some situations where reliable measures are unavailable. For example, psychological phenomena such as intelligence are usually difficult to measure. In cases such as these, the only solution is to measure more. Thus a typical IQ test comprises many items. By measuring a person's performance on many cognitive items and taking the mean, we achieve an IQ score that is relatively consistent. Physical phenomena, on the other hand, usually can be measured more reliably than psychological ones. Thus, when using a scale to assess weight, we usually measure once only and trust the outcome.

So statistics does what it can to make the researcher's life tolerable. In circumstances where it is difficult to design reliable instruments, it only asks that we measure repeatedly. It does not say: "If you don't have a reliable measure, forget it." But it also suggests that, to the extent possible, we use reliable instruments.

Bias is different. If an instrument yields overestimates consistently, measuring many times will not help. Here again, there are two solutions. If you know the degree to which your instrument is biased, you can adjust for it. Thus, if you happen to know that your thermometer is consistently off by 0.5°C, subtract this much from every result you get. Alternatively, you could use an unbiased instrument.

VALIDITY

The last two assumptions listed earlier deal directly with predicting a drug's effects on living systems—the ultimate goal of the research. Recall that the third assumption stipulates that reactions in test tubes must predict those of animals and humans; the fourth states that what happens to those participating in clinical trials predicts what will happen to those who do not. These two assumptions are conceptually comparable in that they require one circumstance to *predict* another, different circumstance—the circumstance of interest.

In statistical terminology, the researcher's results must be *valid*. They must relate to that which is intended. More formally, a measure's *validity* is the degree to which it predicts what it purports to predict.[*]

In a sense this is not very different from what we said about reliability. Recall that a reliable measure is one that yields similar values in similar circumstances. In other words, the numbers obtained in one situation will relate to those obtained in another. Yet there is a difference. A measure is reliable when it yields similar results in *comparable situations*. A measure is valid when it yields similar results in *situations that are different*.

We can now say in a few words what took us many before. We wrote: "Furthermore, if her results are inconsistent—if they vary within or across laboratories—it is more than likely that they cannot simulate the reactions of animals or humans." Put more concisely, *reliability is a necessary condition for validity*.

Necessary, yes—but this is not enough. For example, to predict whether or not it will rain in Spain, we need to measure variables such as Temperature, Wind, and Cloud Cover. There are many other variables we can measure reliably in Spain, for example, Income, Inflation, and the Height of Basques. But for any particular question, there are only a few variables that will provide us with the answers we seek. Incorporating this into our previous statement we have: *Reliability is a necessary but not sufficient condition for validity*.

Still another way of looking at the two concepts of reliability and validity is this: Reliability relates to measurements *within* similar situations. Validity relates to measurements *between* different situations. Only when we measure consistently within similar situations will we be able to predict across different situations. And this will only occur when we have chosen appropriate measures.

---

[*] In fact, there is more than one type of validity. Here we deal with a single type only—that termed *predictive validity*.

ANOTHER EXAMPLE

Let us use the following example to summarize what we have learned. Suppose that have we measured the IQ of 16 high school seniors. Five years later, we also obtain their overall college Grade Point Average (GPA). Figure 13-1 presents the results. In this graph we also include a line that describes the relationship between these two variables.

Alfred, whose IQ is 115, achieved a GPA of 3.1. Based on this, we predict that other seniors with similar IQs will obtain a GPA of about 3.1 as well. Suppose, however, that every time we measure a student's IQ we get a very different result. Using the graph, we would predict a very different GPA based on each of the scores obtained. Now at least some of these predictions would be very inaccurate. After all, a student has only one GPA. Yet each of his different IQ scores would lead to a different prediction of GPA. In other words, if we cannot obtain consistent results on IQ, it cannot predict GPA accurately. Let us translate this into the language we have learned. Variability on IQ within a person indicates that the measure is

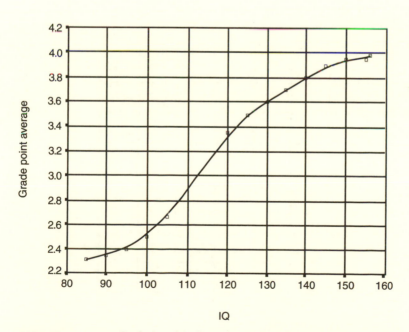

FIGURE 13-1 Relationship between IQ and Grade Point Average in college: Scenario 1.

unreliable. This variability leads to inaccurate predictions of GPA; that is, IQ is not a valid predictor of college performance. Thus *reliability is a necessary condition for validity.*

Now suppose that we measured each senior's IQ twice and obtained the data in Figure 13-2. Based on these data, we conclude that IQ can be measured reliably; that is, IQ scores replicate, more or less, across different occasions. But suppose that we can indeed measure IQ reliably. And suppose further that in relating it to GPA we obtained the data in Figure 13-3. According to these data, we cannot predict GPA accurately based on IQ. For example, one student whose IQ is 95 achieved a GPA of 2.4, whereas another with the same IQ achieved a GPA of 3.4. Based on our line, we would have predicted a GPA of 2.7 for both. This is not a very good prediction for either. Of course, we might have drawn a different line, but no line can predict an accurate score for *both* students. Thus, even though we have measured IQ reliably, we cannot predict GPA very well. In other words, *reliability is a necessary* but not sufficient *condition for validity.*

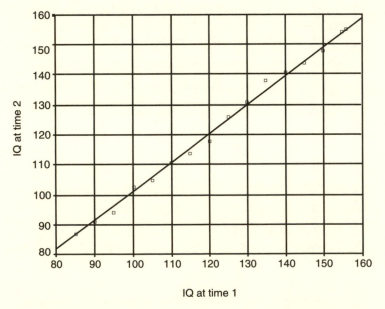

FIGURE 13-2 IQ scores measured at two different times.

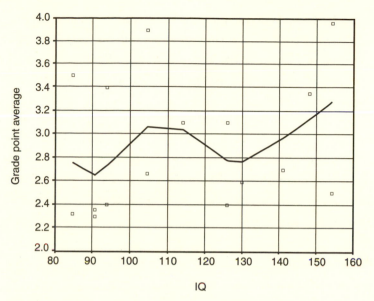

FIGURE 13-3 Relationship between IQ and Grade Point Average in college: Scenario 2.

A NOTE ON ASSESSING VALIDITY AND RELIABILITY

Validity is simple to assess. It is, by definition, the strength of the relationship between two variables we have measured. In the preceding example, it is the degree to which IQ predicts GPA. The better the prediction, the more valid is IQ (as a predictor of GPA). All that is left is the mathematics of computing the strength of this relationship. This is typically done using a statistic we call the *correlation coefficient.**

Reliability, however, is more complicated. Recall that it is defined as the "proportion of truth" in a measure. In other words, it is the relationship between something we measure and the truth, which cannot be known. Still, we are not completely helpless when it comes to evaluating reliability, and in the preceding section we hinted at how this is done.

Take a look again at Figure 13-2. In it we describe the relationship between the outcomes of two tests for each of 16 students. Based on the

---

* More specifically, the *Pearson product moment correlation*, which measures the extent to which two variables are related *linearly*, that is, the degree to which a straight line describes their relationship. When the relationship is better described by another type of line, there are other, more appropriate statistics.

result, we say that IQ scores replicate more or less across different occasions. In other words, IQ is reliable. At the same time, we still do not know each of the student's true IQ. Thus, by assessing the relationship *between a measure and itself*, we get an indication of its reliability. This can be done without actually knowing the truth.

In Figure 13-2, reliability can be quantified by the degree to which the points are near the line*—the degree to which the relationship between different measurements is consistent. But this is precisely what the correlation coefficient, which was mentioned in the context of validity, measures. Thus reliability and validity are not only related conceptually; they also can be assessed using similar mathematics.

---

* And unreliability, by the degree that the points are off it.

CHAPTER XIV

Samples and Populations

GENERALIZATION

The sun has risen every morning since recorded history. It will rise tomorrow as well.

Here, we have extrapolated from what is known to what is not. We *generalized*. This is one method for extending knowledge beyond immediate experience, and it is central to the way we think. It also comprises much of what we do in statistics. Let us begin by showing this with the concepts presented in Chapter 13.

A *reliable* measure produces similar outcomes in different but similarly contrived circumstances. For example, if we reliably measure Alfred's Height at 12:30 P.M., we can expect the same result, more or less, 2 hours later. Knowing Alfred's Height at 12:30 P.M. enables us to know his height at 2:30 P.M. and at other times as well. A reliable measure generalizes across similar situations.

A *valid measure* generalizes to (predicts) different situations. For example, using Alfred's Grade Point Average (GPA) in high school, we might predict his GPA in college. Here we have extrapolated information from a situation we have experienced to a different one that we have not.

LANGUAGE

The single word *dog* expresses a complex constellation of attributes including four legs, man's best friend, and fire hydrant's foe. Generalization is a characteristic of language that enables one to say a great deal with very little.

In Chapter 13 we encountered this aspect of language in a statistical context. There we enumerated four of the assumptions that a researcher makes when conducting research. Using the ideas of reliability and validity, we restated our researcher's assumptions by simply saying that "reliability is a necessary but not sufficient condition for validity." In the preceding section we showed that these two concepts could be compacted even further—that they are both instances of generalization.

This book presents a particular way of looking at things and does so with the aid of statistics' peculiar language. Having journeyed together this far, we can now use our common language to describe all kinds of phenomena. For example, we might communicate the essence of many numbers using one—the mean. And we can describe their numerous differences using another—the standard deviation. Based on a simple graph such as the histogram, we also know how to say when the tale has been well told.

Yet language must be handled with care. It can be used effectively only with those who speak it as we do. So here again we must define our terms precisely. Only thus can we ensure that our words will clarify rather than confuse.

Returning to reliability and validity, we say that both enable knowledge of what we have not seen based on what we have seen. This "learning from experience" is a characteristic of most living things. Although we know it well, in statistics we will have to explicate this experience further.

BOUNDING GENERALIZATION

An advantage of language is that it allows saying a great deal with very little. However, herein also lies a disadvantage. Often, words express more than we would like. Recall the term *uncertainty* (Chapter 11). As commonly used, uncertainty has negative connotations. Yet in statistics it is merely *unexplained variation*—the fact that not all values in a distribution are precisely at the mean. This indeterminate nature of everyday communication led us to distinguish between statistical and linguistic uncertainty. Let us now use a simple example to show in greater detail how generalization works.

Early on, an infant cries and discovers that a parent comes to his rescue. From experience, he learns that crying is worth his while in both daytime and nighttime, and on weekends to boot. The infant also finds that crying in the living room and kitchen accomplishes similar results. Based on this, he generalizes the effects of crying to circumstances beyond his immediate experience. He might, for example, cry in the den for the first time and know exactly what to expect.

But the term *circumstance* is very broad. After all, even in an infant's existence there are many different circumstances. Getting more specific, we say that the infant has extended his conclusions across the variables Time and Location. He may not, for instance, have learned to do this across Person. This is so because he twice cried in the presence of his older sister and was surprised by the result.

The child grows older. The number of situations he encounters multiplies, and the behaviors of those around him change. He finds his conclusions lacking and learns to narrow their scope—painfully. At home he may still cry at will, but repeating the exercise at a restaurant gains him little attention—at least not of the kind he hopes for. He also discovers that it is not prudent to cry on Saturday mornings. If he is clever, he will deduce that Sundays are not all that different. This he does without ever having tested it out. He learns that Location has a more limited meaning now, and so does Time.

This narrowing of scope is a tricky business, however. In Chapter 3 we described a study in which a scientist made lesions in some rats' brains and not in others. He then compared eating in the two groups of rats and concluded that the part of the brain in which he made lesions—the ventromedial hypothalamus—controls food intake. We then asked whether the scientist could extend his conclusions to circumstances where the rats are placed in different cages or fed other types of food. We answered that he cannot actually *know*. You see, our scientist can never be sure that his results replicate across situations unless he tests them all. But this is impossible. Still, this did not stop him from concluding that the ventromedial hypothalamus controls eating—in general.

Clearly, it was *reasoning*, rather than empirical findings, that led our scientist to generalize his conclusions. Thus one link between the known and unknown is thought—a link rooted in logic and obtained by sitting in an armchair and speculating. We are familiar with both activities.

Without the ability to extend our knowledge in this way, science would be little more than a trivial pursuit. And life would be very confusing. At the same time, when generalizing, we had better be careful. We might, for example, find that crossing the street on green works well in Seattle. But extending this to Rome could be a grave mistake.

Despite the difficulties, this kind of reasoning works well for us. And while we may have never articulated its mechanism, we have a good sense of how it works. As long as "things" are "similar," we are comfortable learning about one from the other. To the extent that they differ, we bound our conclusions—limit our generalizations.

We say that we have a sense of how this works, but we do not know exactly. In fact, for about 150 years the discipline of psychology has been looking into the process in the hope of discovering its precise mechanism. Other areas have dealt with the question as well. Thus philosophers such as Berkeley and Hume speculated on this process tirelessly.* Today, neuroscientists try to understand the process by actually looking inside our brain. We do not propose to provide a chronology of these efforts. It is enough that we agree that acquiring knowledge can be done in the abstract—by thinking rather than doing.

Indeed, the ability to generalize is essential to life itself. So much so that when impeded, it can cause serious damage. A child who cannot discover the rules governing his environment is in trouble. If parents and teachers react inconsistently to his crying, he will end up weeping a great deal. As it turns out, much of psychopathology—of disordered thinking—results from the inability to learn about one situation from another. Apparently, being powerless in this way can lead to mental disorder.

---

*And tiresomely.

Returning to the issue at hand, we contend that at least some knowledge is not grounded in direct experience. Rather, it is derived through a kind of reasoning that we term *generalization*.

FROM SAMPLES TO POPULATIONS

A pollster wishes to predict the winner of an election based on a survey of several hundred people. In statistical terminology, the pollster uses a *sample* of several hundred people to estimate the *population* of several million. She extends her knowledge from a sample that she has measured to the population she has not.

What she does is this:

1. *Define a population.* In this particular instance, the population is "all who will vote on Election Day."

2. *Select a sample from the population.* The pollster seeks out individuals who intend to vote on Election Day.*

3. *Measure the variable of interest.* In this case, the pollster measures Voting Preference.

4. *Summarize the results.* The pollster computes the proportion of those who say they will vote for Smith. In statistics, we call this proportion a *sample statistic.* In other investigations, we might be interested in different statistics. For example, when measuring Height, the statistic of interest may be Mean Height; when measuring Income, it may be Median Income.

5. *Estimate the value in the population.* The pollster generalizes the sample statistic, Proportion Voting for Smith, to the population. In statistics, we term the value in the population a *population parameter.* Thus, if the pollster finds that 53 percent of her sample will vote for Smith, she will estimate this to be the outcome on Election Day.

---

* Typically, this is done by first asking those surveyed whether they intend to vote. The ones answering "yes" are assumed to belong to the population. Of course, there are some who answer "yes" and will not vote (and the reverse). This leads to *measurement error*, which we will deal with in time.

Here, the pollster has engaged in *estimation*—has estimated a population parameter from a sample statistic. Put another way, she has generalized from what she has seen to what she has not seen.

In *The Longest Journey*, E. M. Forster tells the story of Ricky, a quiet young man who dreams of being a writer.[1] Ricky was born lame and orphaned young. Despite his difficult beginnings: "He believes in humanity because he knows a dozen decent people." The young man has been fortunate enough to attend Cambridge, where he has made good friends. The experience convinces him that humanity is good.

At the risk of being trite, let us formalize Ricky's thought process. He selects a sample of several people and measures the Goodness of each. He then computes the sample statistic Mean Goodness. Finally, Ricky extends his findings. He concludes that this is also the mean in all of humanity; he decides that the value he has obtained is that of the population parameter Mean Goodness.

But really Ricky has not done what we have attributed to him. People do not actually *think* this way. Ricky has simply met a few good people and decided that all people are good—intuitively. So let us examine how, in this context, statistical thinking both differs from and resembles that of everyday.

STATISTICAL VERSUS EVERYDAY TERMINOLOGY

In both statistical and everyday thinking, a population is defined as *a collection of objects that have something in common that others do not*. For example, we might speak of the population of Japan, whose members share characteristics that others do not. At the very least, they live in Japan. Still, there are several differences between the statistical term and the one commonly used. First and foremost, a statistical population exists only because someone has decided that this is so. If a researcher chooses to call people whose Height is between 6 feet 0 inches and 6 feet 2 inches a population, that is what they are—by definition. After all, only those in the range share this attribute.

Now, you might say, "Granted, you've defined a population, so that's how it is. But it's a pretty useless definition." If the researcher respects your opinion, he will justify himself to you—will tell you why he believes that people in this height range are different from others. Your natural reaction would then be, "Prove it." Indeed, this is what science is all about—making statements about how the world operates and providing evidence for them.

Once again, we have strayed. Recall that our aim in this section is to examine how the term *population* in statistics relates to its use in the everyday. Still, we have made an important point, and it is concerned with our reason for specifying populations in the first place. Neither scientists nor we specify populations for their own sake. We do this because we hope to gain information. Thus we circumscribe the population voters because we want to predict the outcome of an election. Similarly, our scientist defines the population of persons between 6 feet 0 inches and 6 feet 2 inches because he wishes to investigate whether they are different from others on his parameter of interest. In future chapters we shall explore the uses to which statisticians put populations. But for the moment, let us remain with the point that in statistics a population exists only because someone has decided on it.

Based on what we have said so far, it would seem that statistics differs little from the way we think ordinarily. Earlier we gave the example of the Japanese population, which comprises a distinct group. This is so because its members share at least one characteristic that others do not. In principle, this is how we define populations in statistics as well. Yet, with regard to the Japanese, the word *agree* makes all the difference. In everyday language, populations are self-evident—they delimit reality in ways that are *obvious* to those with whom we communicate. In statistics, the partitioning is arbitrary. It depends on someone's particular need at a specific time. Others may agree, but this is not necessary.

An example: Suppose that a pharmaceutical firm wishes to test a potent medication for reducing blood pressure. Being potent, the drug also can cause severe side effects. Because of this, the company intends it only for those with uncontrollably high blood pressure—patients for whom no other medication has done the job. Thus the company selects for study only hypertensives for whom nothing else has worked. This particular partitioning is done for the purpose of the research at hand and may never be repeated again. It is not apparent in the way that the population of those who live in Japan is.

This leads us to a second, related distinction. Because "statistical populations" are not necessarily obvious, they must be delimited precisely. Otherwise, those with whom we communicate may not know what we mean. In the preceding example, a company specified that the patients in its study must have (1) high blood pressure and (2) an inability to control it with conventional medication. But this is not enough. What, for example, do the researchers mean by *high* blood pressure? Is it a systolic reading of 165 torr and above, or must it be at least 170 torr? And what do they mean by *uncontrollable*? Are they saying that the blood pressure cannot be controlled *all* the time, or will 60 percent of the time do?

Circumscribing a population in statistics entails defining the characteristics its members share exactly. This is critical because it tells us just how far we can generalize. Put differently, delimiting a population *bounds* our generalization. It is like saying

> There is a group of people out there who share *x, y,* and *z*. Because they have these characteristics in common, they are a distinct group—a population. I will now obtain a limited sample from this large group and measure something on it, say, Blood Pressure after they have received my medication. I will then compute the parameter, Mean of Blood Pressure. Finally, I will claim that this value applies to the larger group as well, that is, to all who share *x, y,* and *z*. *But only to them.*

Thus our precise definition has a very important function. It determines just how far we will extend our knowledge from the instances we have observed to those we have not. It will *bound* our generalization.

Such careful definitions are not common in everyday language because we typically understand one another more or less. And "more or less" is usually enough. Not so in statistics.

There is also a third distinction. It is the least important but also the hardest to get used to. A statistical population can be *any* collection of "things." It is limited neither to humans nor to living things, which is usually the case in everyday language. For example, in statistics, each of the following might be defined as a population:

- Planets

- Journalists

- Pills produced during the graveyard shift

- Vipers

- Scholastic Aptitude Test scores in 1981

To summarize, the concept of population is similar in statistics and in everyday life. In both, we refer to a collection of things that have something in common that others do not. At the same time, the statistical designation differs on three points:

1. *The partitioning need not be obvious.* It is often arbitrary in the sense that it is based on a specific need at a specific time. This particular partitioning of the world may never be repeated.

2. *The partitioning must be defined precisely.*

3. *Members of statistical populations can be anything*—animate, inanimate, or simply a collection of numbers.

SUMMARIZING

An individual has seen the sun rise many days in a row and concludes that it will continue to rise in the future. A child observes his parent's reaction in the living room and concludes that the parent will react similarly in the bedroom. Finally, a pollster surveys a limited number of individuals and uses the data to predict the outcome of an election. In statistical terminology, if not in the everyday, all these instances involve estimating the population from a sample.

Remember Ricky? He observed a few friends and concluded that all humanity is good. As you might expect, Ricky lived to learn the error of his generalization. Apparently, the road from sample to population has numerous potholes, and Ricky fell into several. In Chapter 15 we explore how Ricky might have made his ride a bit smoother.

CHAPTER XV

Estimating Right

OF RATS AND MEN

I shall devote this paper to a description of experiments with rats. But I shall also attempt in a few words at the close to indicate the significance of these findings on rats for the clinical behavior of men. Most of the rat investigations, which I shall report, were carried out in the Berkeley laboratory. But I shall also include, occasionally, accounts of the behavior of non-Berkeley rats who obviously have misspent their lives in out-of-State laboratories.[1]

Striving for insight into humans, E. C. Tolman spent much of his life trying to understand lower animals. Thanks to him and others, we now know a great deal about rats. In a typical experiment, Tolman placed hungry animals in a maze at the end of which was food. In some situations the rats seemed unsure of themselves, engaging in a kind of "hesitating, looking-back-and-forth, sort of behavior." Tolman called this "vicarious trial and error (VTE)." He wrote:

> But what, now, is the final significance of all this VTEing? How do these facts about VTEing affect our theoretical argument? My answer is that these facts lend further support to the doctrine of a building up of maps.[2]

Tolman claimed that rats running a maze construct a "cognitive map" of its layout. Running repeatedly, they consult the map before making decisions. Tolman believed that "VTEing" is an outward sign of their inward deliberations.

Clark Hull at the University of Iowa felt that Tolman's explanation was needlessly complex. He believed that animals' behavior can be explained more simply by what is termed "stimulus-response learning." According to Hull, it works like this: At each point in the maze the rat senses unique stimuli. Based on previous runs, the animal connects these stimuli to a specific response. It is like the rat saying, "I sense x and y but not z. Last time I encountered this particular combination and responded by turning left, I reached food. I had better go ahead and do that again now." At another point the rat might say, "I sense z as well, so I better turn right."

Yet Hull would have taken issue with our quoting of rats, which implies *thinking*. For him, stimulus-response connections are hardwired into the brain and do not constitute thought in the conventional sense. Once the connections are established, behavior is mechanical. It is like reflexively executing the following lines of code:

```
If (x and y) = yes
  and                    } Stimulus
  z = no
Then
  turn = left            } Response
```

According to Hull, learning is the process of establishing such hardwired connections.

In the brains of both rats and humans are cells that communicate with one another and the rest of the body. Stimulus-response psychologists believe that, through experience, some of these connections strengthen while others weaken. They believe that brains evolved to retain those connections which lead to reward and discard those which do not. In responding to stimuli, neither humans nor lower animals know why they behave as they do. Their muscles merely react to established mechanical connections.

In a sense, Hull claimed that "the brain has its reasons that the brain does not know." His is a more straightforward explanation than Tolman's, which requires

1. Constructing complex cognitive structures (maps)

2. Actively consulting these structures before responding

In science, there is a principle known as *Occam's razor*. It states that among competing theories for the same phenomenon, the simplest should win. Based on this principle alone, we should prefer Hull's explanation to Tolman's.*

For many years now psychologists have been arguing about these alternative mechanisms of learning. Variations on each of these themes have been proposed as well. And the scientists are still arguing.

BIAS

Tolman's rats at Berkeley differed from Hull's. They may have been brighter or duller. Perhaps Hull's rats were not the "VTEing" type. At the very least, Iowa rats misspent their lives in out-of-California laboratories.

Despite their animals' peculiarities, both scientists felt that their samples represented the population of rats in general. Otherwise, they would not have proposed general theories based on them. If their findings were specific to the rats they tested, however, their generalizations were unjustified.

Samples that systematically differ from the population they purport to represent are said to be *biased*. The data we obtain from them will not well represent the population in general. Thus, if we wish to learn about rabbits in general, we ought not to select all our rabbits from Tasmania. Rather, we should place the world's rabbits in a hat and pull out a sample at *random*. In a random sample, each member of the population has an equal chance of being selected—by definition.

When we sample randomly from a population, we aim to obtain a subgroup that is similar in its makeup to the larger group—the population. If all has worked as it should, the information gleaned from the sample can be extrapolated to the population. *Random sampling* eliminates the kind of error we call *bias*—by definition. But it does not necessarily eliminate other kinds of error.

---

* Another principle of scientific explanation is that the more phenomena a theory explains, the better it is. Based on *this* principle, Tolman's explanation is superior. Here, however, we are concerned with sampling and will not delve any deeper into the issue of how learning happens.

KNOWING THE TRUTH

The only way to *know* the truth about a population—to know the population parameter exactly—is to measure all its members. In most cases, this is impractical. In many, it is impossible. Take, for example, a market researcher who wishes to gauge consumer attitudes toward her company's yogurt. She randomly selects for study individuals who have bought the product and expects her findings to apply to all who have bought it. But she also hopes that her results will represent those who will buy the yogurt in the future. Yet this latter group is simply unavailable at the time of her study. Thus, even if she had wanted to measure the whole of the population, she could not have.

So it seems that we are forever destined to extrapolate from samples to populations. And as long as we do this, we will continue to be uncertain of our results. It has been said that "being a statistician means never having to say you're certain." But really, this is a characteristic of life in general.

BACK TO RICKY

Ricky observed his friends and found them good (see Chapter 14). He then concluded that this is true of people in general. Unfortunately for him, his Cambridge friends misrepresented humanity—at least on the parameter Mean Goodness. As a result, Ricky obtained a biased estimate of Mean Goodness.

In Chapter 5 we noted that statisticians distinguish two types of error. *Random error* goes either way. *Systematic error* tends in one direction only. *Biased sampling* is a form of systematic error and, as in Ricky's case, is a common occurrence. Some examples:

1. Alfred is a Teamster. A few days before an election, he attended a barbecue with friends. In casual conversation he discovered that most of them would vote for Smith. Alfred concluded that Smith would win the election.

2. The Associated Physicians HMO has many older members and wanted to know what it could do to attract younger clientele. To this end it commissioned a survey of those visiting its clinics.

3. Boutique, Inc., considered opening one of its exclusive outlets on the Gold Coast. It conducted a survey whose participants were selected at random from the Gold Coast telephone book.

Most of Alfred's friends have political views that are similar to his. As such, they do not well represent voters in general—their views are biased in Alfred's direction. Similarly, Associate Physician members have different needs from those whom the HMO now wishes to attract. Their views are biased toward those of older individuals rather than those whom the HMO hopes to attract. Boutique, Inc., made the mistake of using the telephone book. Some people's numbers are unlisted, and these, more than others, are potential clients for Boutique. Because of this potential bias, survey organizations often employ machines that dial phone numbers at random. In this way, every existing number has an equal chance of being selected for the sample.

SOME IMPORTANT NOTES

True random selection can be difficult to achieve. For example, an automatic dialing machine will guarantee that each telephone line has an equal chance of being sampled. But not every household. Some homes have more than one line, and their chance for selection is greater than that of those with only one line. Then there are the households with no line at all, and these will not be selected at all. Thus random dialing solves one problem, but others remain. As always, we do the best we can.

A second point is this: Bias does not occur simply because those sampled are different from those who are not sampled. Those who participate in a study *always* differ from those who do not. At the very least, they differ because they are in the study. They must differ systematically *on the parameter of interest*.

Suppose, for example, that we wish to estimate the Mean Height of Frenchmen and select our sample from Paris. Now people in Paris differ from those of the rest of France—*they* live in Paris. Still, our sample may well represent Frenchman in general with regard to Height. This would be true if Parisians do not differ from others on this particular parameter. Therefore, as long as we can expect our sample to be typical of the population *on the parameter of interest*, we need not be concerned about bias.

Finally, even perfectly random selection cannot *guarantee* a representative sample. When randomness is perfect, each individual has an equal probability of being selected. In trusting to probability, however, we trust to luck, and periodically, one gets unlucky. For example, in selecting a random sample to estimate Height, we may end up, by pure chance, with a disproportionate number of tall people. It happens. But while random sampling does not ensure a representative sample, it does

1. Eliminate bias.

2. Increase the likelihood of our sample representing the population well.

In the following sections we explore ways to get lucky.

SAMPLING ERROR

Ricky's sample was biased. But it also was small. And small samples are more likely than large ones to yield very erroneous findings.*

When sampling, we aim to estimate a population parameter such as the population mean. However, most elements of populations are not at the mean exactly. We call this *variation*. Some population members are slightly below the mean, and some are slightly above. Others are further out. And then there are *outliers*—elements that are distant from the mean indeed.†

In any distribution, outliers are few—by definition. As such, their chance of being selected at random is small. But it is not zero. If you are unlucky enough to have selected an outlier, your estimate of the population mean may be off by a great deal. The smaller the sample, the greater is the outlier's effect on your estimate.

Now you may argue that the smaller the sample, the smaller is your chance of coming up with an atypical value. And you will be right. You then reason that it all balances out: Large samples are more prone to outliers

---

* Of course, as long as Ricky's sample is biased, it does not matter how many people he measures. Yet, as we shall see, even perfectly random samples are likely to be flawed when they are small.

† Statistically defining an outlier is not a simple matter. Indeed, there is no single definition that is true in general. This a technical issue we shall leave for another day.

but are less affected by them. Small samples are greatly affected but are unlikely to have them. Well, this is certainly a fine piece of reasoning. But it is wrong. What is more, you know this intuitively. In Chapter 5 we wrote: "For example, we are more willing to label someone a good student if she scored high on several tests than if she scored high on one test. Similarly, we deem a poll more credible when it is conducted on 500 people than on 50 people."

If you still agree with this, then you also should agree that it does not balance out—that, in general, larger samples yield more accurate estimates of population parameters than smaller ones. Proving this mathematically is well beyond the scope of this book. Let us trust our intuition on this.

Another disadvantage of small samples is this: Suppose that you obtain a sample of size 4 and suspect that one of its values is an outlier. One solution is to ignore the suspicious value—to estimate your population parameter based on the others alone. But in a sample of 4, it is virtually impossible to evaluate the degree to which a particular value is atypical of the population. Perhaps the suspicious number truly represents one-quarter of the population. After all, it is a quarter of your sample. In large samples, on the other hand, anomalies stand out more clearly.

Now outliers can greatly affect our estimates of population parameters. But not only they. In a sample of 4 where 3 elements are above the true mean and 1 below, your estimate will be off even if none of the values is extreme. This will be the case as long as the one value below is not sufficiently distant to balance out those which are above.

But, you may argue, one should not worry too much about error per se. It is a fact of life, and we must learn to live with it. Rather, it is the *degree* of error that should concern us. And here you will be right all the way through. As it turns out, the smaller the sample, the greater is the likelihood for substantial error. And while we know this intuitively, statistics will quantify the relationship for us. But not yet.

A simple example: By definition, a fair coin has an equal chance of coming up heads or tails. Yet even a fair coin often will come up heads 100 percent of the time when tossed only twice. Certainly you would not conclude, based on two heads in row, that the coin is not true. But if it came up heads on 30 consecutive tosses, you would likely be suspicious.

Let us approach this example from another angle and incorporate statistical terminology. We noted that the only way to actually *know* the population parameter is to measure the whole of it. Thus, if we toss the coin an infinite number of times and compute the proportion of heads, we know that our parameter is perfectly accurate. If we measure all tosses but one, we will be fairly sure of our estimate—but not completely. Measuring all but 100 tosses will further increase uncertainty. Finally, obtaining a "sample" of size 0 leads to the greatest uncertainty of all.

Now the infinite distribution of coin tosses is a theoretical concept. But it is a convenient one. Using it, we say that as our sample approaches infinity, our estimate approaches the truth. Or, as

$$n \to \infty,\ \overline{x} \to \mu$$

where n = sample size

μ = true mean in the population

$\overline{x}$ = mean of the sample data (termed *x*-bar)

Thus even random sampling will yield inaccuracy. This is so because even random sampling rarely produces elements that represent the population perfectly. We call this *sampling error.* And it belongs to the class of *random error.* This is true because it does not consistently tend in one direction. At times it will yield overestimates and at other times underestimates.

Measurement Error

Ricky decided to marry. Ansel, a Cambridge friend, opposed the marriage and made his opinion known. Sadly, Ansel was right. Ricky's troubles began. He appealed to Ansel for help and did not get it. Apparently, even his friends were not as good as he had thought—as he had measured.

Clearly, even a random and unbiased sample will be useless if our measures are bad or if they are measured badly.[*] Therefore, another pitfall in estimating is *measurement error.* It too can be random or biased (see Chapter 5). Measurements that yield numbers above and below the truth with no particular pattern are said to produce random error. Those which tend to inaccuracy in one direction are said to be biased.

---

[*] Measures can be bad in two ways: unreliable and/or invalid. For an explanation, see Chapter 13.

MISCELLANEOUS ERRORS

The reading on the thermometer is 37°C, but the researcher records 38°C. She has simply hit the wrong key on the keyboard and committed *reporting error*. Then there is *investigator error*, which occurs when a researcher does not correctly follow the procedure specified. For example, he might measure Height without, as the study protocol states, first asking his subjects to remove their shoes.

Both reporting and investigator errors can be either random or biased. For example, if a researcher hits wrong keys at random, the resulting error is random as well. However, if some keys are more likely to be mishit than others, the error is biased—it tends systematically to certain keys.

SUMMARY

Estimation yields error, and to this we must reconcile. Yet we *can* minimize error. Table 15-1 lists some of the more common pitfalls associated with estimation. It also provides strategies to minimize the degree to which each will affect our findings.

TABLE 15-1 SOME SOURCES OF ERROR IN ESTIMATING AND THEIR SOLUTIONS

TYPE OF ERROR	(PARTIAL) SOLUTION
Biased sampling	Use your head: (1) Define the population of interest precisely, and (2) design a sampling strategy that will maximize your chances to obtain an unbiased sample.
Sampling error	Select a large sample. The larger the sample's size, the smaller is the sampling error (on average).
Random measurement error	Measure repeatedly.[a]
Biased measurement error	Use a more accurate instrument, or if the bias is known, correct for it.[a]
Miscellaneous error	Be careful.

[a] See Chapter 13.

CHAPTER XVI

Models

WHAT THEY ARE NOT

The rain stopped pounding on the panes, and looking out the window from across the classroom, Robert could no longer see it. He hoped the rain was there, though. On days like this the yard would be little more than a large puddle, and no games will be played. On days like this, Robert is like the other boys.

Ms Rycoff asks a question, and Robert raises his hand. She calls on a boy in the back. The answer is wrong. Once more Robert raises his hand, and once again she calls on another.

Ms Rycoff appreciates Robert's contributions and has told his parents so. Still, he feels it is unfair that she calls on him only when none of the others offer answers. Once he had resolved to raise his hand only when others are doing the same. After a few days, Ms Rycoff asked whether something was wrong. The following day he resumed as before.

Robert is 13 years old. His bedroom is neater than those of other boys his age, but the posters are the same. On his dresser are four Matchbox series cars. One is always a '58 Olds—the first model he owned. This week, the others are sports cars. Next week, he will replace them with station wagons.

Robert has been collecting Matchboxes since the second grade, when his father decided that there ought to be more to the boy's life than just books and school. Robert now has more than 200 models.

When Robert finds it hard to fall asleep, he stares at his models. They calm him down. But when the Matchboxes on the dresser are sports cars, this does not help.

Robert looks forward to the day when he will present the collection to his son. Staring at the cars, his thoughts turn to Sarah. He hopes she will be the mother.

Robert is a model student. The kind Ms Rycoff thinks others should *emulate*. His Matchboxes are models as well—they are *replicas*. Both these definitions contain some elements of the kinds of models we encounter in statistics. Still, they are sufficiently different that trying to make the analogy may get in the way of understanding. For the time being, therefore, forget what you know about models—do not attempt to relate what you know to the everyday. The connection to the real world will emerge in time.

FIGURING OUT NATURE

Table 16-1 presents simple descriptive statistics for Galton's Height of a Child data (see Chapter 2). The mean and median in these data are similar. This suggests a symmetrical distribution (see Chapter 6). Figure 16-1 shows that this is very nearly the case.

This is a particularly nice histogram because

1. The intervals with the largest numbers of observations are located in its physical center. That is, all three measures of central tendency—the mean, the median, and the mode—are similar.

2. As we move away from the center, the frequencies reduce more or less uniformly in either direction.

TABLE 16-1 GALTON'S HEIGHT OF A CHILD DATA: DESCRIPTIVE STATISTICS

NUMBER OF OBSERVATIONS	MEAN	MEDIAN	STANDARD DEVIATION	MINIMUM	MAXIMUM
952	68.202	68.240	2.597	61.200	74.690

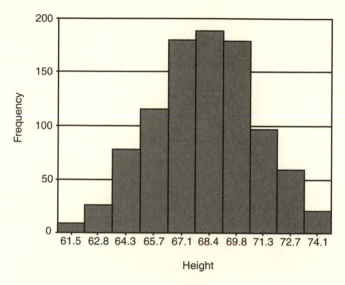

FIGURE 16-1 Galton's Height of a Child data: A histogram.

So far so good. We summarized Height of a Child and found nature to be approximately symmetrical—at least for the 952 children that Galton sampled. But really, we are not concerned with these particular children. We would like to extrapolate our results from this sample to "children in general"—the population of children. So let us move on.

FROM SAMPLE TO POPULATION

There are very many children on this planet, and thank God, each has a Height. For the sake of convenience, we will say that

1. In Galton's time, there was a population of 95.2 million such children.[*]

2. The 952 he obtained were a random sample from this population.

We now ask two questions and answer each in turn.

Question 1: Suppose that Galton had repeated his study. What would his second distribution have looked like?

[*] Within the Age range sampled by Galton.

Answer: We cannot know. Still, we can expect that it would have been similar to the one he actually obtained. After all, both samples would have represented the same population.

Question 2: What would have happened had Galton obtained a sample of, say, 25,000 children?

Answer: Again, we cannot know. But again we can expect that his distribution will have been roughly similar in shape to that presented in Figure 16-1.

While this last answer is reasonable enough, we would like to do better. Well, we can, and it works like this:

1. Have our computer generate a population of 95.2 million heights whose distribution is similar to Galton's.

2. Ask the computer to randomly select 25,000 observations from this simulated population.

A straightforward method to generate the population is to replicate each of Galton's observations 100,000 times. The outcome would be a distribution of 95.2 million heights that is identical in shape to that in Figure 16-1. But this method is flawed, and we used another. We shall explain our reasoning later on.

Table 16-2 provides descriptive statistics for our simulated sample of 25,000 that was obtained from a simulated population of 95.2 million. The mean, median, and standard deviation are similar to those of Galton's sample, but they are not identical. This was expected and is due to *sampling error* (see Chapter 15). When sampling is random, the actual values obtained are influenced, in part, by chance.

TABLE 16-2 DESCRIPTIVE STATISTICS OF A SAMPLE OF 25,000 HEIGHTS FROM A POPULATION OF 95.2 MILLION

NUMBER OF OBSERVATIONS	MEAN	MEDIAN	STANDARD DEVIATION	MINIMUM	MAXIMUM
25,000	68.188	68.194	2.604	56.902	79.628

Yet there is one notable difference between this larger sample and the one that Galton obtained. It is the range. Here the Heights vary between 56.9 and 79.6 inches; in the smaller sample—in Galton's original data—they ranged between 61.2 and 74.7 inches. This should come as no surprise. Most distributions include *outliers*—values that are very distant from the center and occur infrequently. The larger the sample, the greater is the likelihood of discovering such outliers. Take, for instance, a value occurring at a rate of 1 in 10,000. It is unlikely to emerge in a sample of 952. When sampling 25,000, however, one would expect two or three such values.

This, then, is one flaw of the "straightforward method" described for generating a population. Had we used only the values obtained by Galton, our range could not have exceeded the one he found. But Galton's range was probably off by a great deal. The mean, median, and mode can be estimated accurately by a sample. Usually, the range cannot.

Figure 16-2 shows a histogram for our larger sample. Superimposed on the histogram is a bell-shaped curve.

In Figure 16-3 we present two more histograms. Each is based on our larger sample, and each is constructed using progressively more intervals. From these we see that as the number of intervals increases, the histogram approaches the bell-shaped curve.

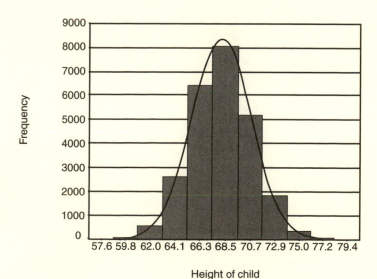

Height of child

FIGURE 16-2 An eight-interval histogram of 25,000 heights.

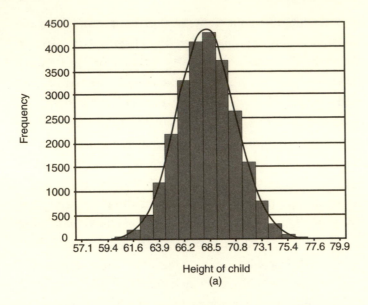

Height of child
(a)

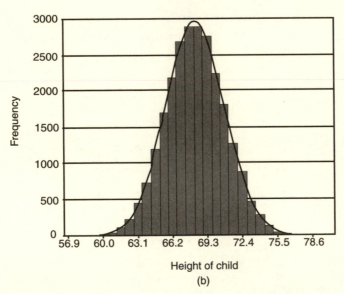

Height of child
(b)

FIGURE 16-3 Histograms of 25,000 heights using (*a*) 21 and (*b*) 31 intervals.

Note that our choice of intervals was arbitrary. We could, for example, have chosen to construct a histogram with 50 or 500 intervals. But had we increased the number indefinitely, our graph would begin to "look funny." This is so because many of the intervals would include no observations. For example, had we constructed 30,000 intervals, at least 5000 would be empty of observations.

INFINITY: A BEGINNING

Suppose that our population were to contain an infinite number of elements. In fact, most populations are sufficiently large that for all practical purposes they can be viewed as such. Suppose further that we constructed a histogram for the whole of the population. No matter how many intervals we chose, none would be empty.* Figure 16–4 describes what would happen as we progressively reduce interval size when constructing a histogram for an infinite population (whose actual distribution is bell-shaped).

A DIFFERENT WAY OF LOOKING

We have been playing an intellectual game. Beginning with a sample of 952 children, we constructed a histogram. We then generated a population of 95.2 million children and selected from it a sample of 25,000. Constructing histograms of decreasing interval size, we found our graphs approaching a bell-shaped curve. Taking the exercise to its logical conclusion, we

1. Introduced the concept of an infinite distribution.

2. Constructed for it a histogram with infinitely narrow intervals.

The outcome was a smooth curve.

So far we have had no special problem with the concept of infinity. But this is about to change. Sometimes, when trying to reason with infinity, strange things happen.

Let us return to Galton's sample and speak of a single child in it. One Alfred J. Malcolm-Hastings.

---

* Technically, this is not completely correct. A population can be infinite yet not have values in a particular interval. In this context we shall dismiss this argument as nit-picking.

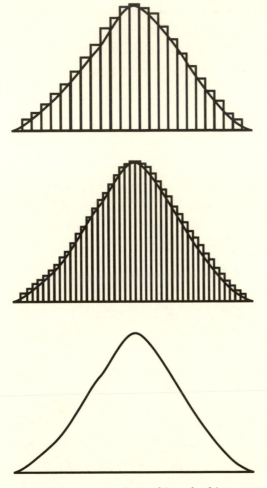

FIGURE 16-4 Smoothing the histogram.

Question: If we randomly select a child from Galton's sample, what is our chance of picking Malcolm-Hastings?

Answer: One out of 952—by definition. In a truly random sample, each particular observation has an equal chance of being selected. Here there are 952 observations, so the probability of sampling a specific child is 1:952. About one in a thousand—not very likely, but not impossible.

Moving on to an infinite population, we ask

Question: Selecting a child at random, what is our chance of obtaining the one and only Malcom-Hastings?

Answer: Using everyday reasoning, our answer is "near 0." Virtually impossible. It is like going to the beach and randomly selecting the same grain of sand we removed from between our toes the preceding day. Using mathematics, our answer is "0"—by definition. Since for all practical purposes "0" and "near 0" are the same, let us remain with the former.

Now, you might accept that obtaining Malcolm-Hastings at random from an infinite distribution is impossible. However, you may argue that selecting his *specific Height* is not. After all, about 1 in every 1000 children in the population is exactly as tall as he is. Recall that when we sample, we are not interested in a particular person—we are interested in all the children this person represents. Thus the probability of sampling his *Height* from the population should be 1 in 1000 as well.

This is where it gets tricky—where the weirdness of infinity comes in. Height is measured on a continuous scale. That is, it can take on *any* value within a specified range. Suppose that Alfred's Height is exactly 70.020738921 inches. We now rephrase the question:

Question: In a sample of size = 1 drawn from an infinite population, what is the chance of obtaining a child whose Height is 70.020738921 inches?

Answer: 0.

If you do not like the answer, add several million digits after the decimal and repeat the question.

The strange part is this: Our reasoning suggests that at any specific point in the distribution there are no observations—that the probability of selecting any particular observation at random is zero. Summing all our "no observations," we obtain . . . nothing. Apparently, our infinite population does not exist. But it does. And you shall have to live with this apparent paradox.

Returning to intervals, we say that a single point on a continuum is akin to an infinitely narrow interval. From the standpoint of probability, there is not a single element of the population in an infinitely narrow interval.

But we *can* speak of wider intervals. And the wider they are, the greater is the probability of obtaining a value in them. What, for example, is the probability of randomly sampling a Height between 70 and 71 inches from our infinite population? Well, we do not yet have the tool to answer the question precisely. But we know that it is not zero.

Let us illustrate the point with, what to some, is a real-world example: Your are watching a rerun of a soccer game that ended 1 to 0. The single goal was scored in regulation time. Sampling one of the game's 90 one-minute intervals at random, what are your chances of witnessing the goal? 1/90. The division into 90 intervals, however, is arbitrary. Suppose that you randomly selected to watch an instant. What are your chances then? Virtually zero (there are, in 90 minutes, an infinite number of "instants"). Now suppose that you watch the whole game. What are your chances then? Well, 100 percent. Thus, as your interval increases, so does your chance of catching the goal.

We are getting ever closer to where we want to be. But we have yet to formally address the issue of probability. In the next section we do this. For the time being, let us simply agree that, in an infinite population,

1. The probability of obtaining a specific observation is zero.

2. The probability of obtaining at random a value from a specified interval depends on the interval's size. The wider it is, the greater is the probability of obtaining a value in it.

PROBABILITY

In mathematics we use the term *probability* to denote *chance*. While chance is often expressed in percentage terms, probability is quantified using values between 0.0 and 1.0. This is merely a matter of convention. For example, when flipping a fair coin, the chance of obtaining heads is 50 percent. That is:

$$\text{Probability of Heads} = P(H) = 1/2 = 0.5$$

Having gotten the terminology out of the way, we return to the histogram in Figure 16-1. It was constructed based on Table 16-3.[*]

---

[*]See Chapter 7 for an explanation of how histograms are constructed.

Question 1: What is the probability that a random sample of one observation will yield a child whose Height is in the first interval?

Answer: Twelve of the 952 observations are in the first interval. Computing probability, we have

P(observation from first interval) = 12/952 = 0.0126

Question 2: What is the probability of obtaining a child from the second interval?

Answer:

P(observation from second interval) = 37/952 = 0.0389

TABLE 16-3 GALTON'S HEIGHT OF A CHILD DATA:
FREQUENCY, PERCENT, AND CUMULATIVE PERCENT
FOR EACH OF 10 INTERVALS

INTERVAL	FREQUENCY	PERCENT	CUMULATIVE PERCENT
60.75–62.15	12	1.26	1.26
62.15–63.55	37	3.89	5.15
63.55–64.95	77	8.09	13.24
64.95–66.35	131	13.76	27.00
66.35–67.75	174	18.28	45.27
67.75–69.15	191	20.06	65.34
69.15–70.55	163	17.12	82.46
70.55–71.95	96	10.08	97.79
71.95–73.35	50	5.25	97.79
73.35–74.75	21	2.21	100.00
Total	952	100	

Question 3: What is the probability of obtaining an observation from *either* of the first two intervals?

Answer:

P(observation from first two intervals) = 12/952 + 37/952 = 49/952
                                        = 0.0126 + 0.0389 = 0.0515

This is the value we find, expressed in percent, in the "Cumulative Percent" column of Table 16-3.

Question 4: What is the probability of obtaining an observation from *any* interval?

Answer:

P(observation from any interval) = 952/952 = 1.0

In this section we have introduced the concept of probability and related it to intervals. More specifically, the probability of obtaining an observation from a particular interval equals the number of observations in the interval divided by the total number of observations.

Area

The total area of a histogram is 100 percent of its area—by definition. For convenience, we shall call this area 1.0. We now return to two of our questions and rephrase them. Note that nothing in our reasoning will change—it is only the language that is different.

Question 1: What is the probability that a random sample of one observation will yield a child whose Height is in the first interval?

Rephrased: What is the proportion of the histogram's total area that is in the first interval?

Answer: 1.26 percent of the histogram's area is in the first interval. The probability of sampling from this interval one at random is 0.0126.

Question 2: What is the probability of obtaining an observation from *either* of the first two intervals?

Rephrased: What proportion of the histogram's total area is in the first two intervals?

Answer: It is the sum of areas of these intervals: 1.26 percent + 3.89 percent = 5.15 percent. Thus the probability of selecting at random from them is 0.0515.

Figure 16-5 illustrates the area just computed.

In any histogram, the height of an interval denotes the number of observations in it. But the area of the rectangle is also meaningful. In general:

P(selecting observation from specific interval)

$$= \frac{\text{area of the interval's rectangle}}{\text{total area of histogram}}$$

Now, recall that in an infinite population

1. A "histogram" with an infinite number of intervals looks like a curve. The rectangles are gone because each interval is so narrow that it is really a point—and even less than this. Connecting these "less than points," we obtain a curve.

2. The probability of selecting at random a specific "nonpoint" is zero.

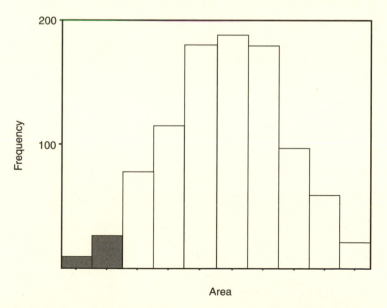

FIGURE 16-5 Proportion of area in the first two intervals.

Thus, when dealing with an infinite population, we do not ask: "What is the chance of obtaining an observation that is exactly x?" The answer is always zero. We ask instead: "What is the probability of obtaining an observation that is from a specific interval?"

From this point on, we shall

1. Deal with curves rather than histograms.

2. Define the total area under a curve as 1.0.

3. Define the probability of obtaining an observation between two points as the area under the curve in the corresponding interval.

Keep in mind that our reasoning for curves is the same as that used for histograms. It is just that curves look a bit different. Note also that computing areas under curves is a bit more involved than doing it for rectangles. But it can be done, and Isaac Newton showed us how. If you would like to do it yourself, pick up a book on differential calculus.

Finally a Model

The title of this chapter is "Models," and we have yet to present a single one. We have, however, introduced several concepts that are crucial to understanding the model we are about to present. That model is called the *normal curve* and is also known as the *bell-shaped* or *gaussian curve*. It is the most widely used model in statistics. For the time being, we ask that you remain impractical. Simply accept the model we present as is. Soon you will see that it is also useful.

The normal curve has the following characteristics:

1. It is perfectly symmetrical and bell-shaped. Indeed, it looks precisely like the curve we superimposed on the histograms earlier.

2. Being perfectly symmetrical, its mean and median are identical.

3. Its mode is identical to the mean and median. That is, the area of greatest *density*—where the largest number of data points reside—is also in the middle.

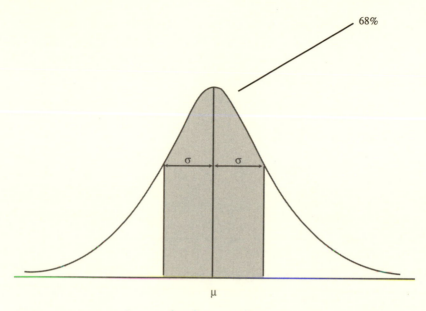

FIGURE 16-6 Area under the curve between −σ and +σ from the mean.

4. The area under the curve within one standard deviation on either side of the mean is 68 percent.[*] This is how the normal curve is constructed. In other words, this is true because we made it so. Figure 16-6 shows this graphically. The shaded area represents the interval whose width is two standard deviations—one on either side of the mean.

Stating the characteristic of the normal curve more formally, we say: *The area under the curve between* $\mu + \sigma$ *and* $\mu - \sigma$ *= 0.68.*

We are now ready to make probabilistic statements about a population described by the normal curve. For example, were we to select an observation at random from it, our chance for a value within one standard deviation of the mean is 0.68. That is:

P(observation between -1σ and $+1\sigma$ from μ) = 0.68

Because the distribution is perfectly symmetrical, we can also say

P(selecting an observation between -1σ and μ) = 0.68/2 = 0.34
P(selecting an observation between μ and $+1\sigma$) = 0.68/2 = 0.34

---

[*] To be more precise, it is 68.26 percent. Throughout, we shall use rounded values.

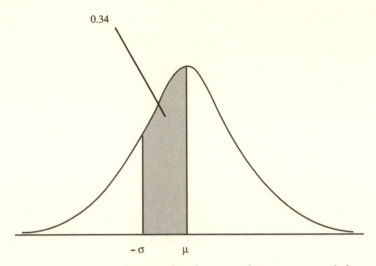

FIGURE 16-7 Area under the curve between -σ and the mean.

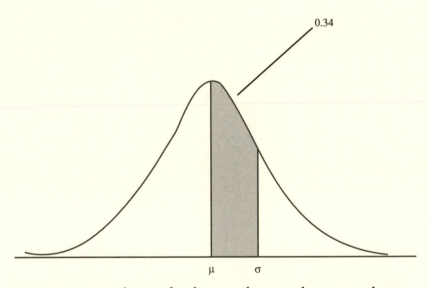

FIGURE 16-8 Area under the curve between the mean and +σ.

We show this graphically in Figures 16-7 and 16-8. Note that, as before, we construct intervals and talk about the areas in them. Recall also that we can choose any width interval we wish. Here we find it useful to construct intervals whose width is a standard deviation.

In the normal model, the following is also true:

1. The area between $\mu - 2\sigma$ and $\mu + 2\sigma = 0.95$.

2. The area between $\mu - 3\sigma$ and $\mu + 3\sigma = 0.99$.*

That is, about 95 percent of the curve's area is within two standard deviations of the mean and about 99 percent is within three standard deviations of the mean.

The normal curve is a model and is generated by a mathematical function. No more and no less. For us, however, a concept is only useful to the degree that it advances our understanding of the real world. In the following chapters you will see that it does.

---

* Actually, it is 0.9974, which we would usually round to 1.00. However, we would like to make it clear that there is still some area beyond 3σ, so we round to 0.99 instead.

Using Models—A Start

GAMBLING

You are driving from Paris to Metz. The sky is clear, and grapes are heavy on the vines. The posted limit is 130 kilometers per hour (kph), but most drive faster. You stop for a rest. Your curious companion takes out her laser gun and clocks the passing cars.

Back on the road, your companion transfers the data from her gun to a spreadsheet on her laptop. She finds that the average speed of the 63 cars she has clocked is 137 kph, and the standard deviation is 7. She tests the data and finds that they are more or less normally distributed.[*] This does not surprise her—many things are normally distributed.

Doing some quick arithmetic, she finds that 130 is one standard deviation below the mean and 144 is one standard deviation above. Based on this and the normal model,[†] she tells you that 68 percent of *all* drivers on the highway—not just those she has clocked—travel at speeds of between 130 and 144 kph (see Chapter 16). Translating this into probabilities, she tells you that if the highway patrol were to clock a car at random, there is a 0.68

---

[*]Using a procedure that is beyond the scope of this book but not beyond her.
[†]And the assumption that the sample mean of 137 that she has found is the true population mean. Although a problematic assumption, we will let her get away with it.

chance that the speed it records will be between 130 and 144 kph (the interval between one standard deviation below and above the mean). This leaves 32 percent of drivers whose speed is below 130 or above 144 kph. Since the normal distribution is symmetrical, she concludes that 16 percent of all drivers on the road drive faster than 144 kph (half of 32 percent). (See Figure 17-1.)

It is 12:15 P.M., and Metz is still a ways away. If you are to arrive for lunch, you had better drive faster. Unfortunately, you have what the Viennese term an "overdeveloped superego." Still, you reason that the French police are sensible—that they cannot possibly consider 144 kph the cutoff for issuing tickets. If they did, they would end up stopping 16 percent of drivers. You increase your speed to 144 kph and engage the cruise control. And you have a decent dinner in Metz.

GEORGE BRUSH

One morning in the late summer of 1930 the proprietor and several guests at the Union Hotel at Crestcrego, Texas, were annoyed to discover Biblical texts freshly written across the blotter on the public writing desk. Two days later the guests at McCarty's Inn, Usquepaw, in the same state were similarly irritated. . . . The same evening a young man passing the First Baptist Church, and seeing that the Annual Bible Question Bee was in progress, paid his fifteen cents and, taking his place against the wall, won the first prize. . . .

THORNTON WILDER[1]

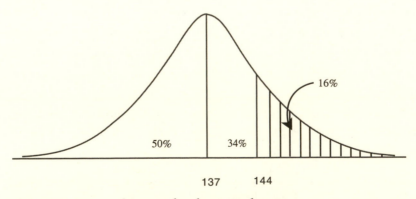

FIGURE 17-1 Areas under the normal curve.

It is the Great Depression, and many are out of work. Many more will lose their jobs in the days to come. This is the backdrop to the story of George Brush, a textbook salesman.

Traveling by train, the young man hocks his employer's wares in small southern towns. He shows his books to education board members and meets with school superintendents. Despite his naïveté, or perhaps because of it, Brush effects the goodwill of those he meets. Some eye him for their daughters, which does not harm sales either.

But George Brush pitches more than books. One day on a train,

> . . . [he] picked up his briefcase and went forward to the smoking-car . . . and chose a seat beside a tall leather-faced man in shirt sleeves.
>
> "Sit down, buddy," said the man. "You're rocking the car. Sit down and lend me a match."
>
> "My name is George Brush. . . . I'm glad to meet you. I travel in school books. I was born in Michigan and I'm on my way to Wellington, Oklahoma."
>
> "That's fine," said the other. "That's fine, only relax, sonny, relax. Nobody's arrested you."
>
> . . . "In beginning a conversation I like to get all the facts on the table."

Preparing his pitch, George Brush says:

> "Brother, can I talk to you about the most important thing in life?"
>
> ". . . If it's insurance, I got too much," he said. "If it's oil-wells, I don't touch 'em, and if its religion, I'm saved."
>
> Brush had an answer even for this. . . .
>
> . . . "That's fine. There is no greater pleasure than to talk over the big things with a believer."
>
> "I'm saved," continued the other, "from making a godam fool of myself in public places. I'm saved, you little peahen, from putting my head into other people's business. So shut your damn face and get out of here, or I'll rip your tongue out of your throat."
>
> "You're angry, brother," said Brush, "because you're aware of an unfulfilled life."

As the conversation progresses, Brush's quarry becomes even more irritated. Finally, the man has had enough. He picks up the young man's briefcase and tosses it out the train window.

George Brush is an attractive young man but not exceptionally so. He is a fine textbook salesman, but here, too, he is not remarkable. But his religious devotion is rare indeed.

Novelists take particular pleasure in exceptional characters and go to great lengths to find them. Where they cannot, they invent them. But for a scientist it is not so simple to discover such rare birds. Being uncommon, the likes of George Brush will not often show up in random samples.

A sociologist explores religious devotion in the United States. She randomly selects 1000 Americans and finds no one remotely like Brush. Based solely on the information at hand, she must conclude that George Brush is fiction. Yet our researcher knows better. She is aware that not finding Brush does not mean that he is not there. It may simply be a matter of sample size. Had she obtained a larger sample, she might have found him. Then again, she may not have.

In statistics, we call this issue *power*. It is the degree to which we are able to discover that a phenomenon exists. Let us take an analogy from Rothbart Laboratories, where a meticulous clinician is examining a blood sample for bacteria. He looks through his microscope and finds nothing. Being a good researcher, he knows that this is not proof that the bacteria are not there. It may simply be that his magnifying power is not enough—that the bacteria are actually there but that he does not have the power to discover them.

In statistics, we describe populations using samples. But samples are mere subsets of the wholes and cannot reflect them exactly. A statistician's magnifying power—her ability to describe the whole of reality accurately—is in great measure determined by sample size.*

So our sociologist has sampled 1000 Americans and has failed to find a George Brush. She does not know what to think. *We* know that somewhere out there George lives. After all, Thornton Wilder has written a book about him (albeit, a short book).

Now there are at least two solutions to our scientist's quandary. The first is to obtain a nonrandom sample. She might, for example, spend a year vis-

---

*Sample size is but one element determining power. Others include reliable measurement, the variation in the population, and mere luck. Here, however, we focus on sample size.

iting the kinds of churches where one is likely to find Brush. If she finds him, she knows he exists. If she does not, she will probably conclude that he is fiction.*

But having obtained a nonrandom sample introduces another difficulty. Suppose that she finds Brush. Indeed, suppose that she has sampled 100 churchgoers and found *three* Brush types. While she can conclude that he exists, she has no way of estimating his true proportion in the population in the United States. It is certainly not the 3 percent she has found.

Her alternative is to obtain a larger random sample, say, 30,000. But this too is a problem. First, sampling so many people is impractical. Second, even the larger sample may not bag her quarry. Remember, her haystack has hundreds of millions of straws in it, and Brush is a mere needle in it.

There is, however, a third alternative, and it involves using models. Let us see how it works. The scientist begins by asking the question, "How inclined are Americans to proselytize?" She defines a variable Propensity to Proselytize, which she measures via questionnaire. Her survey includes 100 questions like the following:

- Should a religious person share his or her religious experience with others?

- Is being a missionary a worthwhile undertaking?

- Do you talk to people about God?

- Do you write biblical texts on hotel blotters?

The sociologist randomly selects 1000 Americans and administers the survey to each. She computes Propensity to Proselytize by counting the number of items answered "yes." Each person now has a score between 0 and 100. Table 17-1 summarizes her results. Here, the mean and standard deviation are sample statistics and so are denoted with Latin letters. Generalizing the data in Table 17-1, our sociologist estimates the population parameters to be

$$\mu = 50 \quad \text{and} \quad \sigma = 10$$

---

*And she may still be wrong.

TABLE 17-1 DESCRIPTIVE STATISTICS FOR PROPENSITY TO PROSELYTIZE

	NUMBER OF OBSERVATIONS	MIN	MAX	MEAN ($\bar{x}$)	STANDARD DEVIATION (sd)
Propensity to Proselytize	1000	19	82	50.0	10

From theory, the researcher knows that George Brush is an 85 at least. Alas, the highest score in the data obtained is 82. Not having found him, she is still asking whether he exists.

Moving on, the sociologist constructs a histogram for her data. Based on the histogram (Figure 17-2), she concludes that Propensity to Proselytize is normally distributed *in the population.*

Our researcher has now extrapolated the following from sample to population:

- Central tendency ($\mu = 50$)

- Spread ($\sigma = 10$)

- Shape (normal)

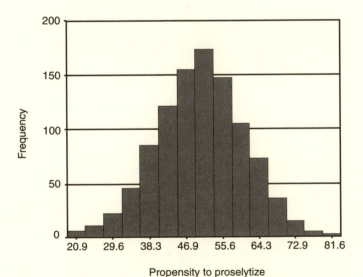

Propensity to proselytize

FIGURE 17-2 Distribution of Propensity to Proselytize.

Using the normal model, she concludes, for example, that[*]

- 68 percent of Americans have a Propensity to Proselytize score between 40 and 60 ($\pm 1\sigma$ from the mean).

- 95 percent have a score between 30 and 70 ($\mu \pm 2\sigma$).

- 99 percent score between 20 and 80 ($\mu \pm 3\sigma$).

And what about George Brush?

Well, George Brush is at an 85 at least—3.5 standard deviations from the mean or above. This value was computed using the formula for standard distance introduced in Chapter 6:

$$z = \frac{x - \overline{x}}{\text{sd}} = \frac{85 - 50}{10} = 3.5$$

Note that in this formula we use $\overline{x}$ and sd rather than the population parameters (μ and σ), which are unavailable.

Our sociologist also knows that the following two questions are equivalent:

1. What is the proportion of George Brush Types in the population?

2. What proportion of the area in the normal curve is at 3.5σ and above?[†]

Statisticians have constructed tables that provide areas under the curve for different values of z. Nowadays, these are programmed into computers. Using such a table, our sociologist finds that the area under the curve from 3.5σ onward is 0.0002. Figure 17-3 shows this area.

She can now conclude that

1. George Brush exists.

2. About 2 of every 10,000 Americans are George Brush types.

---

[*]Actually, extrapolating from the normal model is a bit more involved than presented here, as will be shown in Chapter 21. For the purpose of illustrating our point, let us for now keep to this simplistic (and not completely correct) example.

[†]That is, between 3.5σ and infinity. Here, the maximum possible score is 100, which is in fact a great deal less than infinity. Practically speaking, we can use the normal distribution as is. This is so because 100 is five standard deviations from the mean, and in the normal distribution, this is sufficiently distant from the mean to be regarded as infinity.

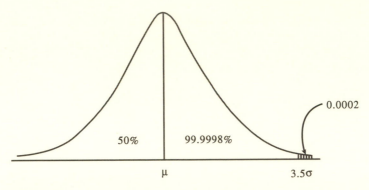

FIGURE 17-3 Area under the curve from 3.5 standard deviations and beyond.

A Fine Point

Our sociologist had two choices for estimating probability. She could, as she did for μ, simply have used the data at hand. For instance, in *her* sample, 67 percent of observations were within one standard deviation of the mean. Generalizing to the population, she could have said: "The proportion of Americans between 40 and 60 *in the population* is 0.67." This is a reasonable generalization.

However, our sociologist did something else. She used a model and obtained 68 percent. Not very different.[*] But the fact remains that she extrapolated with the aid of a model rather than using her data alone. Why?

In Chapter 15 we noted that most distributions include outliers and that samples are not very good at finding them—at least not those points that are very outlying. As a result, our researcher cannot trust her range. Had she obtained a larger sample, her range would have probably been greater.

Statistically, we say that the sample range is a *biased estimate* of the population range. It can, and usually does, err in one direction only—it is smaller. When estimates are biased, they ought to be adjusted. And a model can help us do it .

The mean, on the other hand, is not biased. While samples miss outliers, they miss them equally at both ends of the scale—on average. Thus

---

[*]In another study or, for that matter, in another sample for this very same study, the disparity may have been much greater.

the mean "balances out" as an estimate of μ. Consequently, we claim that $\bar{x}$ is an *unbiased estimator* of μ, whereas the range is not.

What about the sample standard deviation? (*Note:* Statisticians denote sample statistics using Latin letters and population statistics using Greek letter. Thus the sample standard deviation is denoted *sd,* and the population is denoted σ.) On average, the sd as computed in Chapter 7 will be smaller than σ. This is so because it is computed on a sample, which typically will not include the outlying values in the population—the values that are far out and that would increase the sd if they were included. Thus the sd too must be adjusted and is. The *unbiased estimator for* σ is computed as

$$sd = \sqrt{\frac{\Sigma(x_i - \bar{x})^2}{n - 1}}$$

where n is the number of observations in the sample.

In computing the sample sd, we divide by $n - 1$ rather than n, which adjusts our estimate upward.[*] This, then, is our unbiased estimate for σ. Thus our sociologist used a model to correct for bias. Yet we also can look at her thinking from another, perhaps deeper angle.

Samples are designed to estimate the truth. Yet they only provide estimates—different samples from the same population will produce "different truths." But the truth is one. That is, every population has a single, true μ and a single, true σ. As a result, the researcher says to herself: "I must take my estimates with a grain of salt. They are specific to the sample obtained. While they provide me with my best guesses, they may or may not be very good."

At the end of the day, therefore, our scientist decides to put more trust in a model than in her data. Now this seems a strange kind of reasoning. Most people would be more inclined to believe what they see (data) than what they do not (theory).

But really, our theoretical models are based on data as well. Suppose that you have known a person for many years and know him to be honest. Based on many encounters—based on historical data—you have built a model that says, "This man is honest." Now suppose that you have caught him lying once. Would you discard your model? Perhaps not.

---

[*]Note that when the sample is small, this correction greatly increases our estimate (relative to when dividing by n). When the sample is large, it makes little difference.

From experience, we know that when samples behave more or less normally, their populations do as well. *We believe that models work because they have worked*—countless times. We shall continue to trust them until proven otherwise. No less important, models do for us what the data cannot. They tell us about things we have not seen and perhaps never will. Witness our sociologist's inference about George Brush's proportion in the population.

Apparently, choosing to use models is founded as much on utility as on belief. This is a critical point. Models allow for far-ranging *inferences*—such that would be impossible based on data alone.

CHAPTER XVIII

Another Model

CHARGING THE CAVALRY

Between 1875 and 1894, 122 Prussian cavalrymen were kicked to death by horses. This startling statistic is based on data from 10 cavalry corps over the 20 years in question—a total of 200 yearly observations. Table 18-1 summarizes these data.

Using these numbers, we can "predict" the probability of each of these events occurring in 1895 or any other year. That is, we can compute the likelihood for a corps to experience 0, 1, or 2 Deaths, etc. The probabilities are provided in the table's last column.

But computing likelihood based on data alone has its drawbacks (see Chapter 17). Suppose, for instance, that we would like to know the probability of a corps experiencing 5 Deaths in a single year. While we expect this to be a rare event, it is certainly possible. Therefore, it should not be 0. Yet predicting from the data alone leaves us no choice but to conclude that such an event cannot happen. Since it never did, it never will. In Chapter 17 we showed how to use the normal model to extrapolate values that were not observed in a sample. Let us then apply the method here.

TABLE 18-1 DEATHS PER CORPS PER YEAR OVER 20 YEARS

DEATHS IN A SINGLE YEAR (EVENT)	NUMBER OF CORPS IN WHICH OBSERVED	PROBABILITY
0	109	$109/200 = 0.545$
1	65	0.325
2	22	0.110
3	3	0.015
4	1	0.005
5	0	0.000
Total	200	1.000

In the current data,

$$\overline{x} = 0.6 \qquad \text{and} \qquad sd = 0.8$$

These are our estimates for μ and σ. Using them in conjunction with the normal model, we state, for example, that 68 percent of the corps will have between -0.2 and 1.4 Deaths ($\mu \pm \sigma$)—in other words, a probability of 0 or 1 Deaths occurring in a given corps is 0.68.

However, this particular statement is not very consistent with our data, which suggest that the actual likelihood of 0 or 1 Deaths is 0.87 (0.545 + 0.325). When a model does an inadequate job of describing reality, we say that it does not fit the data. That this is clearly the case can be seen in Figure 18-1, where we superimpose the normal distribution on our current numbers.

Therefore, if we insist on using a model, we had better find another. But let us first examine our result from a different angle.

A DIFFERENT WAY OF LOOKING

Standard scores provide *relative distance* from the mean—the degree to which specific data points differ from the typical value of a distribution (see Chapter 8). Computing the standard score for 0 Deaths, we obtain

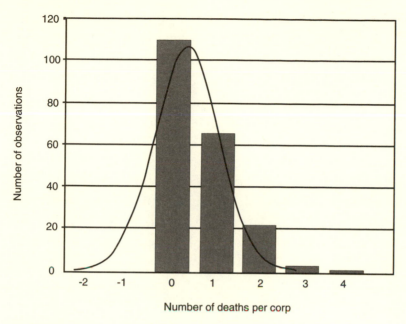

FIGURE 18-1 Distributions of deaths observed with the normal curve superimposed.

$$z_0 = \frac{0 - 0.6}{0.8} = -0.75$$

Computing it for 1, we have

$$z_1 = \frac{1 - 0.6}{0.8} = 0.5$$

Since z_1 is nearer the mean than z_0, we might conclude that 1 Death was more common than none was. In fact, the event 0 outnumbered event 1 by 109 to 65.

This apparent contradiction is explained easily by our having compared apples with oranges. Standard scores provide distance from the mean, whereas the term *common* relates to the mode. Recall that the mode is the most common observation in the data. "0 Deaths" is in fact further from the mean than "1 Death," but it is nearer the mode. Indeed, it *is* the mode.

Now in a normal distribution the mean and mode are identical. So whatever you say about one holds for the other. But as shown in the preceding section, the distribution of Death by Horse-Kick is something other than normal.

In Chapter 6 we wrote that the mean is not robust—that in *skewed* distributions it "gets pulled away" from where most of the data reside toward the extreme values. Well, Death by Horse-Kick is skewed. And it is bounded at the lower end by 0 and is not bounded at the upper end.

To interpret the meaning of distance, we need a context, and for this we compute z. The z transformation turns relative distance into absolute distance by dividing by variation. But in Chapter 8 we noted that this is not enough. To understand the meaning of z easily, we need yet another context—*shape*. Thus the meaning of a standard score depends on the shape of the distribution. Clearly, if we are to specify a model here, we must use one that is something other than normal. Let us then return to the task at hand, which is to find an appropriate model for our data.

POISSON

Siméon-Denis Poisson was born in 1781 in Pithiviers, France. His father hoped he would study medicine and practically forced the discipline on him. In later life, however, Poisson would claim: "Life is good for only two things, discovering mathematics and teaching mathematics."

The child Siméon had a nursemaid. Upon leaving him alone in the house, she harnessed him to a cord attached to the wall. The cord indeed kept the child out of mischief, but the mind is not so easily harnessed. Poisson would later say that his gymnastics on the cord introduced him to the motion of pendulums. As a mathematician, he explored this motion.

In 1809, Poisson became chairman of pure mathematics on the Faculté des Sciences in Paris, and science became his devotion. After Poisson's death, a colleague would say that "His only passion has been science: He lived and is dead for it."

In 1837, Poisson published an important work on probability. In it he set out what became known as the *Poisson model*, which describes the distribution of rare events over time. Some examples include

- Earthquakes

- Power failures

- Lottery wins

- Deaths from horse-kick

Each of these events is relatively rare. But within a given time period, each happens. Using the Poisson distribution in conjunction with historical data, we can make predictions. For example, suppose that we know that a particular power generator fails once a year on average. Extrapolating the Poisson distribution enables us to predict its chance for not failing in a particular year. Or for failing one time or more.

Unlike the normal distribution, of which there is only one, there are many Poisson distributions—one for each mean. Figure 18-2 presents a Poisson distribution with a mean of 0.6. Recall that this is the value for Death by Horse-Kick. Superimposing the model on our data, we obtain Figure 18-3.

In Table 18-2 we show the likelihood of seven types of events according to a Poisson model with $\mu = 0.6$. As can be seen, the model's results are very similar to what actually happened. Now, it is no mathematical tour de force to fit a line to data. Remember, however, that Poisson developed his model long before the cavalry data were collected—and the fit is uncanny.

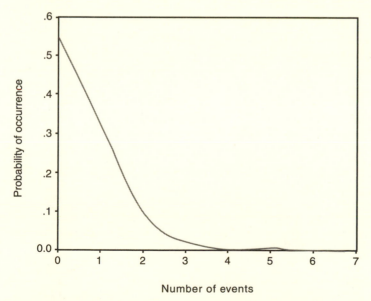

FIGURE 18-2 The Poisson distribution: $\mu = 0.6$.

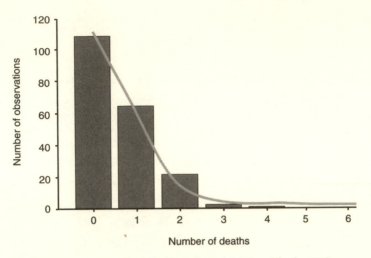

FIGURE 18-3   Deaths from horse-kick with the Poisson model superimposed.

With our newfound knowledge we can now compute the likelihood of events that never occurred. For example, from Table 18-2 we learn that the probability of a corps experiencing 5 Deaths is about 5 in 10,000. Thus we would predict this particular event to happen once every 2000 years. This is a convenient prediction. After all, it will never be tested. This is not the

TABLE 18-2 PROBABILIES DERIVED FROM A POISSON DISTRIBUTION WITH $\mu = 0.6$ CONTRASTED WITH THE PRUSSIAN CAVALRY DATA

EVENT (NO. OF OCCURRENCES)	THEORETICAL PROBABILITY OF OCCURRENCE[a]	"PREDICTION" FOR WHAT OCCURRED OVER 20 YEARS	WHAT ACTUALLY OCCURRED OVER 20 YEARS
0	0.548812	$54.9 \times 200 = 110$	109
1	0.329287	66	65
2	0.098786	20	22
3	0.019757	4	3
4	0.002964	1	1
5	0.000456	0	Did not occur
6	0.000003	0	Did not occur

[a] The sum of these probabilities should not exceed 1.0, and it does, by a bit. This is because of rounding.

case for many other earthly phenomena, such as earthquakes or birth defects, for which the Poisson model is indeed useful.

A NOTE ON THE POISSON

Figure 18-4 shows three more Poisson distributions, each with a different mean. As can be seen, as the mean increases in size, the Poisson distribution

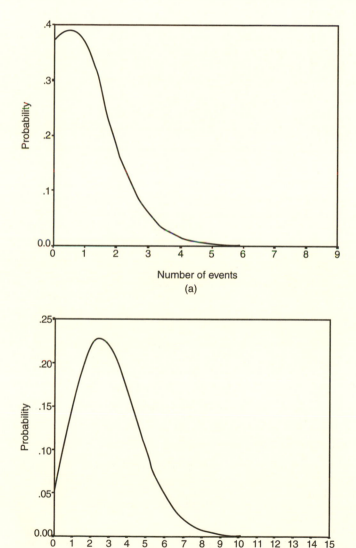

FIGURE 18-4 Poisson distributions for (*a*) $\mu = 1$, (*b*) $\mu = 2$, and (*c*) $\mu = 3$.

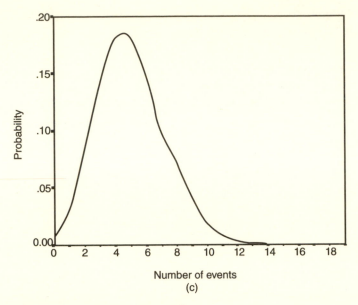

FIGURE 18-4 *(Continued).*

approaches normality. In fact, large means yield Poisson distributions that are approximately normal. Where events occur relatively often—where the mean is relatively large—using either of these two distributions will yield similar results.

Recall that distributions bounded at one end and not at the other tend to be asymmetrical—but not necessarily. For example, Height is bounded at the lower end (0) but, theoretically, not the upper. Still, it is normal. But Height differs from our current example in that its impossible (negative) values are far below the actual mean of heights typically encountered. Not so for Death by Horse-Kick, where the distance between 0—the lower bound—and the mean is less than one standard deviation. Height has a great deal of "room to expand" at the lower end, whereas Deaths does not. Here again, therefore, we see the importance of distance. Its magnitude signifies an observation's uniqueness, and its physical constraints can greatly affect a distribution's shape.

Several chapters ago we described what models are not. Meanwhile, we have shown how to apply two of them. Perhaps it is time to discuss what models actually are.

CHAPTER XIX

What, Then, Are Models?

Returning to Deptford from the Great War, Dunstan Ramsay found a warm welcome and little else. His brother had been killed in the war, and his parents were lost to the epidemic of 1918. Dunstan left his hometown and did not return. As an old man, he recalled his childhood:

> Sometimes on our Sunday walks along the railroad track we were joined by Sam West, an electrician with a mind above the limitations of his work. . . . His detestation of religion and churches was absolute, and he scolded about them in a language that owed all its bite to the Old Testament. . . . His imitations of the parsons were finely observed, and he was very good as the Reverend Andrew Bowyer: "O Lord, take Thou a live coal from off Thine alter and touch our lips," he would shout, in a caricature of our minister's fine Edinburgh accent; then, with a howl of laughter, "Wouldn't he be surprised if his prayer was answered!"
>
> If he hoped to make an atheist of me, this was where he went wrong; I knew a metaphor when I heard one, and liked metaphor better than reason. I have known many atheists since Sam, and they all fall down on metaphor.[1]

Perhaps people are inclined to simplify in their memoirs. Dunstan certainly does when he says that all atheists slip on metaphor's slick surface. And he does it again when he relates his preference for metaphor over reason.

Surely Ramsay must admit to there being at least one atheist who knows a metaphor when he hears it. And even he would concede the odd metaphor's inferiority to reason.

But we are being overly literal—a common failing of scientific thinkers. Dunstan's statements were meant only as general rules, exceptions implied. In statistics we call such rules *models*. Dunstan was not bothered by his generalizations, and neither should we be. For a model to be adequate, it need only be true "on average." If this sounds familiar, it should.

In this book we were dealing with models long before we introduced the term. Thus the *mean* is a model that describes data "on average." And the *standard deviation* models distances in a distribution "in general."

In Chapter 16 we told the story of Robert, a model student—the kind others should emulate. Statistical models are different in that they do not demand conformity. Rather, it is they who must conform to the data. In statistics, we fit curves to numbers and not the other way around. As such, our models describe *what is,* not what should be.

Robert's Matchbox cars are models in the sense of replicas. They are meant to be precise representations. Our models are more modest. While they too are meant to depict reality, they suffer exceptions. When saying that the mean represents the data, we do not say that all the numbers are at the mean exactly. Similarly, when asserting that data are normally distributed, we do not claim that each and every point is on the curve exactly. We only say that the normal curve describes them "adequately."

Therefore, one way to view statistical models is as "rules"—simplified representations of reality. Let us try another view.

MATHEMATICS

The following function generates the normal curve:

$$y = \frac{1}{\sqrt{2\pi\sigma^2}} \, e^{-(x-\mu)/2\sigma^2}$$

This is the normal model.

The following function generates the Poisson curve:

$$\text{Probability of (event)} = \frac{\mu^{ye^{-y}}}{y!}$$

This is the Poisson model.

In this book we have made every effort to avoid complex mathematical statements. Here, we have made exceptions but are not about to explain their algebraic mechanics. Indeed, knowing the algebra will get us no nearer to understanding the concept of model in mathematics.

So why have we bothered with these functions at all? Well, it is to make a point: In statistics, *a model is a mathematical statement*. First and foremost, it is a *definition* in the peculiar language of mathematics. Our first formula above defines the normal distribution, and our second defines the Poisson distribution.

Now mathematics is a language like any other. And while its vocabulary is limited compared with most, it is particularly suited for describing curves. Had we wished, we could have described the normal curve in English, but it would not have been very plain.

Yet this difference in ability to describe curves is not the main distinction between mathematics and English. The fundamental distinction between the two is their attitude toward reality. In English we typically demand that our definitions be grounded in the real world. Not so in mathematics.

Feynman wrote

> Mathematicians are only dealing with the structure of reasoning, and they do not really care what they are talking about. They do not even need to *know* what they are talking about, or, as they themselves say, whether what they say is true. . . . But in physics you have to have an understanding of the connection of words with the real world. It is necessary at the end to translate what you have figured out into English, into the world. . . . This is not a problem of mathematics at all.[2]

The applied statistical approach to definitions is nearer to the physicist's than it is to the mathematician's. For us, a definition is only useful to the extent that it relates to the real world. In this sense it is also similar to our use of language in the everyday.

Webster's defines *pudding* as "a soft, thickened dessert, typically made with milk, sugar, flour, and flavoring."[3] This is a model in the sense that it describes the reality of pudding in general. Its proof is in the eating—in the degree to which it appropriately describes reality. So it is with our statistical models, whose proof is in the degree to which they relate to the way things are.

Notwithstanding, we also use mathematical definitions that were derived theoretically. At the same time, we demand that they describe reality. That this actually works—that theoretical structures of reasoning actually can lead to a better understanding of nature—is one of the wonders of existence.

AN EXAMPLE

> As a rule, Alfred sleeps 8 hours a night.

This is a model-type statement in plain English. Although it reflects reality, it is a simplification as well. After all, it is a rule with many exceptions. Let us now translate this rule into our own peculiar language.

For almost a year now, Alfred has been keeping a diary. In it he has also recorded the times at which he has gone to bed and risen. Since Alfred did not fall asleep immediately on going to bed, his "going to sleep" times are biased. To correct for this, we have subtracted 10 minutes from each Sleep Time that was computed based on "going to sleep" time and "rising" times. Figure 19-1 shows the distribution of 347 times obtained from the diary, and Table 19-1 provides simple descriptive statistics for the data.

These data make up a sample of Alfred's population of Sleep Time and are subject to sampling error. Had we sampled other nights or more nights, our result would have been different. Consequently, in generalizing from these data to the population, we must take our estimates with a grain of salt. Recall that the aim of sampling is extrapolating to the population.

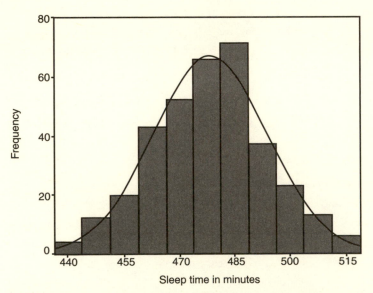

FIGURE 19-1 Distribution of Alfred's Sleep Time.

TABLE 19-1 DESCRIPTIVE STATISTICS OF ALFRED'S SLEEP TIME

	NUMBER OF OBSERVATIONS	MIN	MAX	MEAN $(\bar{x})$	STANDARD DEVIATION (sd)
Sleep Time in minutes	347	436.5	518.3	478.3	15.5

In later chapters we will show how we take our estimates of means with a grain of salt—how we account for sampling error when extrapolating means from sample to population. Here, we are concerned with learning the true *shape* of the distribution of Sleep Time from our sample.

Looking at the histogram, we see that it is not perfectly normal. At the same time, the normal curve is adequate for it.* We are now ready to translate our statement from English into statistics. In English:

As a rule, Alfred sleeps 8 hours a night.

In statistics:

Sleep Time ≈ normal ($\mu = 478.3$, $\sigma = 15.5$)

In statistical English, this reads as "Sleep Time is approximately normally distributed with a mean of 478.3 and a standard deviation of 15.5."

By assuming normality, we have "smoothed" the data—have ignored its deviations from the curve. In addition, we have applied the theoretical normal model to real numbers. In other words, we have used mathematics to simplify our description of the data. This is equivalent to the kind of simplifications we do in everyday language when we use words such as *typically* and *in general*.

Now there is more to this story than meets the eye. As you may have guessed, Alfred does not have a diary. In fact, there is no Alfred. These data were obtained by

1. Having the computer generate an infinite population that is perfectly normal and whose $\mu = 480$ and $\sigma = 16$.

---

* In fact, we have conducted a test for this purpose and found that the data can be considered normal.

2. Asking the computer to randomly select 347 observations from the population.

As evidenced by Figure 19-1, the sample did not reflect the population exactly. This is to be expected. Our point is different and is this: The *true* distribution of Sleep Times is perfectly normal—we constructed it thus. However, the sample obtained did not perfectly conform to normality. Yet, based on the sample, we assumed normality regardless. Thus our assumption using theory yielded a picture that was nearer the truth (that could not be had) than the actual data (that were had). Because of sampling error, *we often believe models implied by data more than the data itself.* In this, admittedly contrived, example we were certainly correct in doing so.

WHAT, THEN, ARE MODELS?

Models, then, are all the following:

- Rules

- Simplified representations of reality

- Mathematical statements

Finally, models suggested by the data are often nearer the truth (in the population) than the data themselves. In statistics, this is typically our working assumption.

CHAPTER XX

Sampling Distributions

THE NUMBER SIX

The *convoy of repentance* reached Jerusalem in 1882 with 1000 French pilgrims. The city was dusty in those days and small. Its few hostels could not accommodate the pilgrims, and they housed in tents instead.

The Russians had done better. By the time the French had arrived, much of their compound was built and offering shelter to compatriot pilgrims. Not to be outdone, the French began building Notre Dame de France in 1884. They completed the hostel 20 years later, its towers surpassing the Russian domes.

The twentieth century was difficult for Notre Dame de France. The Turks evicted its monks in World War I and damaged the building. The monks returned with the British conquest a few years later. In World War II the building was impounded again—this time by the British themselves. But the once-mighty empire was declining, and before long its soldiers left. Soon Israel was born, and the Arabs attacked. The Jews captured the hostel and, between one war and another, in their hands it remains.

Jerusalem is a good-sized city now and almost modern. Notre Dame de France is restored and is once again a hostel. But there is the feel of the ancient about it still. The structure stands on a hillside littered with the kind of stone from which it was built. Thorns thrive outside its fences, and a short distance beyond are the Old City walls. From within the walls emanate the sounds of Moslem muezzins and Christian bells.

Then there is the sound of traffic. The structure stands on a hill above Paratrooper Road, so named for the city's liberators. The din is constant as traffic weaves within and upon itself, which is the way of the East.

Brother Joire has been at Notre Dame for over a year now, but his cassock still smells of the French countryside. Perhaps in a few more months he will finally settle down to the business of being intentionally holy. Maybe it will take another year. But for now he still looks on the city with wonder. He *feels* the holy without trying.

The young man does what he can to subdue his disquiet. He performs his chores with immoderate energy and is excessive in devotion. Early on, he took on Number 6. The schedule indicates that the Number 6 bus arrives at Notre Dame de France on the hour. It mostly does. Except that Jerusalem's hours are not quite those that the brother knows from his watch. Five times every day, six days a week, he stands by his open window and watches for the bus. Observing the stop nearest Notre Dame, he records the number of minutes the bus is early or late. Sometimes the young man is so full of anticipation that he is deaf to both muezzins and bells. Often, he is only vaguely aware of the din of the traffic below.

Brother Joire has been recording Arrival Time for almost a year now. He has filled many pages with numbers and likes looking at their orderly columns. The young man has mentioned this in confession—not so much the activity as his enjoyment of it. His confessor told him not to fret. Brother Joire has not reconciled to the advice but is thankful for it.

When Brother Joire finds the time, he plays around with his numbers. He charts them and computes their many averages. The young man is not a statistician and would be hard put to describe what such a creature does. Still, he does statistics.

After 8 days of observation, he graphed the 40 arrivals recorded and obtained the graph shown in Figure 20-1. Looking at the graph, Brother Joire noticed that there is no pattern to the bus's arrival. That is, it seems as if the bus is as likely to arrive at any point within 15 minutes of the hour as any other.

Brother Joire then came up with another way of charting his data. We

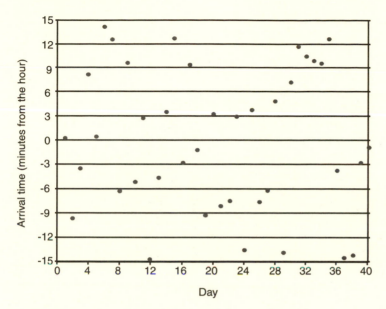

FIGURE 2□-1 Arrival times of the number 6 bus expressed as minutes from the hour: the first 8 days of observation.

call it a *histogram*. Figure 20-2 shows the one he obtained after 52 weeks. In these data he noted the same lack of predictable pattern. Throughout the period, the bus was about equally likely to arrive at any interval within 15 minutes on either side of the hour. For statisticians, this too is a pattern—it is a *uniform distribution*. Table 20-1 presents descriptive statistics for Brother Joire's 52-week data.

Experimenting with his numbers, the young monk computed various means for his data. First, he averaged every two consecutive arrivals. That is, he computed the mean of Arrival Time for his first two observations, his second two, and so on. He obtained Figure 20-3, which plots the 10 means computed from his first 20 observations.

TABLE 2□-1 DESCRIPTIVE STATISTICS FOR ARRIVAL TIMES

	NUMBER OF OBSERVATIONS	MINIMUM	MAXIMUM	MEAN ($\bar{x}$)	STANDARD DEVIATION (sd)
Arrival Time	1560	−15	15	−0.25	8.88

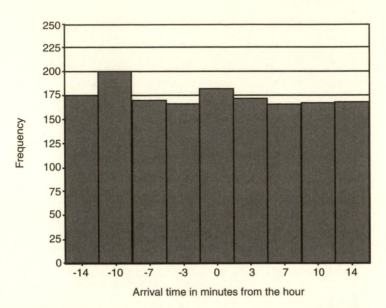

FIGURE 20-2 Distribution of Arrival Tme over 52 weeks.

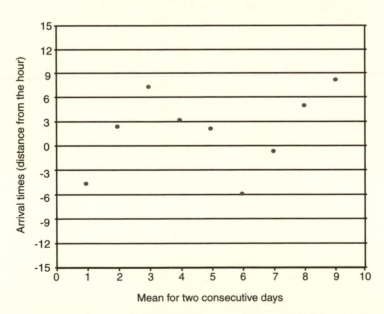

FIGURE 20-3 Arrival Time means for every two consecutive arrivals over 4 days.

Examining the figure, Brother Joire noticed something curious. The points were clustered nearer the hour than his original data. Computing consecutive Arrival Time means for all his observations, he obtained the histogram in Figure 20-4. This last histogram summarizes means for every two observations. As such, it is based on 780 points instead of the original 1560. But it differs from his original histogram in other ways as well. First, the points are generally nearer to the overall mean. That this might happen was already suggested by Figure 20-3. Second, the distribution is no longer uniform. It is denser in the middle and sparser at the edges.

Repeating the exercise for every 4 consecutive days, Brother Joire obtained Figure 20-5. This histogram deviates even further from a uniform distribution—the data are even denser in the middle and sparser at the extremes. Table 20-2 presents summary statistics for these data.

The statistics in Table 20-2 reflect the changes we saw in the graphs. The range is smaller than that of Brother Joire's original data, and the standard deviation is smaller as well. These too indicate that the data are less spread out.

Finally, Brother Joire computed weekly means, that is, means for every 30 consecutive observations. Table 20-3 presents descriptive statistics for

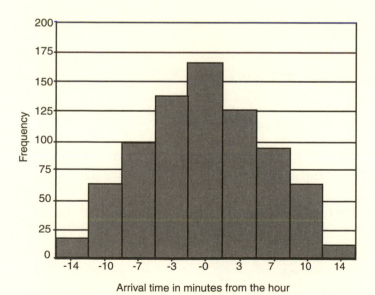

FIGURE 20-4 Distribution of Arrival Time means of every two consecutive arrivals.

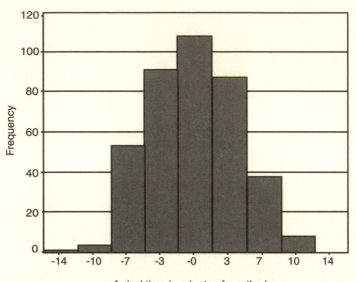

FIGURE 20-5 Distribution of Arrival Time means of every four consecutive arrivals.

these data. The trend continued. Here, the data are even more tightly packed about the mean. The standard deviation of this *distribution of means* is about one-seventh that of the original data.

In the next chapter we will see that the range is not particularly important for our story. Thus from this point we shall confine our discussion to the *standard deviation of the distribution of means*.

WHAT IS HAPPENING HERE?

What is happening is clear: As Brother Joire's means are based on more observations, the standard deviation decreases. The obvious questions are

TABLE 20-2 DESCRIPTIVE STATISTICS FOR ARRIVAL TIME MEANS BASED ON FOUR CONSECUTIVE ARRIVALS

	NUMBER OF OBSERVATIONS (MEANS)	MINIMUM	MAXIMUM	MEAN ($\bar{x}$)	STANDARD DEVIATION (sd)
Arrival Time	390	−12.86	10.16	−0.25	4.42

TABLE 20-3 DESCRIPTIVE STATISTICS FOR ARRIVAL TIME MEANS BASED ON 30 CONSECUTIVE ARRIVALS

	NUMBER OF OBSERVATIONS (MEANS)	MINIMUM	MAXIMUM	MEAN ($\bar{x}$)	STANDARD DEVIATION (sd)
Arrival Time	52	−3.85	2.57	−0.25	1.29

1. Why is this happening?

2. Is this useful?

We shall answer each of these questions in its turn. First, however, let us focus on the pattern itself.

Suppose that Brother Joire were to take his method to the extreme. That is, suppose that he were to compute the mean of all his (consecutive) observations. In this case he would obtain one number—the overall mean. This number would have two characteristics. First, it would be the *true* mean of all his numbers. If we were to treat Brother Joire's data as a population, we would say that he has obtained the population mean. As we know, any population has a single mean only. Second, since there is only one number here—the true mean—there is no standard deviation.

Summarizing what we have seen so far:

1. The greatest variation occurs in the original, raw data—the data based on single observations.

2. The standard deviation of the distribution of means decreases as the means are derived from larger samples.

3. When the mean is based on the whole population, the distribution of means has no variation (there is one number only).

Therefore, this is the pattern. Something else is also happening here, however, and it is a bit odd. Recall that the histogram based on single observations was approximately uniform. Graphing means, the histogram began "looking normal." The greater the number of arrivals for which we computed means, the more normal it looked. Let us show why this is necessarily so using a simpler example.

TOSSING A DIE

You toss a die. On any particular occasion your result is 1, 2, 3, 4, 5, or 6. The die is fair, so your chance for any one outcome is the same as any other. Again, this is a uniform distribution.*

You toss the die twice. On each of your tosses you will obtain a number between 1 and 6 inclusive. Thus, when tossing twice, you will get any one of 36 possible sequences. Figure 20-6 shows them graphically.

We agree, then, that when tossing a die twice the population includes 36 different outcomes exactly: (1, 1), (1, 2), (1, 3), . . . , (6, 4), (6, 5), (6, 6). Moreover, we know that each is equally likely because

1. Every sequence is unique—it occurs exactly once in the population of outcomes.

2. Every outcome is equally likely because the probabilities for each outcome between 1 and 6 are the same on each toss.

Thus, obtaining (1, 1) is as likely as obtaining (1, 2), as obtaining (6, 6), and so on. Stating this more formally:

$$P(1,1) = P(1,2) = \ldots = P(5,6) = P(6,6) = 1/36$$

For some of you, this may not sit too well. After all, an outcome of "snake eyes" is generally considered rare. And it is—1 out of 36. Still, it is no more rare than any other sequence of two numbers. This is so because there is

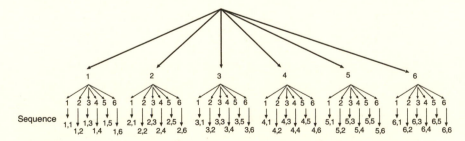

FIGURE 20-6 All possible outcomes when tossing a die twice.

* Since on a single toss only whole values are possible, the distribution is discrete. However, this does not change the fact that it is uniform.

only one each of the 36 possible sequences. If you think about it, you will find that this is perfectly logical. Notwithstanding, it is also correct.

What may be confusing is this. "Snake eyes" are infrequent because there is precisely one way of obtaining it. On the other hand, when ignoring sequence, there are two different ways of getting some of the combinations. For example, (5, 6) and (6, 5) are equivalent combinations when disregarding order. But when we consider the sequence, each is as likely as any other.

Let us move on to means. Again, you toss the die twice, but this time you compute the mean instead of recording the sequence. Once more the possible range is between 1 and 6 inclusive. "Snake eyes" will yield a mean of 1, and two 6s a mean of 6. Any other combination will yield a mean that is between these two extremes. Figure 20-7 describes all possible means of two tosses.

The picture here is clearly different because the distribution is no longer uniform—some of the means occur more often than others. This is so because means "do not care" about sequence—about the order of the numbers that yielded them. For instance, the mean of (2, 3) is the same as that of (3, 2)—different order, same mean. Furthermore, the mean of these combinations is identical to that of (4, 1), which is a different combination altogether. Table 20-4 shows each possible mean when tossing a die twice, the combinations that yield it, and probability of each.

Based on the table, we can, for example, state that

$$P(\text{mean of 1}) = P(\text{mean of 6}) = \frac{1}{36} \text{ (each can occur in only one way)}$$

$$P(\text{mean of 2.5}) = \frac{4}{36} \quad \text{and} \quad P(\text{mean of 3.5}) = \frac{6}{36}$$

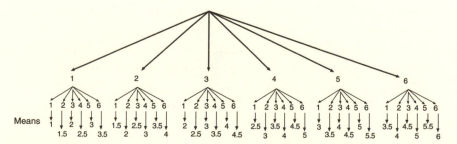

FIGURE 20-7 All possible means of two tosses.

TABLE 20-4 ALL POSSIBLE MEANS OF TOSSING A DIE TWICE AND THE PROBABILITY OF EACH

MEAN	COMBINATIONS YIELDING THE MEAN	FREQUENCY	PROBABILITY
1.0	1, 1	1	1/36
1.5	1, 2; 2, 1	2	2/36
2.0	1, 3; 3, 1; 2, 2	3	3/36
2.5	1, 4; 4, 1; 2, 3; 3, 2	4	4/36
3.0	1, 5; 5, 1; 2, 4; 4, 2; 3, 3	5	5/36
3.5	1, 6; 6, 1; 2, 5; 5, 2; 3, 4; 4, 3	6	6/36
4.0	2, 6; 6, 2; 3, 5; 5, 3; 4, 4	5	5/36
4.5	3, 6; 6, 3; 4, 5; 5, 4	4	4/36
5.0	4, 6; 6, 4; 5, 5	3	3/36
5.5	5, 6; 6, 5	2	2/36
6.0	6, 6	1	1/36

Look at the second column of Table 20-4 and you will see that it looks like a kind of histogram rotated sideways.* As you can see, it has "the beginnings of normality." That is, the outcomes in the middle are more frequent than those further away. And, as you may have already discovered, the exact middle of this distribution is 3.5. That is, it is the mean of all the means. Since the distribution is perfectly symmetrical, 3.5 is also the median and the mode.

From Table 20-4 we see that the nearer the outcome to the true mean, the more likely it is to occur. Thus, while there are six different combinations that yield 3.5, there are five each for the means 3 and 4. However, there is only one combination yielding 1 and one yielding 6. These latter values are as far from the mean as one gets in this particular distribution.

As before, the pattern is this: When tossing a die twice and computing means, the most likely outcomes are those at or near the distribution's

---

* Actually, because this is not a continuous distribution (i.e., not every value between 1 and 6 is possible), it cannot technically be a histogram. But this does not alter the point we wish to make.

mean. The least likely are those at the extremes. This is not so when tossing a die once, where each of our "means" is equally likely and the distribution is uniform.

A NOTE

We have been talking about dice in an effort to better understand how Arrival Time data behave. What we have done is use a relatively simple problem on which to model one that is more complex. Recall that Brother Joire's distribution was only approximately uniform; outcomes of die tosses are perfectly uniform. Also, dice have a limited number of outcomes, and they are known. This is not the case for Arrival Time for buses in the Middle East. Finally, we know everything there is to know about a die even *before* we measure. We do not need to actually toss a die to discover its possible outcomes nor the probability of each. In an effort to simplify, statisticians often toss dice, flip coins, and deal cards. In this they are no different that other mortals.

Think of teaching arithmetic to a child. A teacher employs problems such as 1 + 1 to demonstrate the principles. He then asks the child to apply these to more complicated problems. The child is not taught the theory and immediately asked to sum four-digit numbers.

Here, too, we demonstrate theory using a simple, if unrealistic, case. Once mastered, we shall move on to more practical applications. But there is still a bit more to master.

TERMINOLOGY

A die is tossed twice, the mean computed, and the process repeated. If you wish, you can toss a die twice as many times as you like. And then you can toss it some more. In other words, the population of means of two tosses is infinite.

So what we are talking about now is a *distribution of means that is infinite*. But while the *distribution* of means is infinite—you can keep on tossing twice as much as you like—its outcomes are not. On any given two tosses you will get 1 of 11 possible outcomes only.

Statisticians select samples from distributions. How does one select a sample from a distribution of means? Simple, one tosses a die twice and computes the mean. In other words, the activity of tossing a die twice is equivalent to selecting *a single observation* from a distribution of means. In statistics, we call this distribution a *sampling distribution*. Its elements are means rather than raw data.

In previous chapters we discussed collections of raw data and called them *distributions*. Here, too, we speak of a collection of data points. Except here our points are now means, and we call this particular collection a *sampling distribution*. Do not be misled. A distribution is a distribution is a distribution. Its elements can be data points based on single observations, or they can be means. It makes no matter.

Table 20-4 described the shape of the sampling distribution of two-toss means. It was derived theoretically—we tossed no die. Instead, we used our prior knowledge of the behavior of dice to enumerate their possible outcomes. Usually, we are not so fortunate.

The alternative to find out what a sampling distribution looks like is empirical. To do it, we

1. Toss the die twice.

2. Compute the mean and record it.

3. Repeat this over and over (and over).

4. Count the frequency of each outcome we get and graph our results.

Remember that our die is fair—each outcome between 1 and 6 is as likely as any other is. Therefore, when we get to infinity, our probabilities will look exactly like those in Table 20-4. That is, 1/6 of the means will be 3.5, 5/36 will be 3, 1/9 will be 2.5, etc. This is an important point. When one "samples" the whole population, the truth comes out. Thus, when we get to infinity, which is the whole population, our probabilities will conform to the truth—to what we already know about the behavior of a fair die.

We now have two ways to express what we do when we toss a die twice. We have

1. Selected a sample of size = 2 from the original distribution.

2. Selected a sample of size = 1 from the sampling distribution of means (each computed from two tosses).

Do not leave this section until you have understood why these two statements are equivalent.

WHY IS THIS HAPPENING?

Tossing a die once is like randomly selecting a sample of size = 1 from the distribution of raw data. Your chance of getting a 1 is equal to your chance of getting a 2, etc. The distribution of the raw data is uniform, and its mean is 3.5. That is,

$$\bar{x} = \frac{1+2+3+4+5+6}{6} = \frac{21}{6} = 3.5$$

You should not be bothered by the fact that an outcome of 3.5 cannot happen when tossing a die once. We have already noted that distributions do not necessarily include observations that are precisely at their mean.

Moving on, we say that tossing a die twice is like randomly selecting a sample of size = 2 from the original distribution. But it is also a sample of size = 1 from a sampling distribution. This sampling distribution also has a mean of 3.5, but it is no longer uniform. Your chance of obtaining a result closer to its mean is greater than getting one that is further away.

This is perfectly logical. To get a 1 on a single toss is as likely as to get any of the other outcomes. But to get a mean of 1 on two tosses is more difficult. For this to happen, you need to obtain two 1s in a row—an unlikely event relative to some of the other possible outcomes, which can occur in more than one way.

We can now understand why Brother Joire's sampling distribution of two Arrival Times yielded a smaller standard deviation than his raw data. To get a mean of 15, he would have had to observe two consecutive arrivals that are 15 minutes late. No other sequence will have yielded this exactly.[*] Contrast this with a mean of 0, which can happen in 16 different ways: (15, −15), (14, −14), . . . , (2, −2), (1, −1) (0, 0).[†]

Now think of a sampling distribution based on means of four Arrival Times. Here the value 15 is almost impossible. For it to happen, the bus

---

[*] Assuming that the bus is never late by more than 15 minutes.

[†] And this is true when we talk about whole numbers only. If we allow for fractions, there are even more ways.

must arrive 15 minutes late four times in a row—a very unlikely occurrence where one untimely arrival is as likely as any other. Thus, in general, *the larger the sample, the smaller is the probability of obtaining an extreme mean,* that is, of obtaining a mean that is far from the population mean. More simply, the larger your sample, the nearer its mean will be to the true mean (in general). More simply still, larger samples tend to yield more accurate estimates of the population mean.

Expressed another way, we say that sampling distributions are denser in the middle and sparser at the extremes than the raw data that spawned them. The greater the number of observations on which the means are based, the more pronounced is the pattern.

So far we see that this holds for uniform distributions. But this is also true for all data regardless of the shape of the original distribution. The fact that sampling distributions show this pattern regardless of the original data is, for the statistician, a minor miracle.

CHAPTER XXI

Confidence Intervals

SAMPLING ERROR

Estimating μ with $\bar{x}$ is exactly that. Thus, when we do it, we are anxious to know by how much we are off. In statistical terminology, we wish to assess *sampling error*.

On the face of it, estimating error is impossible. If you do not know the truth, you cannot know by how much you have missed it. Yet there is something that we *do* know, and it is this: In general, the more you measure, the nearer your outcome is to the truth.

Statistically, this works out as follows: Each measurement contains both truth (μ) and sampling error that is random. By definition, random error is equally likely to be above or below the truth to the same degree. Usually, the more you sample at random, the more likely it is that your random error will "even out" (see Chapter 5). That is, as your sample grows larger, its average error will approach zero, and you remain with the truth. We have seen that both statistics and intuition suggest that there is a relationship between sample size and error. Quantify the relationship, and you have quantified error.

An example: In Quinland, the Height of females is normally distributed with

$$\mu = 170 \text{ centimeters} \qquad \text{and} \qquad \sigma = 4 \text{ centimeters}$$

An explorer is about to sample a single Quinlander woman. The woman's Height will be his best estimate of μ. By how much will he be off?

In a normal distribution, 0.95 of the data are within $\pm2\sigma$ of the mean. It follows, then, that 95 percent of the time the woman he samples will be within 8 centimeters ($\pm2\sigma$) of μ. In other words, he has a 95 percent chance of erring by no more than 8 centimeters.

We have just estimated sampling error! That is, we have provided an interval within which the explorer can expect to err. It is like saying, "The explorer can be 95 percent certain that the true mean of heights of Quinlander women is within two standard deviations of the measurement he actually obtained."

This is an elegant piece of reasoning no doubt. But it is completely impractical. To construct intervals in this way we must know σ and μ, which is typically impossible. When it *is* possible, why bother estimating error? After all, you know the truth. Still, we are not about to let such a fine piece of reasoning go to waste.

A (Partial) Solution

It is indeed the case that we can seldom know the population parameters exactly. However, we *can* estimate them. Thus

1. μ is estimated by $\overline{x}$.

2. σ is estimated by sd.

3. Shape is assessed by examining graphs of the data obtained or by using statistical tests specifically designed for this purpose.

Having obtained the necessary information from a sample, our explorer can now say, "I am 95 percent confident that μ is in the interval $\overline{x} \pm 2$ sd." In statistics, we call this statement a *confidence interval*.

The principle underlying *interval estimation* is this: Obtain a sample, compute its sample statistics, and use them to construct a range for the population parameter. In statistics, we contrast interval estimation with *point estimation*, where we provide a single value for the population parameter (e.g., $\overline{x}$ for μ). Unfortunately, there are several difficulties with the reasoning just presented.

DISTRIBUTIONS AND DISTRIBUTIONS

An explorer wishes to compute a confidence interval for μ based on a sample of one woman. To do this, he must

1. Use his single measurement as an estimate of μ.

2. Estimate σ using the sd.

3. Assume that Height is normally distributed.

The assumption of normality is essential because only when we know the shape of a distribution can we know the proportion of the population that is within specified distances from the mean (measured in units of standard deviation). But how is one to know whether the assumption of normality is justified? Well, in the case of Height, this is not a problem because Height is typically normally distributed and can be safely assumed. However, our second condition presents a greater difficulty. Recall that our explorer sampled only one woman. Based on a sample of one, he will not be able to compute an sd.

The solution is both simple and desirable: Select a larger sample. Thus $\overline{x}$ will be your estimate of μ, and sd will be your estimate of σ. Having obtained a larger sample, one also can test whether the assumption of normality was justified. So it seems that obtaining a sample that includes a number of observations is the solution. Well, not quite.

In Chapter 20 we showed that randomly selecting several elements and computing their mean is the equivalent to randomly selecting a single mean from a distribution of means—a *sampling distribution*. This, then, is our explorer's problem: The statement "I am 95 percent confident that μ is in the interval $\overline{x} \pm 2$ sd" is based on estimates for the distribution of Heights. But we are no longer there. The sample mean $\overline{x}$ was sampled from another population altogether—a population of *Height means*—a sampling distribution. And sampling distributions look different from the distribution of raw data.

Recall that sampling distributions are more tightly clustered about the mean than those of the raw data—their values are nearer μ. Also, their σ, that is, standard deviation, is smaller than in the original data. In the explorer's case, he sampled a mean from a distribution whose σ is something less than 4 centimeters.

Yet he may argue thus: "If the sampling distribution is normal and its σ is less than 4, I can say that I am *at least* 95 percent certain the μ is in the interval $\overline{x} \pm 8$ centimeters." And he will have made a good argument. But his statement has three problems with it. First, it assumes that the mean of the distribution of means is the same as that of the raw data. That is, in estimating $\mu_{\text{sampling distribution}}$, he has also estimated μ. Second, he would like to do better than "at least." Finally, the interval he constructed is based on areas under the normal curve. How does he know that his sampling distribution is normal?

The *central limit theorem* will solve all his problems and then some. It states that sampling distributions

1. Have a mean that is identical to that of the raw data. In other words:

$$\mu_{\text{sampling distribution}} = \mu_{\text{original distribution}}$$

2. Have a standard deviation that is

$$\sigma = \frac{\sigma_{\text{raw data}}}{\sqrt{n}}$$

where n designates sample size.

3. Are more or less normally distributed when the sample is large enough.

Let us examine these statements one by one.

The mean of a sampling distribution is the same as that of the raw data. A sampling distribution is a collection of means. Its μ is a "mean of means," which, intuitively, is identical to μ of the original distribution. As it turns out, this intuition is correct.

$$\mu_{\text{sampling distribution}} = \frac{\sigma}{\sqrt{n}}$$

Brother Joire graphed distributions of means based on increasing sample sizes (see Chapter 20). As his samples increased in size, the sd of his sampling distribution decreased. So this is the principle: As n increases, σ of the distribution of means decreases. The central limit theorem quantifies this relationship. For example, when $n = 100$,

$$\sigma_{\text{sampling distribution}} = \frac{4}{\sqrt{100}} = 0.4$$

In other words, the standard deviation of a sampling distribution generated by samples of 100 is one-tenth that of the raw data. While the principle is intuitive, the particular relationship, which involves the square root, is not. But this is the way the mathematics works out.

Terminology. In statistics, we call $\sigma_{\text{sampling distribution}}$ a *standard error.* That is,

$$\sigma_{\text{sampling distribution}} = \textbf{standard error} = \textbf{se}$$

Do not be misled. The se is just another standard deviation—except that it is computed on a collection of means rather than on single elements. The term *se* merely indicates that we are talking about the variation of a sampling distribution rather than of the original data. When $n = 1$, when we are back in the raw data, the formula becomes

$$\textbf{se} = \frac{\sigma_{\text{raw data}}}{\sqrt{1}} = \sigma_{\text{raw data}} = \sigma$$

Sampling distributions are more or less normal. As Brother Joire's means were based on larger sample sizes, their distribution looked increasingly normal. Increasingly, they became dense in the middle and sparse at the edges. This was so despite the fact that the original distribution was far from normal—it was uniform. The central limit theorem tells us that when n is large enough, the sampling distribution is more or less normal. We shall deal with the issue of "large enough" soon.

An important point: The central limit theorem states that sampling distributions are normal and keeps silent on the issue of the shape of the original, raw data. Indeed, sampling distributions are more or less normal *regardless of the shape of the original distribution!* For the statistician, this is another a minor miracle.

BACK TO CONFIDENCE INTERVALS

Let us say that our explorer has sampled 100 women and measured the Height of each. He computes $\overline{x}$ and sd and can now compute a confidence interval. For example, he states with 95 percent confidence that μ is in the interval:

$$\overline{x} \pm 2\ se \qquad \left(\text{where se} = \frac{sd}{\sqrt{100}} = \frac{sd}{10} \right)$$

What he is saying is this: "Suppose that I had repeated my study 100 times and computed a confidence interval for each $\overline{x}$ obtained. I would expect that in about 95 of the cases the interval would include μ." Graphically, this looks like Figure 21-1.

Put another way, our explorer says: "I have conducted my study once and am not about to repeat it. Yet I can state with 95 percent confidence that μ is in my interval."[*] Note that he has used the 95 percent confidence interval but could have used any other. He could, for example, have said with

1. 68 percent certainty that μ is in the interval $\overline{x} \pm 1$ se, or

2. 72 percent confidence that μ is in the interval $\overline{x} \pm 1.08$ se, or

3. 80 percent confidence that μ is in the interval $\overline{x} \pm 1.28$ se

Probabilities associated with intervals are based on areas under the curve. Since we know the curve, we can compute the probabilities for any interval we wish. The actual values can be obtained from tables or computer programs.

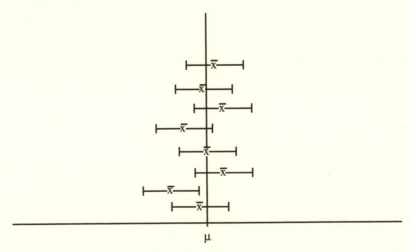

FIGURE 21-1 Estimating μ using $\overline{x}$.

[*] Technically, the earlier statement and this one are not the same. This is a philosophical issue we will not deal with. We, as most statisticians, will treat these statements as equivalent and leave it at that.

YET ANOTHER DIFFICULTY

To compute a confidence interval, we estimate σ with sd. Unfortunately, using sd instead of σ alters our story somewhat. As we have seen, confidence intervals take on the following form:

$$\overline{x} \pm \text{"some number"} = \text{se}$$

This "some number" is derived from areas under the normal curve. For example, within 2 se's of the mean reside 95 percent of a (normal) sampling distribution's elements. However, when σ is estimated from a sample, the sampling distribution is not precisely normal. It has what is termed a *t distribution*. We will not here explain why this is so. Suffice to say that the *t* and normal distributions are virtually identical in large samples.[*] In any event, when constructing our interval, we base our "some number" on the *t* distribution rather than the normal distribution.

The larger the sample size, the nearer is the value obtained from *t* to that derived from the normal distribution. For example, in the normal distribution, 95 percent of observations are between ± 1.96 se.[†] When the sample is $n = 10$, the appropriate *t* value is 2.26; when $n = 30$, $t = 2.05$. Thus, in samples of 30 and above, *t* values and normal values are virtually identical.

This, then, is the form of the confidence interval used in practice:

$$\overline{x} \pm t_{\text{confidence level}} \times \frac{\text{sd}}{\sqrt{n}}$$

$t_{\text{confidence level}}$ is the level of confidence you wish your statement to have. For example, if $n = 30$ and you want to be 95 percent sure that μ is in your interval, $t = 2.05$. If you are content with being 90 percent certain that your interval includes μ, use $t = 1.70$.

Note that as your interval narrows (e.g., ± 1.7 se versus ± 2.05 se), your confidence decreases. We shall deal with this shortly.

---

[*] For each sample size there is a different *t* distribution, unlike the normal distribution, of which there is one.

[†] Here, we provide the exact value rather than rounding to 2, as we usually have done. This is to enable a more accurate comparison to *t*.

A Brief Summary

1. Obtain a sample and compute its $\bar{x}$ and sd. These are your best point estimates for μ and σ.

2. When doing interval estimation, we specify a range of values within which we are fairly certain that μ resides. This is the logic:
   - Randomly selecting several elements and computing their mean is like randomly sampling a single element from a sampling distribution.
   - If we know what the sampling distribution looks like, we also know the kind of error to expect when randomly selecting an element from it.
   - Unfortunately, we do not know what it looks like. But we can estimate. Thus we estimate μ with $\bar{x}$ and σ with sd and use our knowledge of shape to specify an interval that probably contains the truth. Recall that the central limit theorem tells us that the shape of a sampling distribution is normal (regardless of the shape of the original data).
   - Using the parameters above, we construct the confidence interval.

An Application

Products coming off the same production line should be identical. Frequently, they are not. For engineers, this is critical. While they know that variation is inevitable, they can only accept it within certain bounds.

Alfredo Foods produces pasta and sells it in packages of 400 grams. Some packages contain less, and others contain more. The law stipulates that the *average weight* of packages thus labeled must be at least 400 grams.

An Alfredo engineer samples 225 packages and finds

$$\bar{x} = 403 \qquad \text{and} \qquad \text{sd} = 6$$

Computing the 99 percent confidence interval, she obtains

$$403 \pm 2.6 \times \frac{6}{\sqrt{225}} = 403 \pm 2.6 \times 0.4 = 403 \pm 1.04$$

Estimate of μ (from sample)

Value from t distribution to obtain 99 percent confidence

se, estimate of σ of sampling distribution (from sample)

Alfredo's engineer is now 99 percent certain that the true average of the company's packages (μ) is between 402 and 404 grams. Based on this, the company can say that it is 99 percent certain that its production process complies with the law.

SOME ADDITIONAL ISSUES

How Large Is Large Enough?

Recall Brother Joire and his uniform distribution of bus Arrival Times. As his sample size increased, his sampling distribution approached normality. This is the rule regardless of how the original data are shaped. However, the further the raw data deviate from normal, the larger is the sample size needed to yield a normal sampling distribution.

In the case where the original distribution is normal, any sampling distribution derived from it will be normal as well. For other types of data, the rule of thumb often mentioned is $n = 30$. That is, obtain a sample of this size at least and you can assume that the sampling distribution is normal. This is not a bad rule. Still, it all depends on how nonnormal the original data are. Suffice it to say that statisticians have developed a number of ways to deal with this.

Note that this is a critical issue. The confidence intervals we have presented are based on the assumption of normality. If the assumption is incorrect, the probabilities obtained will be wrong.[*]

Which Confidence Level to Choose?

Before she has sampled a single package, Alfredo's engineer can say with 100 percent certainty that μ is between 0 grams and infinity. This is not a very useful statement, but it illustrates an important point: The wider your interval, the more certain you are that μ is in it.

So the principle is this: The wider your interval, the less informative it is, but the more certain you are to have captured the truth. At the other extreme, if you provide an infinitely narrow interval—a single point for μ—you will be very informative but wrong.

The choice of confidence level depends on the circumstance. Specifically, you must answer the following questions:

---

[*] Confidence intervals can be constructed for other distributions as well. But the principle remains. Only when the shape of a distribution is known (or appropriately assumed) will the interval be correct.

1. How narrow is useful?

2. How certain do I need to be (i.e., how serious is the consequence of error)?

Answering these questions has little to do with statistics. Suppose that you are in an emergency room and a woman arrives complaining of chest pains. You test her blood for an enzyme associated with heart attacks. You find that

1. The 90 percent interval for the woman's true enzyme level does not include the mean of that observed in those who have had attacks.

2. Your 95 percent interval, which is wider, includes this mean.

What do you do? Based on the first interval, you say, "I am 90 percent certain that this woman has not had an attack. Send her home." Based on the second, you say, "I cannot say with 95 percent certainty that the woman has not had an attack. If I repeatedly send such people home, I will err in about 5 out of every 100 cases."

We suspect that in this instance the physician will choose the wider interval—the one that is less precise but leads to greater certainty. And the woman will not be sent home. In scientific publications, the norm is typically 95 percent. That is, scientists demand that their intervals have at least a 95 percent chance of including the population parameter of interest. No one seems to know where this confidence level originated. In truth, it does not matter. At the end of the day, it is the particular circumstance, rather than convention, that should determine the level that ought to be used.

CHAPTER XXII

Data and Decisions:
An Introduction

On 15 May, 1796, General Bonaparte made his entry into Milan at the head of a youthful army which but a short time before had crossed the Bridge of Lodi, and taught the world that after so many centuries Caesar and Alexander had a successor.

. . . Very soon a new and passionate standard of manners came into being. A whole nation became aware, on 15 May, 1796, that everything it had respected up till then was supremely ridiculous and on occasion hateful. The departure of the last Austrian regiment marked the collapse of the old ideas.

STENDAHL[1]

Within 2 years, the Austrians returned and sent Napoleon's troops back to France. Several years later the French returned once more but again remained for a short time only.

Many Italians longed for General Napoleon, but his defeat at Waterloo put an end to their hopes. A certain Conte Pietranera of Milan was among Napoleon's mourners. He made his feelings known and was murdered for it. The man's young widow vowed revenge and pleaded with her friend, Limercati, for help. Limercati felt her idea "supremely ridiculous," and the spirited Contessa now turned her wrath on him:

She redoubled her attentions to Limercati; she wanted to awaken love in him, and then leave him in the lurch and fill him with despair. To make this project of revenge intelligible to French readers, I should say that in Milan, in a country far removed from our own [of France], people can still be driven to despair by love.

Stendahl prepares us for such goings on in the introduction to his book. He writes

I will confess that I have been so bold as to leave my characters with their natural harsh traits unsoftened; but, on the other hand—I proclaim it openly—I cast the most moral censure on many of their actions. Where would be the use of endowing them with the high morality and pleasing graces of French characters, who love money above all things, and seldom sin from motives of love or hatred?

The late Professor Bernhard Stiglitz[2] of Heidelberg felt there was a ring of truth to Stendahl's generalization. But while Stendahl's story is set amid events that happened, it is fiction. A scientist, Stiglitz sought proof.

Searching libraries and private collections throughout Europe, the professor and his students obtained 241 diaries written during those turbulent times. For each they computed Love's Despair using a scale that combined the following:

1. Number of Love's Despair experiences mentioned in the diary

2. Average length of the despair periods

3. Average number of adjectives used to describe the experiences

4. Average intensity of the adjectives used*

Table 22-1 summarizes their data.

Looking at the means of the two nationalities, it seems that Stiglitz had obtained the proof he sought. Yet a difference between means cannot by itself prove that a *true* difference exists. *Magnitude* is important as well. For example, had the result been 19.8 to 19.7, Stiglitz would have likely concluded that the nationalities are similar on Love's Despair—this despite their differing means.

---

*Based on the Standardized Adjective Rating Scale (SARS) of the Joint European Committee on Rating (1942).

TABLE 22-1 LOVE'S DESPAIR BY COUNTRY

		MEAN ($\bar{x}$)	STANDARD DEVIATION (sd)	MINIMUM	MAXIMUM	SAMPLE SIZE (n)
Country	Italy	19.8	4.6	6.5	31.5	122
	France	13.4	4.0	3.9	23.6	119
Combined data		16.7	6.4	3.9	31.5	241

And what would have Stiglitz concluded had the means been 19.8 and 18.7? Well, he might have concluded that there is a difference. But then again, he may not have. Clearly, we need a rule for "how large a difference is true."

Suppose that Stiglitz had obtained two samples of Italians. Because of sampling error, his means would differ. This would be so despite "Italians being similar to Italians"—that is, their being only one population with a single, true μ.

In statistics, we distinguish between two possible scenarios to explain an observed difference between means:

Scenario 1: There is only one population with a single μ. Our two $\bar{x}$ values are simply separate estimates of the same thing, and any difference between them is due to chance—to sampling error. There is no true difference.

Scenario 2: There are two populations, each with its respective mean. The difference we observe is due to the fact that one sample mean estimates μ_1 and the other μ_2. A true difference exists.

To see which of the scenarios is the most reasonable here, let us further explore Stiglitz's data. The histogram in Figure 22-1 has several intervals containing relatively large numbers of observations. It is multimodal. In Chapter 6 we pointed out that this typically happens when more than one population is combined into one data set. Multiple modes arise because each of the populations has its own mode. Figure 22-2 shows what happens when we construct separate histograms for the two nationalities.

Each of the histograms has a single mode. What is more, each of the modes is at the nationality's respective mean. It seems, then, that with

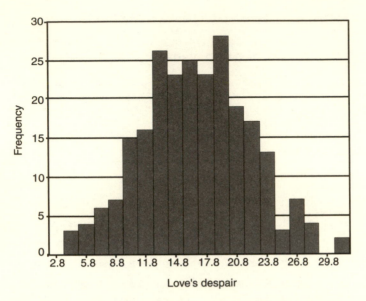

FIGURE 22-1 Distribution of Love's Despair: Italians and Frenchmen combined.

regard to Love's Despair, we have encountered two populations. Stiglitz can conclude that the Italians and French truly differ.[*]

But not all data are as simple to interpret, and a more precise method is needed for comparing means. Such is the one presented below.

BACK CONFIDENCE INTERVALS

An "untrue difference" is one that results from sampling error. Our task, then, is to distinguish between differences that are due to sampling error and those which reflect the truth. Well, in Chapter 21 we showed how sampling error behaves and used our knowledge to construct confidence intervals.

Constructing the 99 percent confidence interval for Italians, we have

$$19.8 \pm 2.4 \times \frac{4.7}{\sqrt{122}} = 19.8 \pm 1.03$$

Based on this, we are 99 percent certain that the true mean for Italians is between 18.8 and 20.8. Computing the confidence interval for the French, we have

---

[*] On Love's Despair. On other parameters they may belong to the same population. For example, they are both Europeans.

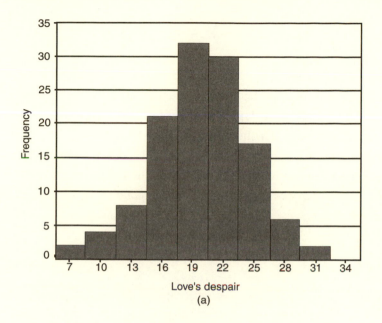

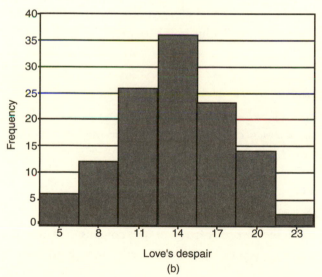

FIGURE 22-2 Distribution of Love's Despair: (*a*) Italy and (*b*) France separately.

$$13.4 \pm 2.4 \times \frac{4.0}{\sqrt{119}} = 13.4 \pm 0.88$$

Graphing these intervals, we obtain Figure 22-3.

Since the intervals do not overlap, we can conclude with 99 percent certainty that the samples obtained represent different populations. In other words, that Italians and French truly differ on Love's Despair.

In statistical terminology, we have obtained a *significant* difference, a difference that we are 99 percent certain is true—not due to chance. *In statistics, saying that two means differ—that there is a significant difference between them—translates into saying that they represent different populations.*

FORMALITIES

The procedure we have just illustrated is called *hypothesis testing*. Let us now work it out formally. You begin with a hypothesis. Typically, it is the one that you wish to disprove. Here Stiglitz says, "I hypothesize that there is no difference between the nationalities." This translates into

$$\mu_{\text{Italians}} \neq \mu_{\text{Frenchmen}}$$

We call this the *null hypothesis*, or H_0. It is the accepted "state of the world" until proven otherwise.

You then specify the *alternative hypothesis, or H_1*—the one you wish to prove. In this case,

$$\mu_{\text{Italy}} = \mu_{\text{France}}$$

The next step is to specify the level of confidence you require. Here Stiglitz said, "I wish to be 99 percent certain of any conclusion I reach." This means that he will multiply his standard error by the appropriate t value. Here, it is 2.4.

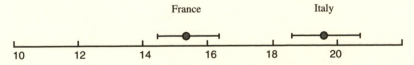

FIGURE 22-3 Ninety-nine percent confidence intervals for Love's Despair.

You then collect the data and compute your intervals. If they overlap, you conclude that the difference you have witnessed may be due to error—you cannot say that the nationalities differ. If they do not overlap, you conclude that they truly differ.

Summarizing the steps of hypothesis testing, we have

1. State H_0 and H_1—the null and alternative hypotheses.

2. Determine your level of confidence—the level of certainty that you wish your ultimate conclusion to have.

3. Collect data—obtain a sample from each of the groups you wish to compare.

4. Construct intervals around each of the sample means you obtained.

5. Decide whether or not to reject H_0 based on whether or not the intervals overlap.

Risks

Random sampling error is exactly that. While we can model what to expect from it, it can surprise us. When constructing a confidence interval for Italians, Stiglitz said that their true mean is between 18.8 and 20.8—but he was only 99 percent sure. That is, there is a 1 percent chance that the true mean is larger than 20.8 or smaller than 18.8.

Suppose that Stiglitz's conclusion was wrong—that the true mean for Italians is much less than 18.8, say, 16.0. If this were the case, his conclusion of a true difference between the nationalities may have been wrong.

Statistical decision making involves probabilistic statements. Here, Stiglitz rejected H_0 (that the populations have the same mean) but added that there is a 1 in 100 chance that he may have been wrong. This is one type of risk we face when testing hypotheses. There is also another. Let us use a simple example to demonstrate our two risks.

Suppose that a coin is fair. That is, its $\mu_{heads} = \mu_{tails} = 0.5$.[*] Flip the coin 10 times and you may not get 5 heads and 5 tails. Indeed, there is a small

---

[*] We designate "tails" as 0 and "heads" as 1. Thus the expected average when flipping a coin over and over is 0.5.

chance that you will get 10 heads. In this case, you might conclude that it is a biased coin. And you will be wrong.

Now suppose that a coin is biased slightly toward heads. That is, μ_{heads} = 0.6 (i.e., the probability of heads is 0.6 and of tails is 0.4). Suppose further that you toss it 10 times and obtained 6 heads. You would likely conclude that the coin is fair. After all, even fair coins show this result often enough. Certainly such an outcome is not extreme enough to conclude that the coin is biased. And you will have erred.

In the first example you made what statisticians call a *type I error*. You reject H_0 (that there is no difference) even though the coin is fair. In the second, you made a *type II error*. You did not reject H_0 even though you should have—the coin was truly biased.

In the first instance the culprit was sampling error. By mere chance, your sample reflected something other than the truth. It is a hazard we are familiar with. This is not so in the second instance, where your result reflected the truth exactly. Here, the culprit was lack of *power*.

To understand the concept of power let us compare two different studies with our 60/40 coin. In the first we flip the coin 20 times, and in the second we flip it 1000 times. Suppose that the outcome of our first study was 12 heads and of our second was 600 heads. Here, both studies have yielded the truth exactly—a proportion of heads that is 0.6. Yet, based on the first study, most people would not conclude that the coin is biased. Based on the second, most would conclude that it is. Because of its larger sample size, the second study had more power to discover the truth. In the next chapter we shall formalize these ideas further.

CHAPTER XXIII

Risks and Rewards

MODELS REVISITED

Lady Bracknell is upset. She says (with a shiver, crossing to the sofa and sitting down):

> I do not know whether there is anything peculiarly exciting in the air of this particular part of Heretfordshire, but the number of engagements that go on seems to me considerably above the proper average that statistics have laid down for our guidance. I think a preliminary inquiry on my part would not be out of place.[1]

The lady has just witnessed two couples become engaged, and nothing has prepared her for it. She suspects that something is amiss—the air, perhaps.

Her rationale is clear. She has a rule—a *model*—of how reality ought to behave. Observing an apparent exception to the rule, she questions the model. But while the gentle lady's reasoning is familiar to us, working it out step by step is a bit more involved. Let us give it a try.

Being a veteran of drawing rooms, Lady Bracknell knows how often they yield engagements. Actually, her knowledge is based on more than experience. It is what "statistics has laid down for our guidance." However she has obtained her model, it is a fact that she has one.

So statisticians have observed Engagement and recorded its distribution over time. In Lady Bracknell's hands, their data become the basis for *expectation*—this, she says, is how Engagement should behave with respect to drawing rooms—at least those which she has discussed with her statistician in their last session.

The lady's model pertains to the behavior of a rare event over time and so is a Poisson model (see Chapter 18). Let us imagine that Engagement happens about once every 10 days in the drawing rooms of minor nobility. Table 23-1 shows the probabilities yielded by a Poisson distribution with a mean of 0.1.

Based on the model, Lady Bracknell expects that on about

1. 90 percent of days the value of Engagement will be 0—there will be none.

2. 10 percent of days there will be one Engagement.

3. 0.5 percent of days there will be 2. That is, once in every 200 days a drawing room will yield two Engagements.

What to do? She has witnessed an unlikely event—unlikely, that is, according to the model. She is now faced with deciding between two scenarios:

H_0: This room is no different than any other. I was just lucky enough to witness a rare event. What has happened is due to chance, and my model still holds (even for this particular room).

TABLE 23-1 PROBABILITIES FOR A POISSON DISTRIBUTION WITH A MEAN OF 0.1

NUMBER OF ENGAGEMENTS	PROBABILITY OF OCCURRENCE ON GIVEN DAY
0	0.9048
1	0.0905
2	0.0045
3	0.0001

H$_1$: This room belongs to a population of rooms that yields more engagements than others do. What I have seen is no fluke at all. This particular room (and others like it) requires another model.

The first scenario, which is her null hypothesis, is the "state of the world" unless proven otherwise (see Chapter 22). When stepping into the room initially, Lady Bracknell had no reason to believe that it was any different from other rooms. The second scenario is what she is testing, that is, whether she has now seen enough to conclude that the room is indeed different, that her initial, null hypothesis is incorrect for this room.

Stating Lady Bracknell's alternatives in the language of hypothesis testing, we have

$$H_0: \quad \mu_{\text{engagements here}} = \mu_{\text{engagements in the rest of Heretfordshire}}$$
$$H_1: \quad \mu_{\text{engagements here}} \neq \mu_{\text{engagements in the rest of Heretfordshire}}$$

In statistics, *testing hypotheses involves selecting between models*. Here, as in most cases, the two models have the same mathematical form. Lady Bracknell only asks whether their mean is the same as well.[*]

ON THE DIFFERENCE BETWEEN DESCRIPTION AND INFERENCE

When doing descriptive statistics, we use models to describe the way things are. There is no opinion involved. We do not say, "Height should be normally distributed with a mean of 174 centimeters." We say that it is. When doing inferential statistics, we use models to state the way things ought to be. And we test them. Here, Lady Bracknell says that if this room is like any other, it ought to display a certain pattern with regard to engagements. If the pattern she actually observes is sufficiently different, she will conclude that it is not like any other. The distinction between describing the world as it is and saying how we *expect it to be* is the essential difference between description and hypothesis testing.

Now it seems that we have done little more than complicate some very straightforward logic. We have our reasons. For the time being, let us only emphasize how common this kind of thinking is. Some examples:

---

[*] H$_0$ asserts a particular value for the population parameter (0.1), whereas H$_1$ only claims that the value is something else. This is typical. However, if one ends up concluding that H$_0$ is incorrect, one's best guess for the mean of the new model is that observed in the data (2 per day).

1. Regina's Grade Point Average was 3.8 in her freshman year. The average in her class was 3.0. Based on this, we model her "a good student." Implied in our statement is that we reject the null hypothesis that her true mean is similar to that of her class. That is, we begin with the hypothesis that Regina is a student like any other—that her true GPA is identical to the average GPA in her class.* Based on data—on our observation of GPA_{Regina} = 3.8—we reject the null hypothesis that GPA_{Regina} = 3.0.

2. On a particular 100-mile stretch of highway we observed 6 Deaths in a month. The mean of most stretches is 1.2. We conclude that this stretch is more dangerous than the population of stretches in general. This one belongs to another population—that of dangerous stretches whose number of Deaths is higher.

3. The first half of the season is over, and a team has lost as many games as it has won. We model it "average." Implied is that we do not reject H_0 that it differs from the average team.

RISKS AND REWARDS

Making decisions based on data has its rewards. At the very least, it is satisfying to be right. In reaching decisions, however, one risks being wrong. Thus it may be that

1. Regina is an average student who got lucky. The truth will emerge once we sample her sophomore grades. In other words, we have incorrectly rejected the null that she is average.

2. The particular 100-mile stretch is as safe as any other is. Sample a few more months and you will discover your mistake.

3. The team you believed to be average is actually strong. Several more games will prove it.

Therefore, if you are brave enough to take a stand based on partial data (i.e., samples), you must be bold enough to risk error. Statisticians are bold

---

* Recall that, until proven otherwise, our best prediction for anyone is the mean (see Chapter 11).

and have learned to live with the consequences. But they are also clever. For them, living with mistakes means taking *calculated* risks—literally. When making decisions, they compute their chance of being wrong. If this sounds familiar, it should. Recall that in Chapter 21 we wrote that we use samples to approximate the truth. At the same time, we also use them to estimate by how much we may have missed the truth. We use our data to estimate error.

Table 23-2 formally presents the possible outcomes of decision making. Using it, we shall calculate the likelihood of risks and rewards. Keep in mind that Lady Bracknell does not know the truth. She will only know it if she remains in the room for the rest of her life and then some. Life is short, however, and drawing rooms are many. So she obtains a sample instead.

Yet whether or not Lady Bracknell actually can know the truth has no bearing on the fact that there *is* one. The room she is now in is, in truth, either the same as others or is different. Let us imagine for the moment that it is truly the same as others—that in reality the null hypothesis is correct. Based on her sample, Lady Bracknell will either conclude

1. Correctly that it is no different (accept H_0[*]) or

2. Incorrectly that it is different (reject H_0).

The first decision places her in cell A and the second in cell B of the table. These two cells are similarly tinted because they "belong to the same uni-

TABLE 23-2 POSSIBLE OUTCOMES OF LADY BRACKNELL'S HYPOTHESIS TESTING

		REALITY—THE TRUTH	
		H_0 IS TRUE, $\mu = 0.1$	H_1 IS TRUE, $\mu = 0.1$
Conclusion based on the sample	Do not reject H_0	A $(p \neq 1 - \alpha)$	C (Type II error; $p = \beta$)
	Reject H_0	B (Type I error; $p = \alpha$)	D (Power; $p = 1 - \beta$)

[*] Technically (philosophically), you cannot prove that H_0 is true. You can only conclude that "I cannot conclude that H_0 is false." This is an unwieldy statement. Therefore, let us remain with the simpler "H_0 is true" and deal with this issue later.

verse"—one in which H_0 is true. They illustrate the only two decision-making scenarios possible in this universe.

The probabilities of cells A and B must sum to 1.0. For example, if the likelihood of reaching an incorrect decision is 0.2, the probability of a correct one is necessarily 0.8. When H_0 is correct, we label the chance of erring α. It follows that, in this universe, the probability of not erring is $1 - \alpha$.* Cells C and D describe what can happen in a universe where H_0 is wrong. Here again, we have only two decision-making possibilities—one correct and the other incorrect.

Let us now return to the case where H_0 is true. Sadly, based on her sample, Lady Bracknell will likely conclude that H_0 is false. Her logic is as follows: "What I have seen happens only once every 200 days if my model is true. My standard model for drawing rooms is false here. In this kind of room, Engagement happens more often. This is why I have seen two in a single day." However, Lady Bracknell also says, "I am only 99.5 percent confident of my conclusion. After all, on 0.5 percent of occasions a standard room will indeed behave thus. In other words, it is 0.5 percent possible that I am in a run-of-the-mill drawing room and have merely witnessed a rare event."

We label the scenario of wrongly rejecting H_0 a *type I error*. And we have just computed its probability α! Lady Bracknell's other possible error is not rejecting H_0 when she should have—when it is wrong. We call this a *type II error*. Computing its probability β is more involved, and we shall forgo it.

CONVENTIONAL WISDOM

In this and the following sections we present the conventional statistical wisdom associated with hypothesis testing. Some of the issues border on the philosophical. We shall not argue with this point or that. Still, you should keep in mind that there are those who do.

What We (Typically) Wish to Find Out

The most common motive for studying a phenomenon is to discover something out of the ordinary, that is, to show that the phenomenon being observed differs from "normal" others. Two examples:

---

* Of course, you can always decide not to decide, but this puts you in another universe altogether—one with its own, separate set of risks and rewards.

1. Scientists compare a novel medication to a standard one when they believe the former is different. They begin with the hypothesis that it is no different—that it is neither more nor less effective as the conventional medication (H_0). And they conduct research in the hope of discovering a new phenomenon—of rejecting the null.

2. Society prosecutes when it believes that a crime has been committed. Kafka aside, we do not randomly select individuals and put them on trial. Thus we begin with the hypothesis that the person on trial is, like ordinary citizens, innocent. We conduct the trial to show that he is guilty—that he differs.*

In general, therefore, the aim of doing research is to land in cell C (of Table 23-2)—to correctly demonstrate an unusual phenomenon. We term the likelihood of landing in this cell *power*. It is the probability of demonstrating a difference when it truly exists. Thus one major goal of research is to maximize power.

On the Conservative Nature of Statistics and Life

One way to increase power is to collect more data rather than less. For example, when a person is truly guilty, our power to discover it increases with more evidence.

The simplest way to maximize power, however, is this: Regardless of the outcome of your test, reject H_0. Do this and you will never miss a new phenomenon. For instance, when putting a man on trial, always decide that he is guilty. Do this and you will never miss detecting guilt. But you also will greatly increase your chance of jailing an innocent man, that is, of making a type I error.

Society has decided to avoid, as much as humanly possible, jailing the innocent, even if it means increasing the frequency of setting the guilty free. In other words, when conducting trials, we most fear making a type I error. Consequently, we will remain with H_0 ("not guilty") unless proven otherwise—beyond a reasonable doubt. In statistics, we quantify this "beyond a reasonable doubt." For example, setting α to 0.01 is like saying, "We will

---

* We may hope that the person turns out innocent, but if we wanted this only, we could ensure it by not conducting the trial in the first place.

only reject the assumption that this man is not guilty when we are 99.9 percent sure of it." Science is similarly conservative. When unsure that it has made a discovery, it will conclude that it has not made one and will remain with H_0.

In statistics, setting criteria for decision making entails balancing between the motivation for discovery with the fear of a type I error. For example, if you relax your evidential requirements for discovery, you increase both

- Power—the ability to discover a new phenomenon when it exists (good) and

- The chance of incorrectly rejecting H_0—of "discovering" a new phenomenon when it does not exist, of making a type I error (bad).

If, on the other hand, you set stringent criteria for concluding discovery, you decrease your chance for incorrect rejection (good). But you also decrease your chance of discovery (bad). In general, both society and statistics agree on this "balancing issue." The fear of type I error is greater than the longing for discovery.

Let us return to Lady Bracknell. Suppose that she had seen only one engagement. Had she concluded that the room is different, her chance of type I error would have been 10 percent. After all, 10 percent of the time normal rooms yield a single engagement in a day. She might have then said, "I cannot accept a 10 percent risk of wrongly rejecting H_0. If I reject H_0, I have a 90 percent chance of being right. But for me, this is *not* beyond a reasonable doubt." And in doing this she has a good chance of having missed detecting a new phenomenon.

So this is the tradeoff: Increase α and you increase both power and your chance for a type I error. Decrease α and you decrease both power and your chance for a type I error. Whatever your choice, the bottom line is that you *can* control the potential risks and rewards of research. But statistics cannot make the decision for you. What it can do is quantify your chances for discovery and error. Once quantified, it is you who must decide what levels of risk and reward are optimal. And these depend on *the circumstance*.

Following are two examples, one of which was already mentioned in an earlier chapter:

1. A woman arrives in the emergency room complaining of chest pains. Suppose that her tests determine that there is a 5 percent chance that she has had a heart attack.* If you send her home—reject the null that she is healthy—you "only" have a 5 percent chance of error. If you send 100 such women home, you will have made a mistake on 5. Is this a risk you are willing to take? Probably not.

2. A scientist has developed a potential cure for a terminal illness. He tests the drug and finds that there is a 90 percent chance that it is effective. Put another way, he has a 10 percent chance of erring if he concludes that it works (i.e., a 10 percent chance of type I error). Since the illness is terminal, the consequences of such an error are not great. In this case he will not be conservative and will recommend that the medication be used.

While extreme, the principles underlying these examples are similar to those in any decision-making situation. You must set α to optimally balance risks and rewards *in the particular situation you are in*. And since situations differ, there can be no single "correct" α.

On Proving the Null

You toss a coin 10 times. It comes up 5 heads and 5 tails. Clearly, you will not reject the null hypothesis that the coin is fair like other normal coins. But will you actually *accept* the null hypothesis? That is, will you conclude that the coin is fair? It would seem so. But conventional wisdom has it otherwise.

Keep in mind that even biased coins "behave fair" every so often. For example, suppose that a coin is biased in that its probability of coming up heads is 60 percent. Still, such a coin will often show 5 heads on 10 tosses. Thus the best that you can say based on a fair-looking outcome is that "I cannot say that the coin is unfair—I cannot reject H_0. But I cannot conclude it is fair. Had I repeated my experiment, with a larger sample perhaps, I might have discovered that it is biased."

---

* For example, based on experience, 5 of every 100 people who have her ECG pattern have had a heart attack, but 95 out of 100 people with this kind of ECG have not had one.

Where Does the Null Come from?

Following are three of the null hypotheses that we mentioned:

1. This part of Heretfordshire is no different than any other.

2. The coin is fair.

3. The Italians and French do not differ on Love's Despair.

Each implies a model, and each generates expectation. But the three originated in different places.

The rule about Engagement in Heretfordshire was based on empirical data, which led "statistics to guide" our expectation. On the other hand, the model for a fair coin is based on the theoretical definition of "fairness." No data are required. Finally, Stiglitz had no prior information on the extent of Love's Despair for Italians and Frenchmen. In his particular case, there was neither previous data nor theory to guide him. Thus Stiglitz chose the conservative view that, unless proven otherwise, the phenomenon of Love's Despair is the same in the two nations. Each of these three methods for modeling the null is legitimate, and each is used in practice.

A Summary

You can consult the stars or common sense. You can ask your family for its opinion. You might as well, since they will give it anyway. But whatever your method, the outcome will be the same. When making decisions, you will be either right or wrong.

Statistics allows you to

1. Classify the kinds of correct and incorrect decisions you can make.

2. Quantify the likelihood associated with each decision.

Based on these quantities, statistics enables you to take calculated risks and receive calculated rewards.

Of all the possible outcomes of decision making, the outcome you typically fear most is that of a type I error. Thus, in research, you typically set α low, and all the other calculations of probability follow.

CHAPTER XXIV

Distance Revisited

QUESTIONS AND ANSWERS

. . . I do not ask any questions, because when a guy goes around asking questions in this town people may get the idea that he is such a guy as wishes to find things out.

DAMON RUNYON[1]

Stiglitz asked whether Italians and French differ on Love's Despair and obtained the statistics we saw in Table 22-1. Comparing the two nations, he found

$$\overline{x}_{\text{difference}} = \overline{x}_{\text{Italy}} - \overline{x}_{\text{France}} = 19.8 - 13.4 = 6.4$$

It would seem that Italians suffer more. But an observed difference between sample means does not *prove* that a true difference exists. After all, even two random samples from the same population will not yield identical means.

Thus Stiglitz then focused on the "magnitude of difference" and asked whether it was sufficiently large to suggest a true difference. He then computed a 99 percent confidence interval for each nationality's sample mean and found that the intervals did not overlap (see Figure 22-3). Based on this, he concluded with 99 percent certainty that the population means differ. Statistically, this was a sound answer.

Yet the question asked and the answer provided do not correspond perfectly. Stiglitz's question related to the size of the difference—is it sufficiently large, he asked, to suggest a true difference. The answer provided was "nonoverlapping intervals." We would like one that deals with the issue of the "magnitude of difference" directly.

ANOTHER KIND OF SAMPLING DISTRIBUTION

The professor discovered an $\bar{x}_{\text{difference}}$ of 6.4. Suppose that he were to obtain two more random samples and compute $\bar{x}_{\text{difference}}$ again. Most likely, it would not be 6.4. Now imagine him repeating his study infinitely and computing a difference on each occasion. Doing this will yield a population of differences—a *sampling distribution* (see Chapter 21).

Like any other, this distribution of differences will have a μ, a σ, and a shape.

- If H_0 is true and French and Italians do not differ, $\mu_{\text{difference}}$ will be 0. Since Stiglitz cannot repeat his study infinitely, he will never know for certain whether or not the true difference is indeed 0. However, he can estimate $\mu_{\text{difference}}$ using the $\bar{x}_{\text{difference}}$ he actually obtained.

- $\sigma_{\text{difference}}$ is the standard deviation of the sampling distribution of differences and is estimated by $se_{\text{difference}}$. The latter is computed using a somewhat complicated formula that we shall forgo. Here, $se_{\text{difference}} = 0.6$.[*]

- *Shape.* According to the central limit theorem, the sampling distribution of means is more or less normal. As it turns out, this is also the case for the sampling distribution of differences between means.

Stiglitz is now in familiar territory. Constructing the 99 percent confidence interval for $\mu_{\text{difference}}$, he obtains:

99 percent confidence interval $= CI_{0.99} = 6.4 \pm 2 \times 0.6 = 6.4 \pm 1.2$

Note that se is multiplied by 2, which is obtained from the *t* distribution. We shall discuss this in the next section.

---

[*] Because we are dealing here with a sampling distribution, our standard deviation is a standard error.

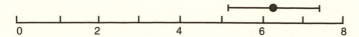

FIGURE 24-1 Ninety-nine percent confidence interval for the difference between the Italians and the French on Love's Despair.

Figure 24-1 shows the interval graphically. The lower bound of the interval is well above 0. Based on this, Stiglitz can be 99 percent certain that $\mu_{\text{difference}}$ is greater than 0. In other words, he is pretty sure that the nationalities differ on Love's Despair.

Statistically, constructing a confidence interval for "mean difference" is equivalent to constructing a separate interval for each mean:

- If in constructing two intervals—one for each mean—we find that they do not overlap, the single interval for the difference between means will be above 0.

- If the two intervals for the means overlap, the single interval for their difference will pass through 0.

Still, constructing a single interval, instead of two, is more elegant. What is more, the interval addresses directly the issue of magnitude of difference; using it, we can estimate in a straightforward manner the true difference between the population means. Stiglitz's single confidence interval ranges between 5.2 and 7.6 (6.4 ± 1.2). Thus he can conclude with 99 percent certainty that Italians are higher than the French on Love's Despair by at least 5.2 and by no more than 7.6.

STILL ANOTHER METHOD

In this section we present yet a third technique for inferring about population means from samples. As before, our method is statistically equivalent to those preceding it. Yet we present this additional method because, historically, it is the one most commonly used for comparing sample means. We have another reason as well, and it will become clear in the next section.

The t statistic is computed as follows:

$$t = \frac{\overline{x}_1 - \overline{x}_2}{\text{se}_{\text{difference}}}$$

$\bar{x}_1 - \bar{x}_2$ is the raw difference between sample means. This is where we begin when comparing two groups that we suspect represent different populations. To truly understand this distance, however, we must place it in context, that is, express it in units of standard deviation (see Chapter 8). We do this by dividing by se. Remember that the se is just another standard deviation. It is merely the notation used to indicate that we are talking about a sampling distribution rather than raw data.* As in Chapter 8, placing distance in context involves translating it into units of standard deviation.

Suppose that H_0 is true and the population means are identical. In other words, under H_0, the distribution of differences has a mean of 0. It also has some standard deviation σ. *This is our null model.* Thus the null model for the distribution of differences has a mean of 0 and a standard deviation of σ. It is normal and its σ is estimated by se$_{\text{difference}}$, which is 0.6 (see preceding section). When σ of a normal distribution is estimated from a sample, our distribution is *t* (see Chapter 21) and looks like the one in Figure 24-2. Note that this distribution "looks normal" because *t* distributions based on large samples (such as the one here) are indeed "virtually normal" (see Chapter 21).

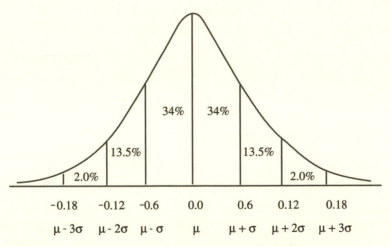

FIGURE 24-2 A *t* distribution with $\mu = 0$ and $\sigma = 0.6$.

* It happens to be smaller than the sd and is computed by sd/$\sqrt{n}$. However computed, it is an estimate of the standard deviation of a sampling distribution.

Stiglitz now asks: "In a *t* distribution with a mean of 0 and an se of 0.6 is

$$\frac{\overline{x}_1 - \overline{x}_2}{se_{\text{difference}}}$$

large or small?" If it is sufficiently large, he will reject H_0 that the true difference is 0; that is, he will say that under the null hypothesis described by Figure 24-2 it is unlikely—it is at the "outer edge" of the curve and will likely not come up in a random sample from this particular distribution. Computing *t*, Stiglitz obtains

$$t = \frac{19.8 - 13.4}{0.6} = \frac{6.4}{0.6} = 10.7$$

This is a very unlikely result under the assumption that $\mu_{\text{difference}} = 0$: In a *t* distribution with a mean of 0, less than 1 out of 1000 points is at a distance of 10.7 standard deviations or more from the mean.* In other words, if this were the true state of affairs, our chance of obtaining the result Stiglitz actually obtained would be less than 1 in 1000. Consequently, it is probably *not* the true state of affairs. That is, the model described based on H_0, and shown in the figure, is likely wrong. Based on this, Stiglitz would conclude that the true difference is greater than 0—that the French and Italians differ on Love's Despair.

Let us take a look at his logic sequentially:

1. H_0 states that Italians and French have identical levels of Love's Despair. That is, the distribution of differences resulting from sampling error alone has a mean of 0 and looks like Figure 24-2.

2. The data yielded $t = 10.7$.

3. Stiglitz now asks whether 10.7 is large or small relative to the 0 he should have obtained if the null is true.

4. The answer is "it is extremely large"—much larger than would be expected by chance. It is virtually impossible to come up with 10.7 in a distribution like the one in Figure 24-2. Notice that in that distribution even 0.18 is very unlikely.

---

* That is, less than 0.1 percent of the *t* curve's area is beyond a distance of 10.7 standard deviations from the mean.

5. He concludes that H_0 is wrong—that the difference observed reflects a true difference between two populations. It is not an artifact of sampling error alone.

FACTORS AFFECTING POWER

In Chapter 23 we said that the typical goal of research is to obtain a significant result—to discover a difference when it truly exists. Our ability to do this is termed *power*. Using the *t*-test formula, we can evaluate directly some of the elements that determine power. This is the other advantage of the formula that we alluded to earlier.

Decrease the size of t required for rejecting the null. In general, the larger the *t,* the more likely the difference observed reflects the truth. However, defining *large* is up to you (see Chapter 23). If you wish, you can set a relatively small *t* as your criterion for rejecting the null. This will increase your likelihood for rejection. In other words, lowering your criterion for rejection increases your power. Of course, this also will increase your chance for incorrectly rejecting H_0—for making a type I error. In any case, the risk you are willing to accept is precisely that.

Increase $\overline{x}_1 - \overline{x}_2$. The means you obtain are estimates of the true means, which you can do nothing about. Thus it would seem that here you are completely at the mercy of your phenomena. They are what they are. At the same time, you *can* choose the phenomena you wish to study. And some are more likely to yield large differences than others are.

Suppose that you wish to assess whether people driving under the influence err more on a driving simulator than those who are sober. You can, for example, give the "under the influence group" 4 shots of vodka or 1. If you select the former, you will likely obtain larger differences than if you select the latter. Thus, in choosing the phenomenon for comparison, you can, to a degree, control the difference you will obtain. In other words, by selecting your phenomenon carefully, you can partially control the chance for obtaining a significant result.

Decrease $se_{difference}$. As the denominator of the *t* statistic (the se) gets smaller, the size of *t* gets larger. This, in turn, will increase your chance for rejecting H_0. Now se is an sd divided by $\sqrt{n}$, where *n* is the sample size. Thus, if you wish for a significant result, increase your sample size. The larger your sample size, the smaller will be your denominator and the greater will be your chances of discovering a difference where it exists. Long ago we noted that this is something you know intuitively. That is, the larger your sample, the better are your chances for discovering the truth. There are other ways to increase power, but we shall be content with these. In the following chapter we present yet a fourth way to test hypotheses, and it is the most general of all.

CHAPTER XXV

Understanding

Any child will tell you that the animals in Figure 25-1 belong to different groups—even without your asking. Classification is instinctive.

Sorting the creatures by species, we obtain Figure 25-2.

We began with a picture in which there was a measure of confusion—of *variation*. Rearranging its elements, we created one that is easier on the eye. But we did not reduce the overall variation. After all, the elements in the two figures are identical, and their differences remain as they were. Apparently, *confusion* and *variation* are not wholly interchangeable.

FIGURE 25-1 Creatures.

FIGURE 25-2 Creatures by group.

The creatures in the figures vary. Some are rabbits, and others are butterflies. Of the rabbits, we can say that they

1. Differ greatly from butterflies.

2. Differ somewhat from one another.

The same is true for butterflies relative to rabbits and one another.

So let us distinguish two types of variation. The first results from there being two different groups and is termed *between-group variation*. The second relates to the differences within each group and is due to neither rabbits nor butterflies being all alike. Naturally, it is termed *within-group variation*.

The statistical attitude toward these two types of variation differs. We say that we *understand* between-group variation—can *explain* it. It is attributed to there being different species. Having explained it, it is confusion no more. Yet the variation among animals of the same species remains unexplained—for the moment.

We can, if we like, go on to separate the within-species variation, and Figure 25-3 does this. Once again, we have *partitioned variation* into between and within. And we did it by breaking up what was once a single population of rabbits into two populations—northern rabbits and southern.

Thus, we began with Figure 25-1, which is disorderly. Explaining some of the variation in Creature by Species, we reduced the disorder and obtained Figure 25-2. Finally, using Figure 25-3, we explained some of the *residual*, unexplained variation of Figure 25-2 by relating Creature to Habitat. *In statistics, understanding involves relating variation in one variable to variation*

(a)   (b)

FIGURE 25-3 Rabbits by habitat. (*a*) Northern rabbit. (*b*) Southern rabbit.

in others, that is, showing that changes in one variable are lawfully associated with changes in others.

Another example: People differ on Love's Despair. Separate them into Italians and French, and you have explained some of the variation in Love's Despair by Nationality. Attempting to understand variation further, we might relate Love's Despair to additional variables such as Gender or Age. As you can imagine, the process is endless. After all, populations contain an infinite number of elements and so can be separated into an infinite number of subgroups. This is what we meant in Chapter 3 when we wrote "This breaking up of things into parts is the essence of analysis. It is the way of science and, for that matter, any formal research. . . . The analytic thinker may begin with the complete picture, but she quickly breaks it up, analyzing each element in its turn."

Thus classification is one form of the activity we call *analysis.* In statistics, it involves breaking up variation into its component parts—explained and unexplained. One formal procedure for doing this is called *analysis of variance* (ANOVA). As it turns out, many statistical procedures do exactly this. But in ANOVA it is most obvious. We say

$$\text{Variation}_{\text{total}} = \text{Variation}_{\text{between}} + \text{Variation}_{\text{within}}$$

In observing a phenomenon such as Love's Despair, we notice its overall variation ($\text{Variation}_{\text{total}}$). We then ask, "*Why* do people vary on this as they do?" By separating overall variation into $\text{Variation}_{\text{between}}$ and $\text{Variation}_{\text{within}}$, we attain a partial explanation.

The formula also tells us that separating into components does nothing to the overall variation. We begin with a "quantity of variation" and end up with the same quantity. Yet partitioning leads to understanding. In statistics, variation that is explained is no longer confusion, and that which remains unexplained is confusion still.

An example: Your desk is piled up with papers—letters, reports, etc. In short, your desk is a mess. To clear it up, you separate the papers into different piles—put some in the inbox, some in the outbox, some in the report box, and so on. Once done, you desk is orderly. The documents—their number and content—remain as they were, but by the act of separating them into piles (within which the variation is relatively small—the documents in each pile are similar in that they belong to the same category), you have created order.

All this is a long-winded way of describing the process of *classification*, which is natural for us. Once again, we have taken everyday thinking and formalized it. And the process has a history. From Genesis:

> In the beginning of creation, when God made heaven and earth, the earth was without form [there was disorder]. . . . God said: "Let there be light," and there was light. And god saw that the light was good and he separated light from darkness.[1]

Time of Day (day/night) explains variation in Light. But not completely. This is so because Light varies within the hours of the day, as it does within the hours of the night.

That we begin this activity early on in life should be obvious. For example, infants classify objects into pacifiers and milk bottles and so make their world more comprehensible. As they mature, they learn to distinguish between toys and dangerous objects. Maturing further, they discover that the population of toys can be subdivided as well. For example, there is a population of electronic toys and another population—that of mechanical toys. In statistical terms, they explain the variation in Toy by Type. *In statistics, classifying is the process of placing objects in their respective populations.*

Piaget, the father of developmental psychology, called this *assimilation*. The human brain, he said, has ready-made categories. When encountering stimuli, it assimilates them into existing categories and so understands. But if an object is of a new type and cannot be readily pigeonholed, a new category must be created for it. Piaget called this "creating of new categories" *accommodation*. Once done, a person can assimilate stimuli into these new classes as well.

Apparently, our brain is biologically built for this type of analysis. Yet often the process is neither simple nor obvious—so much so that for a good time now we have been discussing some involved methods for doing it. We called them *hypothesis testing*. In hypothesis testing, we ask whether two samples represent different populations or are two instances of the same population, that is, whether all the phenomena before us should be assimilated into one category or two.* For example, we asked whether Italians and French are one or two populations with respect to Love's Despair. Similarly, we asked whether a particular drawing room belongs to the class of rooms we know or is a member of one that we have yet to encounter.

In Chapter 14 we defined a population as *a collection of elements that have something in common that others do not.* Applying the definition here, we state that Italians share a mean on Love's Despair that is different from the one shared by the French.

TURNING WEAKNESS INTO STRENGTH

In the preceding section we made an odd statement. We claimed that two nationalities do not share a mean on Love's Despair and so are different populations. But we could have simply computed an overall mean for both and said that they are the same. It would seem, then, that classifying by specifying means is little more than a matter of definition.

Well, it is not as simple as that. Recall that in Chapter 6 we pointed out that the mean has a particular weakness and demonstrated it using the following data:

$$3, 6, 4, 5, 2, 93, 97$$

Computing the mean, we obtained 30 and wrote

> Technically speaking, the number 30 is a measure of central tendency. But really, it does not represent the data's tendency very well. Neither the small values, which range from 2 to 6, nor the large ones, 93 and 97, are near the mean. This example demonstrates a basic weakness of the mean: It is sensitive to extreme values. In statistical terms, it is not *robust*.
>
> A possible solution is to specify two numbers to describe these data—the mean of the small values and the mean of the large. This is a good solution. In fact, this procedure is the workhorse of a number of powerful statistical techniques that we shall discuss in later chapters.

We are now in these "later chapters."

---

* Or three or four, or any number of categories we wish.

In this example it is clear that the number 30 is not a good descriptor of the data. The mean's weakness—its sensitivity to outlying values—makes it inadequate for describing the numbers at hand. In ANOVA, we assess just how inadequate. That is, we select samples and describe them in two ways:

1. Using a single mean.

2. Using as many means as there are samples.

We then ask to what degree specifying several means is more adequate than specifying one. If the answer is "it is more adequate," we conclude that our data represent different populations—that to describe them, one had better specify several means. If a single mean will do, we claim that all our samples represent the same population.

Thus ANOVA is one more method for testing the following hypotheses:

H_0: There is only one population with a single mean. Any differences observed are attributable to sampling error alone.

H_1: There is more than one population. The observed differences reflect true differences.

Yet ANOVA, more than any other statistical procedure, exemplifies the kind of reasoning we use when classifying.

FORMALIZING

To this point we have differentiated between two populations only. Using ANOVA, we can differentiate more. To keep things simple, we shall remain with the two-group case, but our principles apply to multigroup comparisons as well.

An example: You selected two samples and obtained the following values:

Sample 1:　4, 5, 6

Sample 2:　8, 9, 10

You now ask whether the samples represent different populations. Looking at the numbers, it seems that the answer is "yes." Figure 25-4 convinces you of this further.

A second scenario (Figure 25-5):

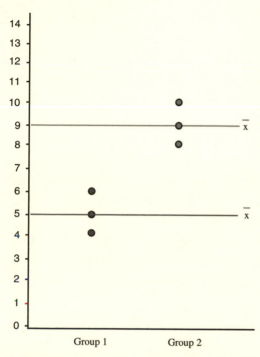

FIGURE 25-4 Two samples: Scenario A.

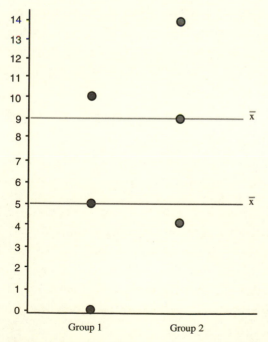

FIGURE 25-5 Two samples: Scenario B.

Sample 1:   0, 5, 10

Sample 2:   4, 9, 14

Examining scenario B, you are not sure what to decide. The means are different, no doubt. In fact, their disparity is the same as in scenario A, but the separation between the groups is no longer clear-cut. Perhaps, you say, there is only a single population. The observed difference between the means is due to sampling error only.[*] Translating into our newly acquired language, we say: "The between-group variation in the two scenarios is the same—the differences between the means are identical. But the within-group variation in the second is larger than in the first."

Statistics allows us to quantify the different types of variations described:

- *Total variation* is a measure of the degree to which all 6 numbers differ from the overall mean. In ANOVA, we call this "overall mean" the grand mean. (Total variation is computed by subtracting each and every one of the 6 numbers from the overall mean, squaring each of these differences, and summing the squared values.)

- *Between-group variation* is a measure of the degree to which the means of the two groups differ from one another [computed by (1) squaring the first mean from the overall mean $(5 - 7)^2$ and multiplying by the number of observations in the first group (3), yielding 12; (2) doing the same for the second group, yielding $3(9 - 7)^2$, which is again 12, and (3) summing the two numbers, yielding 24].

- *Within-group variation* is a measure of the degree to which values in the respective groups differ from their respective means (computed by subtracting each number from its respective mean, squaring each of these differences, and summing the squared values).

In the past, we computed variation using standard deviations. In ANOVA, this is done a bit differently, but the principle is the same. We will not trouble you with the actual computations. Rather, we shall provide their outcomes for our simple example and use these outcomes to demonstrate our reasoning (Table 25-1).

---

[*] We use the term *sampling error only* because even when the differences encountered suggest two populations, the means obtained are measured with sampling error.

TABLE 25-1 PARTITIONING VARIATION IN TWO SCENARIOS

SCENARIO	VARIATION$_{TOTAL}$	VARIATION$_{BETWEEN}$	VARIATION$_{WITHIN}$
A	28	24	4
B	124	24	100

Computing Variation$_{total}$ is like saying that there is only one population, and H_0 is true. Consequently, it is computed on all the observations combined—as if they all originated from a single population. Partitioning is like stating that there are two populations, each with its own mean, and H_1 is true. In partitioning, we compute variation in two parts: between-group (variation of means) and within-group (variation within each of the groups separately). The former we term *explained variation*, and the latter we term *unexplained*.

We are now left to compare between the statements—to test whether partitioning has led to a significant (i.e., true) increase in our understanding of the overall variation. In scenario A, the between-group variation is 86 percent of the total variation (24/28). Having partitioned, we explained most of the confusion with which we began. In scenario B, it is only 19 percent (24/124).

Now Variation$_{between}$ will be 0 only when the two sample means turn out to be identical. We do not expect this to happen *even if our samples do indeed originate from a single population*. This is so because of sampling error. In other words, the fact that two sample means differ does not, by itself, suggest that we have before us different populations.

Thus partitioning will always increase our understanding somewhat. The question now becomes whether this "increase in understanding" is real or merely due to chance (sampling error), that is, whether Variation$_{between}$ is sufficiently large to indicate a true (significant) difference between populations.

ANOVA answers this question by evaluating the relative sizes of the between- and within-group variations. In our current example, we say

1. In scenario A, the ratio of between to within is $24/4 = 6.0$.

2. In scenario B, the ratio is $24/100 = 0.24$.

Thus, in ANOVA, we assess:

$$\text{Ratio of explained to unexplained variation} = \frac{\text{variation}_{\text{between}}}{\text{variation}_{\text{within}}}$$

The actual computations in ANOVA are more involved.[*] The idea behind them, however, is that which we have just shown. When the ratio is small,[†] we conclude that there is a single population only.

Why can we conclude this? Recall that between-group variation represents what we understand—it is explained variation. Within-group variation is what remains unexplained. When the ratio of explained to unexplained is small, we say that our explanation is lacking. Perhaps, we say, it is no explanation at all—it is merely a result of error.

Remember also that our proposed explanation takes the following form: "The means of the groups differ because there are two populations." If this is no explanation—if it is wrong—then there are not two populations, and we remain with H_0.

Quantifying Confusion and Understanding

In ANOVA we have a fine example of how statistics formalizes everyday thinking. And it provides us with a bonus by allowing us to quantify the terms *confusion* and *understanding*.

When we look at a set of numbers that vary, we are "100 percent confused." That is, without additional information, we do not know why they vary. This overall confusion is quantified by Variation$_{\text{total}}$. For example, in scenario A above we began with a "total confusion of 28." By partitioning, we explained 24 of the 28 and gained an understanding of 86 percent of the variation in the data. We are now only "14 percent confused." This is an odd statement, no doubt. Still, it nicely expresses the degree to which we understand why the data look as they do.

---

[*] The actual "*F* statistic" tested in ANOVA involves computing ratios of *mean squares*, which are derived from the values presented. Once again, we shall not trouble you with the actual derivations.

[†] Sir Ronal Fisher, who developed ANOVA, showed how this ratio is distributed. Based on his *F* distribution, we can evaluate just how "large is true," that is, the size required to conclude that two sample means do indeed represent different populations.

In life you often say, "I understand," and rarely mean "understand completely." Yet in everyday life you are rarely called on to state just how complete your understanding is. Formal research is different. Doing it, we not only wish to explain a phenomenon, we also want to know just how well we have explained it. ANOVA enables us to do this.

Thus, by quantifying variables and relating them to one another, we can

1. Assess whether a lawful relationship exists between them.

2. Evaluate whether there is a single population or many.

3. Understand *and* quantify the degree to which we understand—the degree to which we have explained variation.

STATISTICAL EXPLANATION

Variation in Time of Day "explains" Variation in Light. While this is an accurate observation, most people would agree that it is not a *causal* explanation. For this, we might relate variation in the Earth's Position to variation in the Sun's Position.

As used here, the term *explain* can be misleading. Statistical methods do not pretend to indicate how conceptually sound explanations are. Nor do they pretend to determine what causes what. They simply are meant to discover relationships and quantify them. Just how useful are the discoveries we make is something we must decide for ourselves.

Afterword

A story well written is a story complete. Not so with the process of analysis, where questions multiply with each answer.

In this book we have presented some basic statistical methods. And even here we have been less than exhaustive. But more than presenting the methods themselves, our aim has been to describe their logic—to show how statistics, which is a product of our psychology, reflects it. In a small way we have attempted to meet the challenge that Einstein presented to physicists when he wrote:

> The whole of science is no more than a refinement of everyday reasoning. Accordingly, the physicist cannot proceed without considering critically a much more difficult problem, the problem of analyzing the nature of everyday thinking.[1]

Introduction

1. Barrett, W. 1958. *Irrational Man: A Study of Existential Philosophy.* New York: Doubleday, p. 30.

Chapter I

1. Forster, E. M. 1927. *Aspects of the Novel.* New York: Harcourt Brace Jovanovich.
2. Agnon, S. Y. 1977. *To Here.* Tel-Aviv, Israel: Shocken.
3. Kahneman, D., and Tversky, A. 1973. On the psychology of prediction. *Psychological Review,* 80:237–257.
4. Jones, T. O., and Sasser, W. E. 1997. Why satisfied customers defect. *Harvard Business Review* (November–December):88–99.

Chapter II

1. Darwin, C. 1859. *The Origin of the Species by Means of Natural Selection or the Preservation of Favoured Races in the Struggle for Life.* London: John Murray. Reprint: New York: New American Library, 1958, p. 59.
2. In Willerman, L. 1979. *Individual Differences.* San Francisco: W. H. Freeman.

3. In Porter, E. 1986. *The Rise of Statistical Thinking: 1820-1900.* Princeton: Princeton University Press, p. 129.
4. Galton, F. 1869. *Hereditary Genius: An Inquiry into Its Laws and Consequences.* London: Macmillan, p. 23.
5. Op. cit., p. 25.

Chapter III

1. Hamsun, K. 1892. *Mysteries.* London: Pan Books (1976).
2. Teitelbaum, P. 1955. *Journal of Comparative Physiology* 48:156–163.

Chapter IV

1. Kotov, A., and Yudovich, M. 1961. *The Soviet School of Chess.* New York: Dover Publications.
2. Goetz, C. 1994. Charcot: A scientific Janus. *Review of Neurology (Paris)* 150(8–9):485–489.

Chapter V

1. Chandler, R. 1949. *The Little Sister.* New York: Ballantine Books.

Chapter VI

1. Kissinger, H. A. 1957. *A World Restored.* London: Victor Gollancz, Ltd., p. 10.
2. Bureau of the Census. 1992. *Current Population Reports,* Table 29, pp. 60–184. Washington, D.C.: Bureau of the Census.

Chapter VII

1. Mann, T. 1934. *Joseph and His Brothers.* New York: Alfred A. Knopf.
2. Böll, H. 1965. *The Clown.* New York: Avon Books.

Chapter VIII

1. Böll, H. 1965. *The Clown.* New York: Avon Books.
2. Ibid.

Chapter X

1. Watson, J. B. 1927. The weakness of women. *Nation* 125:10.

Chapter XI

1. Dostoevsky, F. 1864. *Notes from the Underground*. New York: E. P. Dutton, 1960.

Chapter XII

1. Marquand, J. P. 1949. *Point of No Return*. New York: Bantam Books, p. 1.
2. Kohler, W. 1957. *The Mentality of Apes*. London: Pelican Books. In Koestler, A. 1964. *The Act of Creation*. New York: Dell, p. 101.
3. Ibid. p. 233.
4. Ibid.
5. Feynman, R. P. 1965. *The Character of Physical Law*. London: Penguin, 1992, p. 57.

Chapter XIV

1. Forster, E. M. 1907. *The Longest Journey*. Middlesex, England: Penguin, 1967, p. 66.

Chapter XV

1. Tolman, E. C. 1948. Cognitive maps in rats and men. *The Psychological Review,* 55(4):189.
2. Ibid. p. 200.

Chapter XVII

1. Wilder, T. 1934. *Heaven's My Destination*. Garden City, NY: Doubleday.

Chapter XIX

1. Davies, R. 1983. *Fifth Business*. In *Deptford Trilogy*. London: King Penguin, pp. 58–59.
2. Feynman, R. P. 1965. *The Character of Physical Law*. London: Penguin, 1992, pp. 55–56.
3. Webster's Universal College Dictionary. 1997. New York: Gramercy Books.

Chapter XXII

1. Stendahl. 1840. *The Charterhouse of Parma*. London: Penguin Classics, 1958, p. 19.

2. Stiglitz, B., Oester, L., and Ebbinghaus, T. L. 1972. Love's despair in 19th century Lombardy. *Archives of Sociological Anthropological History,* 31(2):1046–1059.

Chapter XXIII

1. Wilde, O. 1899. *The Importance of Being Earnest.* In *The Complete Illustrated Works of Oscar Wilde.* London: Chancellor Press, 1996.

Chapter XXIV

1. Runyon, D. 1956. "The Lily of St. Pierre." In *Guys and Dolls and Other Stories.* London: Penguin Books, 1997, p. 127.

Chapter XXV

1. *The New English Bible.* 1972. New York: Cambridge University Press, p. 1.

Afterword

1. Albert Einstein 1950. *Out of My Later Years.* London: Thames and Hudson, p. 58.

Absolute zero   The 0 point on a ratio scale, indicating a complete absence of the attribute being measured. For example, 0 on the Kelvin temperature scale indicates a complete absence of heat.

Alpha (α)   In hypothesis testing the probability of inappropriately rejecting the null hypothesis. Most commonly, it is the chance of concluding that different samples represent distinct populations when they do not, that is, when the samples have actually been drawn from the same population. In setting α, one sets one's risk for a type error.

Alternative hypothesis   In hypothesis testing the alternative statement to the null hypothesis. For example, when the null hypothesis states that two samples represent one population, the alternative hypothesis states that the samples represent two populations (which have different population parameters).

Analysis of Variance (ANOVA)   A hypothesis testing procedure used to assess whether means obtained from two or more samples ($\bar{x}$'s) represent means of distinct populations (μ's).

Arbitrary zero   The 0 point on an interval scale, which does not necessarily indicate a complete absence of the attribute being measured. For example, a child may score 0 on a test of arithmetic, yet have at least some arithmetic ability (which is the attribute the test is intended to measure).

Between-group variation   In Analysis of Variance, a quantity expressing the degree to which group means vary—the extent to which they differ from one another. When divided by Total Variation, it quantifies the proportion of the overall variation that is explained or understood.

Bias Systematic or nonrandom error. Error that is not due to chance and so tends in one direction relative to the truth (e.g., systematically overestimates the truth).

Biased measure A measure that will systematically yield errors in one direction. For example, a thermometer that is off by +0.5⁰, is a biased measure of temperature. On average, it will overestimate the true temperature by 0.5^0.

Biased sample A sample obtained using a biased sampling procedure.

Biased sampling A sampling procedure that yields sample statistics that are biased—that systematically overestimate or underestimate population parameters. For example, polling in traditionally Democratic neighborhoods to predict Proportion Voting for John Smith in a national election constitutes biased sampling. On average, the proportions obtained will be biased in the "Democratic" direction.

Bimodal distribution A distribution that has two modes, or two frequently occurring values.

Boxplot A kind of graph for describing a distribution. A boxplot provides information on a distribution's quartiles and outlying values.

Categorical scale A scale that provides information on class but not on rank. For example, an Eye Color scale categorizes into classes such as brown, blue, and green. At the same time, it says nothing about these classes' standing relative to one another (e.g., which is "better"). Also called *nominal scale*.

Central limit theorem The central limit theorem states that a sampling distribution of means (1) has a mean that is identical to that of the raw data—the original distribution; (2) has a standard deviation that equals that of the raw data divided by the square root of the sample size (on which the sampling distribution's means are based—i.e.,

$$\sigma_{\text{sampling distribution}} = \frac{\sigma_{\text{raw data}}}{\sqrt{n}}$$

and (3) is more or less normally distributed when the sample size is large enough.

Central tendency *See* Measures of central tendency.

Coefficient of variation The standard deviation expressed as a percent of the mean. For example, in a distribution where the standard deviation is 2 and the mean is 10, the coefficient of variation is 20 percent.

Confidence interval of the mean   A range that contains the true population mean (μ), with a specified likelihood. For example, saying that the 95 percent confidence interval for the mean is between 7 and 9 is like saying: "I am 95 percent confident that the true population mean is between 7 and 9." This is the standard interpretation of the term in statistics. Technically, it is the interval within which we are certain, to a specified degree, that our sample means ($\bar{x}$'s) will fall when repeatedly sampling from the same population. Confidence intervals can be computed for statistics other than the mean (e.g., σ).

Continuous Scale   A scale that can take on any number of values between any two values in it. For example, between 1° and 2° on the Celsius scale there is an infinite number of values.

Correlation coefficient   A measure of the strength of the relationship (association) between variables. The most commonly used correlation coefficient is the Pearson Product Moment Correlation. It measures the degree to which the relationship between two variables is appropriately described by a straight line.

Cumulative distribution   A distribution in which each entry equals the number of cases, or percent of cases, at each point and below it.

Density   In a distribution, the extent to which a part of it contains more observations than others. For example, a positively skewed distribution has its greatest density at its negative end (on its left).

Descriptive statistics   The area of statistics concerned with providing summary information about distributions (e.g., using statistics, such as the mean, and graphs, such as a histogram). When doing descriptive statistics we aim to show "the way things are" rather than to explain "why they are as they are." (*See also* Inferential statistics.)

Dichotomous scale   A scale that can take on two values only. For example, a Gender scale takes on the two values of male or female; and Election Outcome scale takes on the values of win or lose.

Discrete scale   A scale that takes on a finite number of values between any two values on it. Typically it refers to scales on which only whole numbers are possible. For example, Number of Children in a Family or Number of Monopoly Games Bought are measured on discrete scales. (*See also* Continuous Scale.)

Distribution   A collection of values. The values can be quantities or categories. For example, one can talk about the distribution of Daily Temperature as well as the distribution of Hair Color.

Error   The difference of an obtained value from the truth. (*See also* Measurement error and Sampling error.)

Estimation   The area of inferential statistics that is concerned with learning about populations from samples. For example, one might estimate the population mean (μ) from a sample mean ($\bar{x}$'s).

Estimator   A sample statistic that is used to estimate a population parameter. For example, the sample mean, $\bar{x}$, is an estimator of the population mean, μ.

Explained variation   Variation in a variable that is lawfully related to the variation in another variable. It is "understood variation" in the sense that something else explains it. For example, the variation in Height of Children is partially explained by the variation in the Height of Parents; that is, there is a relatively lawful relationship between the two. Explained variation is a statement of a mathematical association and keeps silent on the meaning of the relationship (e.g., whether it is causal).

Generalization   Extrapolation from something we have experienced or measured to something we have not. For example, when using a sample to generalize to the population we extrapolate from the sample we have measured to the population that we have not.

Histogram   A kind of graph used to describe a distribution. On the histogram's horizontal axis are marked intervals, and its vertical axis denotes frequency or percent. The height of each of the histogram's bars represents the frequency (or percent) of the values in the interval on which each bar is placed. The area of a bar, divided by the total area of the histogram, indicates the proportion of values in the distribution in the bar's interval.

Hypothesis testing   A form of inferential statistics that tests the validity of a hypothesis regarding the value of population parameter (or parameters) based on sample statistics.

Inferential statistics   The branch of statistics that is concerned with extrapolating information about populations from samples. Estimation and hypothesis testing are two forms of inferential statistics.

Interquartile range   The range in which resides the middle 50 percent of the data in a distribution. It is a robust measure of spread.

Interval estimation   Estimating a population parameter (e.g., the population mean, μ) using a confidence interval.

Interval scale   A scale of measurement whose values provide meaningful information on rank *and* distance. The value 0 on interval scales is an arbitrary zero in that it does not indicate a complete absence of the attribute being measured.

Latent variable The true value of a variable, which cannot be known exactly because of error. For example, one's latent Height is one's true Height. Because the measurement of Height is imperfect (because it yields at least some error), the value of Height obtained through measurement is not one's exact Height.

Mean A measure of central tendency. The mean is the arithmetic average in that it is computed by dividing the sum of the values in a distribution by the number of values in it.

Measurement The activity of assigning values to things (e.g., rocks, tests, people, etc.).

Measurement error The deviation of a value obtained through measurement from the truth.

Measures of central tendency Measures that describe the "typical" value in a distribution—the location in the distribution where the numbers "tend to be." The mean, median, and mode are measures of central tendency. In specifying a measure of central tendency we summarize and so simplify; that is, we describe a distribution with something less than all the information in it.

Measures of variability Measures that describe the extent to which scores in a distribution differ from central tendency, and so from one another. The standard deviation, range, and interquartile range are measures of variability.

Median A measure of central tendency that is the 50th percentile, that is, the point in a distribution above and below which half of the values in the distribution fall.

Mode A measure of central tendency. The mode of a distribution is its most frequently occurring value.

Model A description or mathematical statement typically used to represent reality more simply. For example, the normal distribution is a mathematical statement used to describe the shape of some distributions.

Multimodal distribution A distribution that has at least two modes.

Multivariate method Formally, denotes a method in which at least two variables are explained by one or more other variables in a single procedure. It is typically (and less than correctly) used to describe methods in which more than two variables are related to one another at once.

Negatively skewed distribution A skewed distribution whose scores trail off (are less dense) at its negative end (on its left).

Normal distribution A theoretical model, or mathematical statement, used to describe the relative frequencies of values in some distributions. It is bell shaped.

Null hypothesis   In hypothesis testing, it is the initial statement of belief about the value of a population parameter or parameters. It represents the accepted state of things until proven otherwise. For example, when comparing the mean effectiveness of two medications we typically hypothesize (assume) that the means are the same until proven otherwise. This then is our null hypothesis.

Observed variable   The measured values of a variable—the values that can be empirically had. (*See also* Latent variable.)

Ordinal scale   A scale of measurement that provides meaningful information on rank but not on distance. For example, Olympic Medal is an ordinal scale with three values—gold, silver, and bronze. Using it we know who came in 1st, 2nd, and 3rd (rank), but we know nothing about the distance (e.g., meters or seconds) between the ranks.

Outlier   A value whose distance from central tendency is especially great; that is, it is great relative to the distance from central tendency of the other values in the distribution.

Partitioning variance   Separating the variation in distribution into components. For example, in analysis of variance we partition variation into explained and unexplained components. One can also partition variance into different explained components. For example, the variation in Success at School can be partitioned into that explained by (1) Hours Spent Doing Homework and (2) Extent of Help Given by Parents.

Percentile   A point that divides a distribution according to the percent of values that fall above and below it. For example, 60 percent of the values in a distribution are equal to or smaller than the 60th percentile, while 40 percent are larger.

Point estimation   Estimating a population parameter with a single value. For example, estimating the population mean (μ) with an obtained, sample mean ($\bar{x}$). This is in contrast to interval estimation.

Poisson distribution   A theoretical model or mathematical statement that describes the relative frequency of values in some distributions. The Poisson distribution often does a good job of describing the relative occurrence of rare phenomena over time (e.g., earthquakes, power failures).

Population   A collection of elements (people, places, things, numbers, etc.) that have at least one characteristic in common. For example, all those belonging to the Population of Hypertensives have in common the characteristic that they have high blood pressure.

Population parameter   A characteristic of a population, such as its mean (μ). Typically, we estimate population parameters, such as μ, using sample statistics such as the sample mean ($\bar{x}$).

Positively skewed distribution A skewed distribution whose scores trail off (are less dense) at its positive end (on its right).

Power The ability to detect a phenomenon that exists—a true phenomenon. In hypothesis testing it is the likelihood of rejecting the null hypothesis when it should be rejected. The probability of this happening is designated $1 - \beta$.

Predictive validity The extent to which a measure predicts what it is intended to predict. For example, in clinical trials Outcome in Rats is intended to predict Outcome in Humans. The extent to which this happens is the extent to which Outcome in Rats is a predictively valid measure of Outcome in Humans. There are other types of validity, and these are not dealt with in this book.

Probability The technical term in statistics used to denote "chance." It is quantified on a scale from 0 to 1, where 0 indicates "no chance" and 1 indicates "certainty." For example, a fair coin has a 0.5 probability of coming up heads on a given toss. It has a probability of 1 of coming up either heads *or* tails on any given toss.

Quartiles The 25th, 50th, and 75th *percentiles* in a distribution.

Random error Error that is due to chance alone—that is equally likely to go above and below the truth to the same extent. This is opposed to bias, that is, error that tends to go consistently in one direction.

Random sample A sample obtained using a random sampling procedure.

Random sampling A sampling procedure in which each and every member of the population has an equal probability of being selected for inclusion in the sample.

Range A measure of variability or spread in a distribution. It is the distance between the largest and smallest values in the distribution.

Ranking Ordering according to some criterion of relative standing.

Ratio scale A scale of measurement whose values provide information on rank and distance, and on which ratios are meaningful. For example, on the variable T-cell Count the value 8 relative to the value 4 is: (1) greater (rank), (2) greater by 4 (distance), and (3) twice as great (ratio). The value 0 on a ratio scale is an absolute zero.

Regression toward the mean Describes the attribute of statistical prediction whereby extreme values predict values that are nearer the mean than they are.

Relative distance A term used in this book to describe distance that is placed in a particular context. For example, the z-score provides distance of an observation from the mean in units of standard deviation, that is, distance from the mean relative to that of the other values in the distribution.

Reliability Consistency in measurement is the extent to which measuring the same thing, under similar circumstances, yields similar results.

Representative sample A sample that represents its population well; that is, whose sample statistics provide good estimates of its population parameters. Random sampling is a technique designed to increase the likelihood that the sample obtained will be representative. However, it does not ensure it.

Robust measure Unaffected by outlying values (outliers). For example, the median is a robust measure of central tendency and the interquartile range is a robust measure of variability.

Sample A subset of a population. Samples are typically drawn to obtain sample statistics, which are then used to estimate population parameters.

Sample statistic A summary value of some characteristic of a sample. For example, the sample mean summarizes one aspect of a sample's central tendency. Sample statistics are typically used to estimate population parameters.

Sampling distribution A distribution that a sample statistic will follow if one repeatedly obtains subsets of the population and computes the sample statistic of each. For example, repeatedly drawing samples of size $n = 10$ from a population, and computing their means ($\bar{x}$'s), will yield a sampling distribution of means.

Sampling error The deviation of a sample statistic from the true value in the population—from the population parameter.

Significance level In hypothesis testing, symbolized by α. It is the probability value that forms the boundary between rejecting and not rejecting the null hypothesis.

Significant difference A difference that at a specified level of probability, reflects the truth. In hypothesis testing it is a difference that leads to the rejection of the null hypothesis. For example, when the difference between two sample means ($\bar{x}$'s) is significant, at a significance level of 0.01, one is 99 percent certain that the samples represent distinct populations (whose means differ).

Skewed distribution An asymmetric distribution in which the scores are bunched up on one side of central tendency and trail off at the other. (*See also* Density; Negatively skewed distribution; Positively skewed distribution).

Standard deviation A measure of variability in a distribution; that is, a measure of how the scores in a distribution are spread. Computationally, it is a "kind of average" of the distances from the mean of all the scores in a distribution.

Standard error   The standard deviation of a sampling distribution. It is computed by dividing the standard deviation of the data in a sample by the square root of the sample's size.

Standard score   *See Z*-score.

Statistic   *See* Sample statistic.

Statistical explanation   Showing that variation in one (or more) variables is lawfully related to *variation* in one (or more) variables. (*See also* Explained variation.)

Statistical significance   In hypothesis testing, the probability that a difference between sample statistics is due to chance, that it is a result of sampling error alone rather than a result of the samples originating from distinct populations.

Sum of squares   A measure of variability computed by (1) computing the distance of each data point in a distribution from the mean, (2) squaring each of the distances, and (3) summing all the squared distances. It is the numerator of the variance.

Systematic error   *See* Bias.

***t*-distribution**   A theoretical sampling distribution that describes a sampling distribution of means for which σ is unknown and estimated from a sample. It describes sampling distributions that originate from populations that are normally distributed.

Total Variation   In Analysis of Variance, it is the sum of within-group variation and between-group variation. It expresses variability when data from all the groups are combined (as though there were a single group only).

***t*-test**   A family of hypothesis testing procedures typically used to assess whether means ($\bar{x}$'s) obtained from two samples represent a means of distinct populations (μ's). The test assumes that the sampling distribution of the means, and their differences, have a *t*-distribution. It is also used to test whether a particular sample mean is truly different from a specified value (there is no example of this application of the *t*-test in this book).

Type I error   In hypothesis testing, mistakenly rejecting the null hypothesis. The probability of this happening is designated α.

Type II error   In hypothesis testing, mistakenly *not* rejecting the null hypothesis. The probability of this happening is designated β.

Unbiased estimator   A sample statistic whose estimate of the population parameter has no bias; that is, a sample statistic whose difference from the population parameter is due to random error alone. For example, the standard deviation of a sample (sd), which is computed with *n* in the denominator, is a biased estimator in that it tends to consistently underestimate the population standard deviation (σ). This bias is corrected by putting $n - 1$ in the denominator instead. In other words, computing sd with $n - 1$ in the denominator provides an unbiased estimator of the population standard deviation. On the other hand, $\bar{x}$ (the arithmetic mean of a sample) is an unbiased estimator of μ (the population mean).

Unexplained variation   Variation in a distribution that has not been shown to relate to variation in another distribution. (*See also* Within-group variation.)

Uniform distribution   A model for a distribution in which any of its values is as frequent (as likely to occur) as any other. For example, the outcomes of fair dice are uniformly distributed—each has $1/6^{\text{th}}$ chance of occurring.

Validity   *See* Predictive validity.

Variability   The extent to which scores in a distribution differ from one another.

Variable   A characteristic of "things" that can take on more than one value. For example, Gender is a variable that can take on the two values of male and female; Distance in Miles is a variable that can take on any number of values.

Variance   A measure of variability in a distribution. The variance is the square of the standard deviation.

Variation   *See* Variability.

Within-group variation   The degree to which the values within a group vary. In Analysis of Variance it denotes the amount of variation in the data that is unexplained.

***z*-score**   A derived score that says how many standard deviations a point is above or below the mean of its distribution. Also called *standard score.*

Joseph Tal received his Ph.D. in clinical psychology from Northwestern University. He was a statistician at the National Institutes of Health in Maryland and at the statistical laboratory of the Technion, Israel Institute of Technology. He is currently managing director of TechnoStat, a statistical consulting firm based in Israel.